Birth Control and Controlling Birth
WOMEN-CENTERED PERSPECTIVES

BIRTH CONTROL AND CONTROLLING BIRTH

Women-Centered Perspectives

Edited by

Helen B. Holmes, Betty B. Hoskins, and Michael Gross

The HUMANA Press Inc. • Clifton, New Jersey

The present work is one of two thoughtfully enhanced and carefully edited volumes that emerged from the conference on Ethical Issues in Human Reproduction Technology: Analysis by Women, held in June 1979 at Hampshire College in Amherst, Massachusetts.

"This book was prepared with the support of NSF Grant #0SS 78 24508. However, any opinions, findings, conclusions, and/or recommendations herein are those of the authors and do not necessarily reflect the views of the NSF, The Federation of Organizations for Professional Women, or the Editors."

Library of Congress Cataloging in Publication Data

Main entry under title:
Birth control and controlling birth.

(Contemporary issues in biomedicine, ethics, and society)
Bibliography: p.
Includes index.
1. Contraceptives—Research—Congresses.
2. Contraception—Congresses. 3. Obstetrics—Technological innovations—Congresses. 4. Obstetrics—Social aspects—Congresses. 5. Childbirth—Congresses.
6. Women's health services—United States—Congresses.
I. Holmes, Helen B. II. Hoskins, Betty B.
III. Gross, Michael, 1948- IV. Series.
RG136.A2B54   614.9′4   80-82173

ISBN 0-89603-022-9

ISBN 0-89603-023-7 (pbk.)

CONTENTS

Ethics of Contraceptive Development and Deployment

Depo-Provera and Sterilization Abuse

Childbirth

Section 1: Childbirth Technologies

Section 2: Social Control of Childbirth

Policymaking and Projections

Preface

Women most fully experience the consequences of human reproductive technologies. Men who convene to evaluate such technologies discuss *"them"*: the women who must accept, avoid, or even resist these technologies; the women who consume technologies they did not devise; the women who are the objects of policies made by men. So often the input of women is neither sought nor listened to. The privileged insights and perspectives that women bring to the consideration of technologies in human reproduction are the subject of these volumes, which constitute the revised and edited record of a Workshop on "Ethical Issues in Human Reproduction Technology: Analysis by Women" (EIRTAW), held in June, 1979, at Hampshire College in Amherst, Massachusetts.

Some 80 members of the workshop, 90 percent of them women (from 24 states), represented diverse occupations and personal histories, different races and classes, varied political commitments. They included doctors, nurses, and scientists, lay midwives, consumer advocates, historians, and sociologists, lawyers, policy analysts, and ethicists. Each session, however, made plain that ethics is an everyday concern for women in general, as well as an academic profession for some.

The conference displayed the power of intense thought, motivated by passionate commitments—to other women, to free and rational inquiry, to the urgency of political action. The most carefully textured philosophical analyses were informed by felt experiences of pain and joy, anger and pleasure, frustration and satisfaction. The most impassioned calls for action were grounded in searching analysis. Yet across barriers, including age, class, race, status, training, sexuality, and politics, women talked together in mutual appreciation.

Early during the Workshop, members of each topic subgroup met together. These new colleagues, most of whom had never met each other in person, discussed the contents of each others' papers and planned together for the session that their subgroup would present. The Workshop was structured around eight sessions: contraception; Depo-Provera and sterilization abuse; diethylstilbestrol (DES); childbirth; prenatal diagnosis; neonatology; sex preselection; and such manipulative reproductive technologies as in vitro fertilization, egg fusion, and cell manipulation. A session on policy became devoted largely to balloting on specific resolutions. Each session here occupies a chapter that includes a brief summary overview of the topic in relation to the work of the panel, followed by the panel's technical, interpretive, and ethical papers. Each chapter concludes with panelists' formal responses to papers and the ensuing (edited) discussion.

Speakers and respondents were asked to direct their remarks toward the specific goals of the Workshop. These goals are:

1. To identify the ethical issues involved in setting priorities in research on human reproduction and in the application of such research.

2. To determine which values have heretofore been considered in resolution of conflicts.

3. To discover any alternative applicable social values that are now being offered by women.

4. To recommend new approaches for assessing values and determining policy.

As befitted a woman-planned, woman-oriented, and woman-conducted conference, the organization and format departed significantly from established practice. In the selection of participants, conventional academic qualifications weighed no more than deep concern, demonstrated interest, and previous personal experience. Each person had a place on the program and received the same honorarium. So that financial status would be less a factor in determining who could come, travel, board, and room were furnished to all. In the same spirit, participants provided for the conference directory a brief biography with suffficient personal background to acquaint participants with one another beyond their specific occupation or credentials.

The aim of many conferences and their ensuing proceedings is to reach closure and to arrive at a level of consistency and agreement. However the principles underlying both this Workshop and these volumes differ from such conventional practice. For decades men have been making decisions in the area of human reproduction technology: women have not been heard from. Hence, the purpose of the Workshop was not to resolve issues but, quite the contrary, to begin the discussion. It aimed to bring forth differences that heretofore had remained unexpressed and, in particular, to highlight the diversity of views that emerges from the varied experiences and situations of women. Therfore, in editing materials for publication, we guided ourselves primarily by the principle of remaining faithful to all contributors' intentions and, insofar as it allowed for a readable and coherent volume, to their exact language. For that very reason we considered but rejected the alternative possibility of a shorter, highly synthesized volume derivative from the multiplicity of views and approaches in the conference.

We intend that the completeness of this work will enhance its interest and usefulness. The technical papers have been written in such a way as to communicate expert information to the layperson, and we hope thereby to reach a wide audience, especially women and readers interested in women's studies. Yet these volumes will have particular interest as well for such professionals as providers of health care and social services, philosophers, and bioethicists. Beyond their immediate topical interest, these books become a critical historical document reflecting the development, at this time, of women's thought. Of most immediate practical importance, however, is that they make available to ethicists and policymakers women's views that hitherto have been ignored. Furthermore, this work establishes the urgency of incorporating many more women into all ethical and policy deliberations on issues of human reproduction.

Helen B. Holmes
Betty B. Hoskins
Michael Gross

Acknowledgments

The EIRTAW workshop climaxed four years of planning, starting with a small group of women who met for the first time at the Workshop on Medical Ethics at Manhattanville College, in June 1975 [sponsored by the Institute of Society, Ethics and the Life Sciences (The Hastings Center), Hastings-on-Hudson, NY]. I am grateful for the inspiration and impetus from those women. The Program in "Ethics and Values in Science and Technology" (EVIST) of the National Science Foundation (NSF) and the National Endowment for the Humanities co-funded the workshop. The Ford Foundation agreed to add supplemental funds as we sought to increase minority representation among the prospective participants. The NSF also funded editorial and clerical work toward the preparation of these volumes. The keen interest and encouragement of the EVIST Program Directors, first Dr. William Blanpied and, recently, Dr. Arthur Norberg, meant a great deal. Criticisms and suggestions by anonymous reviewers of the proposal contributed to the outcome of the project. Dr. Linda Atkinson and Ms. Jacki Ans of the Ford Foundation facilitated discussions with that organization.

Concrete assistance from officers of the Association for Women in Science—Dr. Judith Ramaley, Dr. Anne Briscoe, and Dr. Ellen Weaver—helped get the project rolling at its commencement. Later, our sponsor, the Federation of Organizations for Professional Women, gave indispensable aid: its officers, Dr. Naomi McAfee, Dr. Julia Lear, Ms. Ilene Wolcott, and Dr. Margaret Dunkle; and those who handled our finances so expertly, Ms. Louise Ott, Ms. Carolyn Feinglass, and Ms. Ruth Scott. Dr. Marie Cassidy, who served as the official representative of the Federation, handled critical paperwork in Washington, DC, which was crucial to the success of this project.

Useful suggestions in composing the grant proposal came from Dr. Malcolm Willison, Ms. Melissa Fountain, Dr. Mila Aroskar, and Dr. Judith Ramaley. From the Hastings Center Dr. Daniel Callahan, Ms. Margaret Steinfels, and Dr. Rosalind Petchesky gave useful advice during early planning stages. Dr. Robert Murray, Jr., Dr. Charles Lance, Dr. Joan Sieber, and Dr. Sally Kohlsted also helped in early shaping of the project. During the workshop, at its conclusion, and in a post-conference followup report, our evaluators—Dr. Ben Barker-Benfield, Dr. Claudia Card, and Dr. Maureen Flannery—offered keen insights and useful criticisms.

I am especially indebted to the dedication and creativity of Co-Director Dr. Janice Raymond, and the devotion and hard work of my interdisciplinary advisory planning and executive committee: Dr. Michael Gross (history of science), Dr. Betty Hoskins (biology and bioethics), Ms. Gerene Major (nursing), Ms. Norma Swenson (women's health and sociology), and Dr. Caroline Whitbeck (philosophy). Committee members, joined by Dr. Marie Cassidy, organized the panels, playing a principal role in the selection, and at times the recruitment, of its members, and in the advance coordination of their presentations. In addition, the convener of each panel gathered the papers for this publication, undertook their initial editing, and contributed a summary overview.

The creation and execution of the Workshop and the preparation of these books would have been literally impossible without the dedicated labor and loyalty of Ms. Flora Johnson Josephs, Administrative Assistant. Her enthusiasm and spontaneous contributions went far beyond any reasonable expectations. Our Conference Assistants, Ms. Vivian Gabor and Ms. Julie Melrose, gave competent assistance during the Workshop, transcribed Workshop discussions, and typed early drafts of many manuscripts. Ms. Gale Storum's help with final manuscript preparation was indispensable. We are also grateful to the people at Humana Press for their kind assistance throughout the period of the book's accouchement.

Associate Editors, Dr. Michael Gross and Dr. Betty Hoskins, devoted long hours of painstaking, dedicated attention to each and every manuscript, with deep concern that each author's own ideas would come across clearly to our readers. Despite all this good advice, in a controversial, developing area such as this, errors, indiscretions, misinterpretations, and awkwardnesses invariably slip in. For them I take responsibility.

Finally, this project would have been totally impossible without the dedicated support and loyalty of my husband, Francis. Besides such customary husbandly duties as preparing meals, keeping the household running, and typing, he became a cheerful and competent volunteer whenever there was a deadline or job to do and no one to do it: providing office assistance before imminent deadlines, chauffering, advancing funds, proofreading, and reviewing of proposals and manuscripts. Whenever there were rejections, frustrations, disappointments, or cutting criticisms, his encouragement spurred me on and raised my spirits.

Helen B. Holmes

Birth Control and Controlling Birth

WOMEN-CENTERED PERSPECTIVES

Reproductive Technologies

The Birth of a Women-Centered Analysis

Helen B. Holmes

Women have been the bearers of the next generation since human beings first existed. Yet today human reproduction hardly seems to be a natural process—a clutter of biomedical technology surrounds it. Drugs, devices, and instruments besiege us—to block or ease conception; to foster or terminate gestation; to monitor or hasten birth. And recently emerging uses of technology include the design of progeny to meet specifications, as well as the creation of embryos outside the human body.

Vast sums of money are spent in the development and marketing of such technologies. The public is expected to absorb these costs and to generate profits, but the public at large may not benefit. Sophisticated treatments may be available only to the rich, to the well-insured, or to the experimented-upon poor. Meanwhile even minimal medical care is unavailable to many ordinary people. Moreover, some do not know how to seek what is there, and others cannot afford what they find.

Women, although they are the principal consumers of reproductive technologies, have scarcely been involved in making the decisions about which technologies to develop and when and where to deploy them. The collective impact of the accounts of these technologies unveils a picture of inappropriate and distorted priorities, as will be seen in texts of the articles here printed. Our focus on the issues is entirely different from the usual one. Many questions that society considers to be major issues and dilemmas dissolve when the underlying patriarchal assumptions are brought to light, only to reveal entirely different sorts of questions.

The following synthesis is based on an analysis of some key ideas from the thoughtful papers and stimulating discussions presented in these books. I have tried to reflect accurately many of the valuable insights of our authors. However, I take full responsibility for my choice of the points to enlarge upon and, insofar as I have gone beyond their data, for my interpretations, my inferences, and my opinions. I shall begin with one example of the way in which women's perspectives evoke new questions. Next I shall enumerate existing values motivating the use of reproductive technologies and then shall present alternative values offered in the contributions to these volumes.

THE NEED FOR A NEW APPROACH

A contraceptive drug or device is developed to be powerful and effective. It is deemed essential that it be easy enough for use by poor women and women in developing nations who are judged to be the cause of overpopulation. It has a raft of side effects: documented immediate effects and suspected long-range effects, some inconvenient, some debilitating, some lethal. Currently society approaches the decision of whether to deploy this drug or device with a risk/benefit calculus such as this: the risk of death in childbirth for this population is greater than the risk of death from the contraceptive. Or, overall, the benefit to society from having fewer poor persons is greater than the benefit to society from avoiding morbidity among poor women.

We detected other motivations behind such an analysis. To us, mortality risks in childbirth and mortality risks from contraception do not belong in the same equation. They are not parts of the same dilemma.

In some cultures the risk of a woman's dying in childbirth is simply a necessary assumable risk. For her, the production of a child may well lead to her receipt of financial benefits from a man, to a rise in her social status, to support in her old age, and to the joy of having someone totally dependent on her for a few years.

In our analysis we approach the childbirth mortality problem in a variety of ways: on the one hand, through such policies as better prenatal care, health and nutrition education, training of midwives; on the other hand, through expanding opportunities for women by creating new ways for legitimating women's existence. *Our* ethical question would begin with individual respect: Which approaches are best for the women concerned? What do the women themselves want? Which methods would have the most input and leadership from the women at risk? Which choices would involve the least outside control from (male-dominated) political and business interests?

As for the question of risk from the contraceptive itself, in no way would we as women analysts condone the chance of death or disability in the service of contraception. Nor are women willing to accept what have been quoted as "inconveniences" (such as a disrupted menstrual cycle, loss of libido, a perforated uterus) as side effects of contraception. Furthermore, potential dangers to a fetus in case a woman happens to be pregnant when she receives the drug or device must not be risked. And a drug powerful enough to stop fertility should never be taken by a nursing mother.

Our values here are total—physical, mental, emotional—health and well-being, and concern for future generations.

Thus it is often clear that old questions are not valid questions to our participants, and that nonmeaningful values are being weighted heavily in the traditional methods of analysis. Now I shall point out those values that actually motivate current decision-making and then shall clarify our own set of values in order to define issues in new terms.

EXISTING VALUES

What are the desirable and worthwhile principles that heretofore have been considered in the resolution of ethical conflicts and in the setting of policy in reproductive technologies? Standard lists include: honesty, promise-keeping, truth-telling, justice, loyalty to patients, impartiality, obligations, and duties. I do not deny that these values *do* function in our health care system. Many individual physicians (hospital administrators, researchers, and others) *do* pattern their lives and orient their practices toward the above values. The warm and concerned physicians who are authors in this book serve as examples. And most other physicians believe in these values. However, I propose that, in most conflicts and dilemmas, the above values can be and often are overridden by other values such as the six to be described below. The overall impact of the American health care system on people's lives reveals these other motivations. Although policymakers may claim that decisions are made "in the best interests" of women, they do not *know* what is best; therefore they cannot be excused for failing to attempt to involve in their decision-making the input of the women at risk.

As we studied policies around each aspect of reproductive technology, the same underlying values were revealed over and over again. The actual principles used in making present-day decisions and choices were not those in the list above. Among the operative values, six salient ones turn out to be: technology, domination, objectification, exploitation, hierarchism, and profit.

Technology as Intrinsically Good

We discover that **technology serves as an end as well as a means.** All problems are expected to have technological solutions. Should a given device or machine fail to perform as expected, this is not taken as a refutation of the general aim of finding a technological solution. Simply, a better device must be produced. The "right" course of action is to develop a replacement, or a device to use with the first to correct its imperfections, or a new machine to monitor the first to tell whether its performance is satisfactory. Nontechnological solutions to problems are not sought: these are not intrinsically good. Furthermore, the emphasis is on finding solutions rather than on identifying causes.

Consider the electronic fetal monitor (EFM): Devised to monitor the fetal heart rate and display it on a screen, the EFM requires that the mother lie very still in a prone position with electrodes strapped to her abdomen. This position is unphysiologic for labor and delivery. The lack of movement of the mother and the pressure on the vena cava may adversely affect the baby's heart rate. As a result, women have been rushed for cesarean sections when their babies actually were not in distress; conversely some babies' real distress has gone undetected.

And so, a new technology was sought and found: internal monitoring. Rupture the amniotic sac, insert electrodes through the cervical os, and attach them to the baby's scalp. Result: still some false positives, some false negatives.

The next technology found was fetal scalp sampling. Through a cone inserted in the cervical os, a bit of blood is removed from the baby's scalp and tested for pH (acidity). The pH correlates with oxygen content, which, in turn correlates with fetal distress. Result: still some false positives, some false negatives. What will come next? Allowing the mother to sit up or move around does not fit the paradigm.

If technology is applied to the comfort and convenience of people (obviously I exclude military technologies), it may well make our lives fuller and richer, enhancing the inner quality of life, extending a productive life, reducing pain, and improving our relationships with each other. But we need to be vigilant critics about even the life-enhancing technologies. Often technology comes imperceptibly to control us and to turn us into slaves of our machines. And when do the negative aspects of any invention outweigh the positive? Negative aspects are seldom considered when the technology itself is assumed to be an intrinsic good.

This notion that technology is intrinsically good has several corollaries. Some of these are:

—A limited budget is better spent on a spectacular new machine than on public health measures.

—A hospital is better, the more machines and devices it has.

—A physician is better, the more technological solutions he uses.

—A patient is better cured, the more pills, the more injections, the more X-rays, the more tests, the more operations she has.

These latter two corollaries may well explain why the chemical diethylstilbestrol (DES) continued to be prescribed for threatened miscarriage long after some literature reported that it was less effective than a placebo; and why now DES is given to *terminate* pregnancy (the Morning-After Pill), with essentially no followup.

Efficiency is prized over working things out carefully and thoughtfully; speed, over a deliberative process. This translates to a preference for using machines instead of human beings to solve problems. Another consequence of short-circuiting deliberation is that only those problems with technological solutions are identified as real problems. Furthermore, experts are defined as those with technical competence.

Domination

A second current value is **domination,** by which I mean power over other human beings. It implies competition, putting out effort to be "better" than others. Physicians, hospitals, and pharmaceutical houses demonstrate that power over others is a primary value, as they compete for prestige or profit.

Only minimal health care information is made available to consumers and to health care workers low in the echelon, so that the physician remains indispensible. Consumer groups and women's health advocates have had to struggle to get patient package inserts for drugs and medications. Essentially each new drug requires another battle. When the medical system is finally forced to comply, the inserts they create are of little value. English fails to inform non-English readers; medicalese keeps most patients still ignorant; legalese protects physicians and pharmacists from malpractice suits. Language has been used to obfuscate.

Similarly, after the struggle to make informed consent forms mandatory before all surgery and experimental procedures, a victory seems to have been turned into a partial defeat. Those in power have learned how to use the forms to retain their power, by obtaining signatures when the patient is: in extreme pain or about to have an abortion; or intimidated by an atmosphere of authority; or under the guise of haste and urgency, without the legally required opportunity to get information.

The medical system also creates power for itself by defining nonmedical events as medical, i.e., with an emphasis on disease and cure. Birth control, pregnancy, and childbirth are three such areas. The plastic specula that many lay women in the women's health movement are using have been classified as prescription devices in some states, in order to make them no longer available without the hassle, cost, and subordination of a visit to a physician.

Another aspect of power is blind loyalty, meaning unthinking loyalty to the attitudes and individuals who constitute the network of the higher echelon in the health care system. Often this is unconscious because it flows out of shared values in a closed community. Or, it is manifested as a professional ethic of always speaking well of others in the same profession. It excludes those who differ in race, in class, in sex, in profession. Occasionally, it may slip over the line into cronyism and conspiracy, for instance, when FDA bureaucrats "summarize" a drug company's experimental data in such a way that negative results are not evident.

Objectification (Reification)

The professed value is "objectivity," "an attitude uninfluenced by personal prejudices and based on observable phenomena." But what is actually found is, "an attitude that turns persons into objects, that depersonalizes"; this is **objectification.**

Consider cost–benefit analysis. Should a certain drug be used? In the choice of what to count as costs and what to count as benefits, the personal is removed. Mortality is estimated for groups of people. The cost to the hospital is counted, but not the ultimate personal costs to individual patients. Suffering from side effects or pain during the procedure is rarely considered.

Also, the language used serves to depersonalize. The expression "target population" cancels out individual humans; "patient management" implies the nonexistence of a sentient brain; "target organ" focuses narrowly, blotting out the fact that the organ is part of a whole, living, feeling human being.

Women, who in fact are highly diverse, are lumped together as a class. The role for this class is wife/mother, a role that is assigned responsibility, but given no control. "The classic perception of woman as *Matter* becomes even more reified and objectified, because women are now biomedically manipulable."[1]

Exploitation of Nature

The earth is viewed as existing in order to be **exploited** by humankind. The consequence is a possessive, yet detached and callous, attitude toward the natural world: plants, animals, and minerals are here to serve us. As many resources as possible must be extracted; if we run out, we search for a technology that can extract even more, or that can extract something else. Furthermore, current practice seems to assume that nature is poorly designed or sick and needs to be controlled, that natural processes can and must be "improved" by technology (for example, that Similac is better than mothers' milk). And short-term consequences may receive concern; long-term consequences tend not to be considered.

Hierarchism

Values, ideas, and persons seem to be viewed as occupying rungs on ladders, with some of them higher than others in a **rank-ordering.** When two values conflict, the one that outranks the other is chosen. When two human beings present their concerns, the person with the higher status is heard.

Invidious ways of ranking people are by their "normalcy" and by their culpability. Often, this means blaming a lower-status victim, for example, blaming rape victims and mothers of defective children for their own suffering.

Profit

This sixth value may underlie all of the others. Our health care system is a business run for **profit.** We see this in so many ways. Here I mention only five: unnecessary surgery, contraceptive development, attacks on lay health groups, patenting of techniques, and the short shrift given to preventive medicine and public health.

Surgeons are paid by the operation; surgeons have the highest income among physicians. From these two facts, even if we did not know of specific examples among our friends and relatives, we could conclude that there would be unnecessary surgery. Most pertinent to the subject matter of this book are the breast removals, the hysterectomies, the episiotomies, and the cesarean sections that may sometimes be unnecessary. Even if federal funds or private insurance pay the surgeon and the hospital, the patient pays physically in risk and discomfort, and financially in lost work time and convalescence expenses. And all of us will pay for her unnecessary surgery through higher taxes, higher insurance premiums, and general inflation. Surgeons and insurance companies grow richer while lower-level health workers and consumers grow poorer.

After World War I the pharmaceutical houses moved into the wide open field of contraceptive development; they foresaw, correctly, the huge profits possible. Nowadays, however, private industry in this country has essentially discontinued the development of new contraceptives: they cannot make enough profit because of the lengthy testing procedures currently required by the FDA. In the past, methods that seemed to have low profit possibilities, such as the cervical cap, did not get developed.

So that profits will keep coming, power and prestige must be maintained. Not only have those in control kept most lower status health workers semi-ignorant; they have also fought, sometimes viciously and violently, against lay health centers and workers, and against women's self-help procedures. Women who choose to have their babies at home have been accused of child abuse.[2]

Obvious examples of profit-orientation are the techniques for sex preselection recently developed by Ericsson and by Bovenkamp. Each has patented his invention and is selling it to clinics. The new in vitro fertilization clinic in Virginia is another example.

Public health physicians are the most poorly paid and have the least power and prestige. Public health programs get minimal support funding; is it coincidental that their goal is to help people take care of their own health, to prevent disease, and thus to keep people *out* of the medical system?

EMERGING WOMEN'S VALUES

Different indeed are the values offered in these books as the basis of moral action. Many of these women-centered values are described below.

Respect for the Individual

Each person has worth: first, simply because she is a human being, and second, because she is unique and different from every other human being. Her value priorities and her blend of values are unique, for they relate to her particular life experiences. In the selection of a contraceptive, her wish for a large, for a small, or for no family is a pertinent factor. In genetic counseling, her values should be the primary consideration.

Her physiology is also unique. Thus, before prescribing medicine for her, one should solicit information about her experiences with her own body and then proffer possibilities. A diversity of approaches should constantly be sought. "The best health care for a pregnant women simply allows the discovery of her particular physical and emotional needs, and ensures a dignified, self-directed resolution to those desires, wishes and needs."[3]

The method of women-controlled (patient-controlled; consumer-controlled) research nicely illustrates individual respect. In this method, the same women design the experiments, participate as subjects, have full access to the records, and have input to modify or to withdraw from the experiment at any time. Clearly, this meets no definition of experiment that we learned as The Scientific Method. There is no blind-control group, no randomized design. Essentially, this type of experimental design serves to acknowledge that total objectivity is impossible. Such a design can be ethically—perhaps even scientifically—superior to current and past clinical experimental practices, which have had some widespread problems. For example, control groups may have been chosen to deny a treatment to some, or to enhance anticipated experimental results. Sometimes when data were disappointing, they were conveniently forgotten. Also, the ethical dilemma of how to give equity to both experimental and placebo groups often cannot be resolved.

Respect for the individual implies that individual differences are to be fostered, sought, and encouraged. Richness of the policy debate is to be expected from diversity. Ethical dilemmas are the better resolved, the wider the spectrum of inputs.

Respect for the individual further implies, of course, that we should not stereotype people according to class, race, sex, occupation, or educational attainment. This principle was, unfortunately, not uniformly followed by some of the Workshop participants. Thus, on occasion, a sort of reverse discrimination took place when speakers seem to have been condemned in advance because of their male sex, their white race, or their professional degrees. We have picked up pigeonholing and categorizing from our patriarchal society, and the habit is hard to break.

The Personal is Political

Every individual comes from a particular background, the influence of which she brings into every situation. This background stems from her personal experiences in life that modify the important effects of membership in a particular race, sex, and economic class. Therefore, for her policy proposals to be meaningful and valid, the listener must know from where she comes. This may not make the stance more true, but it increases its informational value. So, for good analysis, the analyst must bring all necessary factors out into the open. This also counters any tendency toward objectification and towards the blind application of any single ethic.

Let us take in vitro fertilization (IVF) as an example. Imagine how each of the following individuals could be of the same race and class, but could have her policy stance toward IVF shaped differently: an infertile woman whose marriage had broken up for this reason; a neonatologist who has worked with severely deformed infants; a developmental biologist who regularly in the daily course of her work discards mouse embryos. To take examples from the workshop, Judith Luce, as an advocate for birthing women, tells about the moment after the birth of her first child when she was scolded for trying to touch him.[4] Mary Ampola, defending the use of prenatal diagnosis, describes the joy and relief she felt after amniocentesis when she learned that her second child would not have Down's syndrome.[5] And Wendy Carlton,[6] before reporting on her sociological study of the training of medical students, lets us know that she was a rescued premature baby, and that, during her teen-age years, her eyesight was saved by high technology.

Facing up to one's biases and revealing them is quite in contrast to the practice of medical science. Researchers claim "objectivity," but seldom acknowledge their biases and interests.

Also, that which is usually condemned or treated as anecdotal or trivial is the personal, but the personal energy and passion that we commit to our work and to our lives may well be as important as or more important than the concrete results.

The Political is Ethical

Power is an ethical issue. Those in power define what is right and wrong and punish the deviant. Yet the demands made are contingent and idiosyncratic: fifteen years ago in a given hospital it may have been forbidden for a mother to touch her newborn right after delivery; today, it may be required.

As we in these books seek what is morally right, we automatically also perceive what ought to be done. Thus, an ethical discussion creates a political policy stance. For us, ethics is not negative (refrain from doing wrong), but positive (go out and see that what is right gets done).

Autonomy and Choice

Anyone who is affected by a policy or by a technology ought to have authentic choice of whether to submit to it and ought to be able to participate in controlling it. There was consensus about this value; this theme surfaced repeatedly in all sessions. This kind of autonomous control was proposed as a solution to the problems left with us by a patriarchal society, and as a means for preventing new problems from occurring.

At the personal, individual level, autonomy means that we may choose in an informed context whether, for example, to have home birth, to have the fetal monitor, to be sterilized, to have amniocentesis. Of course, we must have full access to pertinent information given by someone without a vested interest. Consent forms must be written clearly and presented well ahead of the moment for signature. It must not be made difficult for us to assert our choices. Also, since personal control is such an important value, user education for a self-help procedure would be ethically preferable to a high technology solution to a medical problem.

Autonomy extended to the group level means that policymaking groups working on the development or on the deployment of a technology should always effectively include persons on whom the technology has been used and/or include some who are at risk for its future use. For example, population planning for underdeveloped nations ought to involve the *poor women* of those nations. In fact, most of us believe that policymaking boards should include a *majority* of potential consumers. Some make the case that *all* members of these boards should be such consumers and that specialists and scientists should merely testify before these boards.

There was consensus that consumers at risk would be competent to cope with technical details and to make involved decisions. Determining an acceptable contraceptive, for example, is so complex an issue that it *requires* input from consumers. Judgment of the acceptability of risks is a social decision that can be made validly *only* by the consumer.

If we have autonomy to make and act on decisions about our reproductive lives, we shall be empowered. This is not power over others in a hierarchical sense. We wish to use power differently—to hold our own as strong equals, to pass it on to others who need it.

Wholeness of the Individual

No focus on a particular organ or on a particular disease should leave the entire body out of consideration. Wholeness of a person includes her psychological, physical, and emotional aspects. It takes into account her entire life span. A primary concern for *safety* stems from this value.

For example, the first priority in selecting a contraceptive is total well-being. Non-invasive techniques that leave the body intact are preferable. Depo-Provera with its numerous, diverse, and often irreversible side effects—psychological, emotional, as well as system-wide physical effects—clearly is unacceptable under this ethic.

And in childbirth, the choice of who should be present at birth obviously depends on considering the psychological, emotional, and physical wholeness of the mother-to-be and the baby.

Wholeness of the Community of Women/ Women-Centeredness

A sense of community leads us to strengthen our bonds with women everywhere. It leads us to be concerned about minority and disadvantaged women, and to avoid objectifying classifications about any of us. Actions that one takes for her own benefit should not serve to harm others.

Some of us believe that ending the isolation of women from one another will foster basic self-knowledge about our fertility. This knowledge, shared among women, may be far more liberating and empowering than any imposed contraceptive technologies. It may also be more effective—but effectiveness seems not to be an overriding value.

One of the ways in which our authors openly state their biases is in their clear and refreshing pro-woman stance. Some deplored the presence of even a few men; they yearned for the special exchanges that can take place in woman-only space. Woman-centeredness is a very positive, buoyant, conscious effort to bring us from the periphery of a man-centered world into a core together with each other. It is inspiriting and empowering. For it is essential that women have self-regard; it is valid for women to give ourselves first priority when we have been denied this for so long. The nurturing done by women, their calling-forth of persons, has kept our species in existence on the earth's surface in spite of the repeated scenarios of total destruction planned and partially executed by men. It is long past time for us to come together, for by doing so we may well save the human species.

Although we approach each issue with the question, "What is really in the best interests of women?" rather than with the question, "What is in the best interests of society?" correct answers to the first question will automatically answer the second.

Wholeness of the Human Community into the Future

We have a deep concern for the unborn, including those whom we shall never see, generations hence. We must not leave a legacy of disability. Taking an untested drug when one is pregnant or leaving radioactive wastes buried in salt deposits both conflict with this ethic.

We do believe that children must be chosen and cherished. Most of us would support the choice of a woman not to carry a particular fetus if she ascertains that she cannot parent well at a particular time in her life.

Many contributors note that they would avoid drugs, food additives, caffeine, alcohol, X-rays, and nicotine when pregnant or when nursing their babies. We seem to be fanatical about avoiding repetition of the DES and thalidomide tragedies.

Wholeness of the Ecosystem

We have a responsibility to the earth, a one-ness with nature. Our actions should disrupt as little as possible the other forms of life with which we share our planet. Furthermore, the inanimate parts of nature also should not be wantonly wasted.

This concern was especially deeply felt by the midwives, and eloquently expressed by Katsi Cook: "Feminists need to understand...the suffering of our Mother Earth...She's being raped for her natural resources...The process that provides the ability for a human being to get to the moon requires a rip-off...The reproduction of the four-leggeds—who is thinking about them? These plants outside—they are our medicine. And who's thinking about them?"[7]

Each part of nature has value. Each should be respected.

And note that I have come full circle, back to *respect*. Note the connectedness of values, without ranking them in priority. Thus we come to:

Connectedness and Nonhierarchism

Connectedness can be applied to persons and to our values. There exists a circle, not a rank-order.

Persons are connected one to another. This is egalitarianism but not the atomized view of everyone as separate; rather it is tempered by concern for and commitment to others as valued inviduals. Is there ever a need to have hierarchies? Expertise cannot be compared or scaled because it comes in different forms—it is not institutionalized within certain professional or quasi-professional groups. Each of us is an expert in a different way—by study, by concern, by experience. A woman who has had a C-section and a surgeon who has done 100 sections both have expertise valuable to the policymaking process. A dilemma can be truly resolved only if all affected persons participate in determining the course of action.

Similarly, no one value in our circle is independent of any of the others. Each is influenced by and blends into the others. No one value automatically takes precedence over any one of the others. If two or more values seem to conflict over a given issue, then more ramifications need to be explored so that a real solution, an inclusive solution, is found.

THE PERSPECTIVE WIDENS

With these values as our frame of reference, we begin to see that issues in human reproduction technology encompass more and more elements of our lives. We cannot follow standard techniques of acknowledging that all social issues are related, and then ignore this relatedness in order to deal only with the bits and pieces. We strive to uncover all ramifications.

Take contraceptive choice and development as one example. Although most of us would favor offering any woman many options leading to an informed choice of contraceptive method, we were clearly biased toward nontraumatic, non-invasive methods with little chance of long-term side effects. Still, a safe, nontraumatic method of postcoital contraception is needed in case of failure of other techniques and in case of rape. However, most postcoital methods are risky and future technological solutions may well be also. Therefore, confronting the context of rape becomes an issue in contraceptive technology. Educating about rape, setting up rape crisis centers, caring for battered women, stopping pornography, and curbing violence in men are *all* issues in human reproduction technology.

Protection of the chosen fetus is another example. We see that potential person as a link to the future. We are concerned about possible harm to the fetus during pregnancy, especially during the first trimester when many women may not know that they are pregnant. We urge avoidance of X-rays with their known harm, and microwaves and ultrasound with less well documented ill effects. But there is an even more serious environmental insult: radioactivity. We are concerned about pregnant women who live near nuclear waste disposal areas, or whose houses are built on tailings, or whose husbands work in uranium mines. An increase in the number of nuclear power plants or in our stockpile of nuclear weapons leads to more waste disposal, more tailings, and more uranium miners. For some the question of nuclear power is seen in isolation as simply a matter of energy policy. But to us, these so-called "energy" issues become issues in human reproduction technology.

Furthermore, as we consider any particular technology for its effects on women, we also realize that the more technologies there are, the more the need for energy. Patriarchal society has assured us that the need for energy is at present a need for more nuclear power plants. Safety, the wholeness of individuals now and in subsequent generations, remains secondary to technology as an end in itself.

Another example is the dangerous contraceptive, Depo-Provera. We agreed that no woman should be given Depo-Provera, unless she gave truly informed consent. But we face our country's policy of not giving economic aid to underdeveloped countries unless they prove that they are tackling their "overpopulation," even if it be with an unsafe contraceptive. International economic policy thus has become an issue in human reproduction technology.

For a fourth example, consider the several biomedical technologies (some quite effective) that are now available to preselect the sex of a child before that child is born. Two stark realities hit us: the nearly universal preference that firstborns be sons, and the great advantage that any firstborn has in society. Therefore, strengthening bonds among women so that we *like* our own sex, expanding opportunities for women, and supporting the ERA *all* become issues in human reproduction technology.

SOME UNRESOLVED DILEMMAS

Clearly emerging from the values delineated above and from our wider perspectives were general recommendations for improved ways of setting policies dealing with reproductive technologies, so that these policies could better serve the interests of consumers at risk. These general proposals surfaced repeatedly and, in their essentials, were unanimously endorsed at the Workshop. As explicitly formulated for the final session and as voted in the form of fourteen "general resolutions," they can be found in the Appendix of our companion volume, *The Custom-Made Child?*.

We also agreed on many specific policy proposals. These recommendations and the level of agreement reached on each follow the general resolutions in that Appendix.

However, our method of analysis also revealed ethical problems, dilemmas, and disagreements. Some of these are presented below. In each, a conflict appears between two or more of our women-centered values. Here the dialogue has just begun. I propose that, in each case, it will be possible, with continuing input from affected consumers, to resolve these dilemmas without resorting to the sacrifice of one value in favor of another. For as one maximizes one value in the circle, one ought to try to maximize all. Sustained discussion may reveal an underlying harmony of values or a novel approach.

The Contraceptive Cafeteria

The concept of a "cafeteria of contraceptives" provoked one issue. Increasing the number of options in order to respect individual differences and give autonomy to individuals seems to conflict with the concern that some contraceptives may entail such risks to the whole body and/or to future generations that they ought never to be offered. In short, the conflict is between regulation and free choice. Perhaps we began to resolve this dilemma with one observation that so far the cafeteria has been male-supplied, and that its problems might vanish if the cafeteria were to be female-supplied. Suppose profit and objectification were replaced by our women-centered values in motivating the development of contraceptives?

DES Daughters

Another dilemma was how to determine policy toward our sisters who happen to be DES daughters. We want to identify them in order to help them, but we do not want to stigmatize them. Emotional scars in addition to physical scars are not needed. We want them to get good medical care, but not unnecessary surgery and frequent, painful physical examinations and tests. Do we turn them back into the system that created the problem? As we groped toward a solution, we wondered if lay women could learn to examine and counsel DES daughters, considering that the cytological changes in their vaginas are so difficult to interpret that only a few—if any—gynecologists are now competent to do so. Only when we determine to answer *all these questions at once* will new answers emerge.

Records and Registries

We raised questions about potential harmful sequellae from just about every procedure, drug, and technology we considered. For each of these procedures and drugs, what sorts of medical records should be kept and by whom? To whom should they be made available? National registries may allow us to uncover long-term effects many years from now. Future mothers-to-be may benefit from these data. But such registries may violate autonomy and respect for the individual. Keeping our own records to assume personal responsibility and/or allowing women-centered health groups to set up registries were two suggestions to start the dialog in reaching an equitable policy on this issue.

EFM When Needed

How can we provide the option of electronic fetal monitoring for the few women whose babies will truly benefit from it, without making it routine for all women? If we apply EFM only to "high risk" mothers, since socio-economic factors are involved, the labeling process becomes racist and classist. Labeling may also become a self-fulfilling prophecy. Can we shift the emphasis toward minimizing the factors that lead to high risk pregnancies in the first place, by ensuring adequate nutrition and whole-body medical attention?

In Vitro Fertilization

Is the development of in vitro fertilization in the best interests of women? On the one hand it appears to help our sisters who are infertile and wish to become biological mothers. But on the other hand it binds us more tightly to the male-controlled medical system and legitimates our assigned roles as child-bearers.

Reproductive Ability as a Measure of the Worth of a Woman

How can we reconcile our advocacy for drug-free, technology-free childbirth with our view that the worth of a woman ought not to be tied to her reproductive ability? I fear that we are going to demand that our sisters "perform" well during labor and childbirth. Will a woman feel guilty if she fails to have a drug-free delivery, chooses not to have her husband present, or leaves decision-making to others? If *choice* becomes the norm, how much personal responsibility *must* the mother take (for the well-being of the child), and how much *may* the mother delegate completely to professionals? Society currently blames the mother for a defective or stillborn child. My concern is that we women may do so also, as well as blaming her for an unjoyful or nonstoical childbirth performance.

This sparks a broader concern. We demonstrate quite well in this book that it will be better to remove the control of all aspects of human reproduction from the overwhelmingly male policymaking boards. But, we need to be careful that in so doing we do not just reconfirm the male typecasting of us as the sex partners of men, existing essentially to bear and rear their children. The women's movement has struggled long and hard to extend the roles of women. There is no easy solution to this dilemma. If women can acquire a larger share of control over (rather than simple assignment to) this formerly traditional female role, we shall then be able to guarantee, for the women who choose to reproduce, the freedom to add other dimensions to their lives and to guarantee that they do not sacrifice their physical, mental, and emotional health in order to reproduce.

A LOOK AHEAD

We have major suggestions to make about new approaches in determining policy for research directions and for application of research results in reproductive technologies. Clearly, old questions need to be reframed and old solutions need to be scrutinized for the actual values used in reaching decisions. To facilitate this rethinking there should be diversity in the membership of policymaking boards. A variety of viewpoints will make it more likely that the ramifications of a given policy be ascertained ahead of time.

Women ought to be included in every group where policy decisions are being made in the areas treated in these books. All levels of policymaking should include women: preparing budgets; reviewing research proposals; carrying out research; applying research; disseminating information; advertising; composing consent forms; composing patient package inserts; designing clinical trials; evaluating clinical trials; setting up FDA policy; compensating victims; and so on.

Furthermore, involved lay persons should be included in all such groups. "Involved lay persons" means active lay health workers, consumer advocates, and consumers at risk. Such consumers include those who in the future may be subjected to a given technology, as well as those who have had it used on them—both the disappointed victims and the enthusiastic advocates of that procedure. These lay persons should serve such roles as: community representatives on medical school admission committees, members of hospital policy review boards, monitors of HEW regulations, composers of patient package inserts, keepers of voluntary registries of drugs and procedures.

It is evident that the new debate has just begun. We have started to clear away the underbrush in breaking a new trail. There are many points of view, many issues to be examined, and many unresolved dilemmas. These volumes are the record of the gropings of one group toward a new synthesis. I have faith that there will be more struggles together toward the just, equitable, and woman-affirming policies we envision.

Ethics of Contraceptive Development and Deployment

Organized by

Michael Gross

Introduction

Michael Gross

In no way is reproduction experiential for men as it is for women who bear and rear children. Yet men essentially control the development and distribution of contraceptive methods, while women suffer their consequences. To dissolve this paradox of patriarchal society, those who bear the major burden of reproduction should determine how and when to control their fertility. How are women to win that power? Practical political questions are woven seamlessly into ethical considerations. With all the other inequalities that riddle American society—class, race, income, opportunity, education, access to health care, and so on—the problems of patriarchal control of contraception affect different groups of women with varying emphases.

The articles and discussions in this chapter document and explore the implications of the above perspective. Patriarchal authority and values prevail from the very outset of the modern period of public, popular contraceptive advocacy. Joyce Berkman notes that women practiced some form of birth control long before contraceptive agitation reached the political realm. When it did, in the 1930s, patriarchal political values molded advocacy of particular techniques. Indeed, technique itself was part of the ideology even of this early movement. It disparaged women's folk knowledge of abortifacients and lay abortionists, and condemned the nontechnological means of withdrawal and periodic abstinence, emphasizing instead the technology then available—diaphragm and pessary—and the power of male physicians to regulate their use. Then, as now, the middle class was induced to support contraception for immigrant and working class women because it offered an "effective means . . . to halt their own [middle class] racial demise." If anything, the emphasis on female reproductive autonomy waned. The movement gathered strength with its emphasis on smaller families for the sake of stable marriage and better mothering. Likewise, today it compromises female autonomy with a male-centered concept of "sexual freedom." After World War II contraceptive development and promotion—in the hands of the pharmaceutical industry, physicians, and the popular media—became even more fully entrenched in male-controlled political and economic institutions. Only in the new women's health movement does Berkman find "new questions and values about contraceptives.... A woman's well-being is the first priority," which includes not only safety and efficacy, but also "greater bodily pride, control, and freedom."

The current pattern of men doing research to control female fertility emerges dramatically from data presented by Belita Cowan. For example, in 1977, only six of eighty-two federally funded contraceptive development projects dealt solely with male contraception and one of those was for reversibility of contraceptive effects; only nine of fifty-five steroid hormone projects focused on the male. Research on contraceptives for women may ignore informed consent and even employ agents known to be harmful. Research on male methods shows drastically different priorities: all twelve of the projects on sterilization concerned men, and most of those had to do with safety—short- and long-term side effects of vasectomy. Describing the directions of contraceptive research, Carol Korenbrot shows that it is essentially manipulative or invasive. In order to develop methods that are patentable and profitable, much of the research involves neurohormones, prostaglandins, or antibodies. Or else it seeks physiological delivery systems that minimize the need for sustained medical follow-up to Third World women who are a major target of the population control movement. In contrast to user-centered questions of ease, comfort, and safety in application, the main biochemical/pharmaceutical problems concern delivery, efficacy, and adaptability to factory production.

For women the value of personal control of reproduction suggests locally acting barrier, or reliable ovulation detection, methods. Still, Linda Atkinson and Jacki Ans observe, barrier methods have risks: known (e.g., a higher risk of pregnancy from user or method failure), suspected (e.g., potentially harmful spermicides absorbed through vaginal mucosa), and unknown. Asserting the continuing need for "high technology," they judge that "inputs from contraceptive users are necessary to the development process." Korenbrot calls for a shift in funding priorities away from high technology. For instance, non-invasive methods can be improved not only by intensive technological development, but also by improved user education.

Women have increased their control over the processes of development and deployment in two examples from women's self-help: women-controlled research and group study of the ovulation method of birth control.

In Laura Punnett's description, research on menstrual extraction grew from the values of the women's self-help movement: cooperative, respectful treatment of one another's health needs. Conversely, the outstanding feature of patriarchal "objective" research is the treatment of women as objects—to be experimented upon, coerced, manipulated, and controlled. Instead of the legally-imposed adversarial system that demands minimally informed consent to protect women from scientists (and scientists from lawsuits), each subject in women-controlled research "formulates her own criteria for deciding whether she wishes to experiment on her own body, aware of the potential risks of the procedure." Indeed, the distinction between researcher and subject collapses since subjects are also investigators, and in a cooperative self-help context they retain control of the project. Patriarchal research assumes that all bodies are equal and that the first consideration is technical feasibility. Women, experiencing themselves as intact organisms, emphasize an appreciation of individual differences and seek methods that are, fundamentally, nontraumatic: "Women who have full control of the research would not perform an experimental procedure on themselves that they had reason to believe was unsafe." Side effects are not just "subjective" problems that interfere with the applicability of a method but, for women, are what one feels and how one's health is compromised. Research in the context of women's self-help is small in scale, integrated into the community, and oriented toward women's autonomy. Patriarchal research institutions are isolated from the community. Costly in their technical requirements and in their application of experimental agents to large numbers of often unwary subjects, they aim towards profitability. Ultimately, they foster the goals of racist population controllers.

Instead of deploying a universally generalizable formula or uniformly applicable agent, natural birth control, as shared in self-help groups at the Cambridge, Massachusetts, Women's Community Health Center, encourages women to appreciate their individual differences. Instead of a division between professional and patient, group process encourages woman-to-woman sharing. Instead of a fetishization of method that isolates contraceptive choice from the rest of a woman's experience, the groups explore a range of contextual issues concerning sexuality, relationships, and control. Although Church-supported promoters of the ovulation method teach it in the service of a patriarchal religious code, self-help groups "actively work against making assumptions about how women will use the information," and do not use the term "abstinence" to refer to forms of sexual activity other than phallic-centered penile/vaginal intercourse.

Still, neither the millions of dollars of advanced technological research nor the underfinanced efforts of community self-help groups have been able to meet the special difficulties faced by poor and Third World women. For each woman the choices and the known and potential risks may be overwhelming. Yet here paternalistic physicians intervene to remove choices and options when they are most badly needed. Poor women experience still more urgent desperation: at one extreme they undergo involuntary sterilization; at the other they may seek from a clinic drugs or devices with health risks but, in Byllye Avery's words, "... you look at the other side and say, 'What is life worth, anyway?'"

Complementary to the value of maximum freedom of choice is maximum diversity—of approaches, techniques, research contexts, and delivery systems. Yet here diversity does not mean more of the same approaches set according to patriarchal priorities. As illustrated by women-controlled health research and health care environments, full participation by women in the setting of research priorities and guidelines will change the very meaning of research contexts and delivery systems.

Historical Styles of Contraceptive Advocacy

Joyce Avrech Berkman

The May 25–June 7, 1979, issue of *New Women's Times* reported that the British Pill Victim Action group was planning to sue American drug companies for damages running into millions of dollars. The group had on file more than 300 cases alleging the pill to be responsible for incidences of brain hemorrhage, paralysis, and death. Alongside that item was another one about a trial opening in Sweden, the first of an expected 100 cases involving pill-induced deaths and injuries. The mounting evidence in the last decade about the dangers of the contraceptive pill, and the inadequate information furnished to users about hazards, have sparked a legal and political attack on irresponsible contraceptive advocacy, an attack of historically unprecedented proportions.

Earlier in this century birth control advocates, eager to establish the medical safety and effectiveness of the diaphragm or pessary, vigorously attacked the purveyors of unsafe, unreliable condoms and douches. They were confident that once doctors and government authorities approved contraceptive use, and once doctors were responsible for prescribing products, only safe and effective products would be marketed. Their confidence, women have learned with great pain, was ill-founded. The increasingly prevalent suspicion of authorized as well as unauthorized contraceptives marks a new chapter in the history of birth control.

Critical doubts about the motives and procedures of producers, dispensers, and promoters of contraceptives coincide with a far wider and unparalleled disillusionment with applied science in general and medical technology in particular. Ours is the pollution-conscious, post-thalidomide sensibility, far different from the wonder drug optimism of the 1950s. The accident at Three Mile Island, the subjection of Puerto Rican women to experimental Depo-Provera treatment, the coercive sterilization of welfare recipients, asbestos-induced cancer, DC-10 crashes—examples could be rattled off *ad nauseam*—are all of a piece and have gone far to shatter our trust in scientific and medical experts, a crisis in trust that is highly salutary, but at the same time terrifying.

The disenchantment with the medical safety and effectiveness of modern contraceptives converges with a sharpening perception of the failure of contraceptives to usher in the reproductive and sexual liberation touted by its advocates throughout this century. The much vaunted sexual autonomy has little reality for women subject to male decision-making, from lovemaking to job placement. Nor does it truly exist for countless minority and poor women whose personal and economic options are circumscribed by class and race. Nor do contraceptives assure reproductive and sexual freedom to the millions of adolescent women who were denied genuine sex education and are particularly vulnerable to social pressures to be "hip." We have learned over the past two decades that although contraception can help women exercise greater control over their lives, there are deeper, far-reaching social conditions that must be altered for that control to become meaningful for most women.

This disillusionment with scientific technology and contraceptives comes at the very time historians and demographers are challenging the belief that modern contraceptives are responsible for population decline in America and Europe. Studies in national fertility clearly demonstrate that the decision to limit family size long preceded the energetic contraceptive campaigns of the period between World War I and World War II—the interwar years. Examining demographic trends in 19th and 20th century America and England, scholars conclude that some form of birth control was commonplace in the 19th century not only in middle and upper class families, but also among the poor.[1] By 1900 the average family size in America and England had dropped from a little over seven per family in 1800 to a little over three. By the 1930s both countries had approached zero population growth.

The labeling of interwar campaigns for contraceptives as simply birth control movements is misleading. They were in fact campaigns for specific modes of contraception: the diaphragm (Margaret Sanger, English Neo-Malthusians) and the check pessary (Marie Stopes). From the late 1930s onwards, Sanger, joined by newcomers to the contraceptive movement, promoted the development of chemical means of extricating sex from procreation.

In propounding specific contraceptive technology, birth control advocates aimed not only to establish the virtues of the technique they championed, but also to discourage the use of alternative modes of contraception that statistics verified were effective. The array of contraceptive and birth control options included various syringes and douches, which were sold under the euphemism "feminine hygiene" or "marital hygiene"; rubber condoms, which enjoyed booming sales since the mid-19th century under the guise of prophylactics against disease; and, of course, abortion. The primary methods of birth control prior to the widespread use of diaphragms, however, were periodic abstinence and withdrawal (*coitus interruptus*). These nineteenth century practices had generally replaced infanticide and lactation as techniques of family limitation.

In opposing the various 19th century birth control methods, 20th century birth controllers challenged their efficacy and safety. Margaret Sanger, in her forward to Elizabeth Garrett's tract, "Birth Control's Business Baby," charges, "The adulteration of drugs and the traffic in quack nostrums is a scandal smelling to the heavens." She adds, "In a test of more than one hundred of these so-called 'contraceptives,' undertaken by our Birth Control Clinical Research Bureau in New York City, forty-five were discovered to be utterly unreliable."[2]

Abortion was a remedy taboo to almost all interwar contraceptive advocates. Eager to cloak their position in respectability they took pains to distinguish contraception from abortion. (Opponents of contraception commonly equated the two.) They formed a chorus bewailing the horrors of abortion, its hideous and fatal dimensions. Contraceptives were advanced as a preventative to the abortion nightmare.[3] Stella Browne, an active worker for socialist feminism in England, was unusual in endorsing both contraceptives and legal, safe abortions, founding the Abortion Law Reform Association in 1936.[4]

For generations working class women had turned to abortion as the cheapest, easiest form of birth control, one that, unlike sheaths, abstinence, and withdrawal, did not require male compliance. Sheila Rowbotham, in her historical analysis of the English experience,[4] observes: "Against the stereotype of the sinister quack, luring women to have unwanted abortions for large sums of money, the picture which emerges from the Interdepartmental Committee on Abortion in 1938 is of women who aborted themselves or relied on someone known and trusted within the community. Drugs were obtained from herbalists, chemists or stalls in market places. Women heard of them by word of mouth or advertisements or booklets... Women passed enema syringes round the village or about the factory. This hidden history of control over reproduction could well have been transmitted from generation to generation."[5] Linda Gordon's study of the 19th century American abortion practices comes forth with similar revelations.[6]

Interwar contraceptive advocates were hardly sympathetic to the existence of a traditional female subculture. Word of mouth remedies were deemed fatal gossip; irregular folk medicine was attacked as reactionary and mortally dangerous. The contraceptive campaigners looked to medical professionals to rescue women from peddlers profiteering in pseudocontraceptives and female folk practices; thereby they hoped, as well, to secure medical prestige and authority to the birth control movement.[7]

With studies of contraceptive behavior in interwar England and the United States disclosing that periodic abstinence and withdrawal were, even in the 1930s, the most widely adopted birth control methods,[8] contraceptive advocates focused intensively on the undesirability of those options. In order to challenge long-standing reproductive customs, birthcontrollers looked to new authorities, the progressive social theorists, sexologists, and doctors of the early 20th century. These authorities condemned periodic abstinence and withdrawal as physically and psychologically injurious, as thwarting natural bodily energies, as hangovers of Mrs. Grundy.[9]

Their attack on periodic abstinence assumed that all sex is coital sex. Because couples were not engaging in intercourse is no reason to believe that they were not experiencing sexual excitement and orgasm. Although much 19th century prescriptive literature condemned masturbation, mutual petting among married couples was not deemed masturbatory. Even if it were, we have evidence that actual human erotic behavior often defied or circumvented prescriptive literature,[10] perhaps partly because most people were not familiar with the literature.

The assumption that without coital orgasm women are frustrated rests on questionable premises regarding the normal nature and frequency of sexual activity. Birth control advocates, desperate for support from professional theorists, swallowed the phallic-centered logic of Freud's followers. Normal sex was accepted to be heterosexual coitus accompanied by vaginal orgasm, occuring roughly twice a week. Recent research by Masters and Johnson, and by Hite, questions whether coital orgasm is as keenly gratifying to women as noncoital sexual play. Elizabeth Janeway, Sheila Rowbotham, and others underscore the relativity of human sexual need in accordance with each individual's temperament, work satisfaction, quality of personal relationships, channels for effective release of anger, other sources of ego gratification, and susceptibility to media and advertising's sexual sell.[11]

Periodic abstinence as an alternative to contraceptive devices does require male cooperation and can be less reliable than the diaphragm. But the sweeping 20th century assault on periodic abstinence belies a profoundly masculine conception of ideal sexual expression, an ideal women have to a large extent internalized. Numerous sources though there may be for the acculturated focus on male penetration needs, it is clear that if men felt no loss in virility through mutual manual orgasm then various forms of periodic abstinence might well be a more popular option.

Withdrawal need not preclude orgasm, either, though that is the premise rampant in birth control literature.[12] Although advocates attacked withdrawal as ineffective and unreliable, it did work for many, many families. A more persuasive argument against withdrawal was that it placed women at the mercy of their male partner's control. Both Sanger and Stopes stressed this point strenuously and for the same reason opposed the condom. However, in placing exclusive reproductive responsibility on the women's shoulders, they perpetuated the double standard of sexual morality whereby women must control while men can be irresponsible and carefree. Moreover, they failed to realize that the diaphragm simply shifted female dependency from her male partner onto the male physician who prescribed the device.

Although originally upholding as primary the reproductive self-determination of women, Sanger, like most social activists in America and England, recognized that abstract theories of right and justice are not as persuasive to large numbers of people as is more practical reasoning: contraception not as a fundamental right, but rather as a means to other ends. Reproductive self-determination could be compatible with a woman freely choosing a family of ten children. This was far from the minds of contraceptive proponents, who defined birth control strictly as family limitation. Just as female suffrage triumphed when set adrift from its radical, idealistic moorings, so too with contraceptives.

The practical advantages of small families are, of course, relative to social and personal circumstances. Even a feminist might decide that a large family was compatible with her life goals if she lived in a society with humane childcare services of high quality, where extensive women's health clinics were supported, where shared parenting with her mate and friends was routine, where she was not penalized for maternity leaves, where economic insecurity did not haunt each birth, and where she did not depend on male economic protection. Most birth controllers rarely considered these dimensions of genuine reproductive choice, and, instead, pragmatically campaigned within the parameters of given social and economic institutions.

By and large, feminist ambitions did not figure prominently in birth control arguments between 1920 and 1970. Stella Browne was exceptional in her ardent interwar insistence that "our bodies are our own."[13] In campaigning for birth control from the 19th century to the present decade, contraceptive advocates made every effort to remove what might be construed as selfish arguments for reproductive freedom. Contraceptives were advanced as a means to better motherhood. Healthier women would breed and raise healthier children; mothers who could space their births would not be harassed by the demands of many youngsters, would be calmer, more attentive parents, more capable of training the moral character of each child.[14]

Contraceptive advocates promoted the diaphragm and, later, the pill also, as ways to cement the marriage bond, again advising women to adopt a technique not for their own "selfish" ends, but for the sake of their marriage. A principal motivation for Robert Latou Dickinson's decision as President of the American Gynecological Society to ally the medical profession with contraceptive use was his belief that it would stem the growing divorce rate. Similarly, a primary explanation for the interwar conversion of various Protestant denominations to approval of contraceptives was the belief of church leaders that sexual adjustment and family limitation would stabilize the nuclear family and arrest the alarming increase in infidelity and divorce.[15]

Many of the leading turn-of-the-century advocates of contraceptive birth control were inspired by a vision of heterosexual intimacy, a vision of ideal love and marriage starkly at odds with the brutal realities of many marriages. Their vision of intimacy involved much more than sheer physical compatibility. Often waxing rhapsodic, these pioneering 19th century writers on sexuality and marriage, such as Edward Carpenter, Havelock Ellis, and Olive Schreiner, glorified a heterosexual communion that profoundly mingled spiritual and physical experience. Margaret Sanger and Marie Stopes shared this vision.

But as the twentieth century advanced, this ideal of total, ecstatic union was reduced to mutual, hopefully simultaneous, orgasm. The contraceptive advocates of the mid-twentieth century were harnessed to a sexual revolution dislodged from the sexual idealism of a number of its nineteenth century forerunners.[16] Functioning in a pervasively secular, materialistic, and pleasure-oriented society, these proponents marketed their wares in terms of erotic intimacy as an end in itself and as a social panacea. The equation of the goals of contraception with the various advantages of small families, the desirability of stable marriages, and the simplistic definition of heterosexual intimacy all testify to the shrinking importance advocates after World War I placed on female reproductive autonomy.

Scholars debate the wisdom of Sanger's shift from a socially visionary to a sheerly practical campaign for contraceptives, and challenge her decision to court the support of professional and social elites. For example Elizabeth Fee and Michael Wallace contend[17] that Sanger's expedient politics were not genuinely effective and had damaging long run effects, neither guaranteeing quality controls nor providing easy, inexpensive access to contraceptives. They propose as a possible alternative strategy, the mobilizing of masses of women to pressure the government and establish clinics.

Mass mobilization, however, assumes the presence of a sufficient number of feminists and socialists prepared to facilitate effective organization. Fee and Wallace do not appreciate how feeble both movements had become in interwar America. But even in interwar England, where feminism and socialism were far healthier, the extensive grass-roots campaigns to gain Labour Party endorsement for contraceptives involved a long, strenuous, uphill struggle. Nor did these British socialist and feminist-inspired campaigns assure an alliance of the sexual revolution to social transformations indispensable for female self-determination. In short, if, even in England where the circumstances were so much more favorable for a genuinely democratic and feminist birth control movement, one did not fully materialize, I cannot share Fee and Wallace's optimism about the possibility of preserving in interwar America the pre-war radical social vision of contraceptive advocates.

In the late '30s with the winning of public support and court approval in the United States for the distribution of information about contraceptives, contraceptive advocacy passed from the hands of birth control organizations with their daring and pugnacious leaders to profit-hungry pharmaceutical companies, government and social service agencies, physicians, and sex therapists. After World War II, a proliferation of periodical items, advertisements, television programs, and so on readily informed the public as to the latest "advances" in contraceptive technology. In 1957 and 1958, *Fortune, Reader's Digest, Time, Newsweek, Scientific Digest, Coronet, Mademoiselle,* etc. featured articles favorable to the pill. During the years 1963–1965, a similar media blitz accompanied the release of the IUD.

Simultaneously, drug companies distributed to physicians free samples of the latest contraceptive, and bought national circulation for colorful, catchy advertisements that never mentioned the physical side effects and risks. The ads stressed effectiveness, reliability, safety, ease, and sexual spontaneity. Doctors, eager to appear up-to-date, but too busy to study the medical literature, distributed the latest product to their female clients with reckless enthusiasm.[18]

Gena Corea, in a scorching, highly documented exposé, reports that the AMA even opposed the inclusion by pharmaceutical companies, in their contraceptive packages, of information on the risks of the pill, lest they alarm patients unnecessarily and intrude on the patient–physician relationship. Corea speculates that the unspoken AMA motive was very likely fear of malpractice suits. So effectively did organized medicine, combined with population control groups and drug companies, push for less complete information on hazards that the FDA cut its insert for packages of pills from 600 to 130 words, noting only one serious complication—blood clotting.[19] Apparently, unethical advocacy of contraceptives still characterizes the distribution of contraceptives, as surely as it did during the interwar years.

What are the trends in contraceptive advocacy today? Do they reflect the emergence of a revitalized women's movement?

On the one hand, continuities with past advocacy practices are evident and disturbing. According to National Fertility Study reports, contraceptive sterilization has surpassed the pill in popularity among poor and middle class women,[20] and yet most women, especially poor women, are not told about the risks of tubal ligations and laparoscopies, or given ample opportunity to weigh their long-term personal consequences.[21] While women continue to serve as guinea pigs for questionable biomedical experimentation in contraceptives, research into male contraceptives proceeds warily and with far fewer advocates. When, for example, male prisoners became ill from combining alcohol consumption with the use of amebicide, the experimental contraceptive was quickly withdrawn.[22]

Leafing through the June 1979 issue of *MS* magazine I was struck by two advertisements on contraceptives. One ad features the suppository Semicid. No comment is offered as to the possible side effects of nonoxynol-9 "the spermicidal ingredient in products doctors recommend most." The only caution is the blithe "use as directed."[23] The other ad features Conceptrol Shields, declaring in bold print across the midsection of a poised, urban, casually "liberated" Ivy-league male, "more and more doctors are recommending his birth control to her."[24] Condoms are very much back in style, and this ad, like the ads for other contraceptives, invokes the authority of doctors advising women to switch to this method. In the corner of the ad is a

50¢ discount coupon for Conceptrol Shields with an image of male–female interaction of the sort that Erving Goffman in his book *Gender Advertisements* labels "ritualized subordination".

Fortunately there are strenuous counterforces to traditional forms of contraceptive advocacy. Rather than cite the many excellent books, pamphlets, and periodical articles, or the many new women's health groups expressive of the vitality and wide ranging concerns of the feminist renaissance, I want to conclude by focusing on a particular essay that appeared in the April 1977 issue of *Sparerib,* the leading radical feminist and socialist–feminist periodical in England.[25] The article is titled, "If the cap fits..." and consists of interviews with a variety of women about the diaphragm. The article is preceded by a full-page, illustrated, and detailed explanation of the proper use of the diaphragm. Unlike interwar advocacy, the diaphragm here is not presented as an alternative to abortion; rather, the article concludes, "If we are to use the diaphragm, and it seems many of us *must,* we have to have free, easily obtainable abortion on demand." Nor is the "cap" hailed as part of a mystique of heterosexual erotic ecstasy; the same article promotes lesbianism as a valid and joyful alternative. Nor does the article suggest that clinics and physicians are flawless experts; it cites a few disturbing stories of women's experiences in clinics where they were misinformed about diaphragm use. Moreover, the socialist–feminist persuasion of the periodical guarantees that readers do not harbor the naive notion that contraceptives augur genuine reproductive autonomy. What is explored in a complex fashion are the psychological and feminist issues surrounding diaphragm usage.

Some women interviewed spoke of their difficulty in simply touching their genitals, an act the pill does not require. For other women, the diaphragm enhanced their sense of owning their own body: the act of inserting the diaphragm furnishing a sense of self-assertion. Although many women complained that the diaphragm inhibited their sexual spontaneity, aroused sexual uncertainty, depended on initiative they were loathe to exert, and heightened an unpleasant sense of preparing to meet male needs, other women preferred the premeditation with regard to coitus. "For Jo, the check on spontaneity isn't a problem. Comparing the pill and diaphragm she found the pill 'coercive.' 'It was developed to enable women to be sexual at *any* time, but to me it was like a statement that I had to be sexual at *all* times. The pill seemed less to do with not getting pregnant than with being sexually available'." For Margaret "'It means I have to make a conscious decision as to whether or not I want to make love. It makes me feel I control my sexuality'... And Alice, looking back to her marriage, said the diaphragm made her confront the fact that she no longer enjoyed sex with her husband, "When you're on the pill, it's easier to have sex than not.'"

What emerges from such articles as this one in *Sparerib* are historically new questions and values about contraceptives that transform the context for advocacy. A woman's well-being is the first priority. This requires not only safe and effective contraceptive techniques, but as well methods that promote the feminist growth of women toward greater bodily pride, control, and freedom. Questions of erotic roles, such as who assumes initiative, and issues of personal assertiveness and independence become central. Maybe the historical style of contraceptive advocacy in the 1980s will be dominated by women in the interests of an authentic reproductive and sexual freedom for women of all social classes and races.

Ethical Problems in Government-Funded Contraceptive Research

Belita Cowan

Because the federal government is a major source of funding for contraceptive development, it is useful for women to analyze the government's priorities. Unlike private agency research or drug company research, American women are providing direct support for contraceptive development through our tax dollars.

The National Women's Health Network undertook a study of government-funded contraceptive research projects as the basis for our testimony before the House Select Committee on Population and the US Senate HEW Labor Appropriations Subcommittee hearings in 1978. What we discovered is that the developers of contraceptives for women, and the federal officials who approve them for marketing, have apparently changed the definition of the word "safe." Whereas Webster's dictionary says that "safe" means "free from harm," the drug companies, our doctors, and federal regulatory agencies tell us that "safe" really means that "the hazards will likely be outweighed by the benefits."

I'm reminded of the birth control education efforts of a small health group in Fayetteville, Arkansas—the Mari Spehar Health Collective. Mari Spehar was a young farm woman who, after seeing several different doctors for abdominal pain over the course of many months, died, finally, in a hospital, surrounded by her close friends, of massive infection caused by a Dalkon Shield IUD that had perforated her uterus. The doctors had assured her that the pains would go away, since they could not locate the IUD by X-ray or physical exam, and assumed that it had been expelled. The coroner's report concluded otherwise. The Mari Spehar Health Collective was formed for the sole purpose of educating women to the hazards of cetain types of birth control. They had learned, through this tragedy, the needless death of a dear friend, that today's contraceptive technology—with its emphasis on hormones, devices, implants, and injectables—has, in the ultimate sense, betrayed us.

Federal population research activities described in the *Inventory and Analysis of Federal Population Research*[1] are coordinated by an Interagency Committee on Population Research, which reports to the HEW Deputy Assistant Secretary for Population Affairs (Irvin Cushner) and is chaired by the director of NICHD's Center for Population Research (Philip Corfman). Also on the Committee is R. T. Ravenholt, ex-director of the Office of Population, US Agency for International Development (AID). Until recently, the Interagency Committee consisted of 17 white, middle-aged males. Three years ago a token female was added, and today only 5 of 29 committee members are women. Consequently, one of the most critical areas of ethical concern for women in the field of contraceptive development is that the scientists, researchers, developers, physicians, drug company executives, and vendors of contraceptives will never have to subject themselves to the very pills, devices, implants, and injections they are promoting.

Indeed, the decisions concerning which contraceptive technologies are given priority reflect the values (and fears) of men. This is evident from the *Inventory* itself. According to the *Inventory,* "population research" has two major areas:

—Male and female fertility and, in the female, fertilization, zygote transport, preimplantation, and implantation.
—Contraceptive development, including new steroids and hormone drugs for women, new intrauterine devices, and sterilization techniques.

Within HEW, NICHD has the largest budget for contraceptive research because of its Center for Population Research, which accounted for over 50% of the $91.5 million spent in fiscal '77, and $12 million in fiscal '78. Almost 40% of all government funds spent on contraceptive research were directed toward research in reproductive endocrinology in the areas of hormone regulation, ovulation, egg transport, uterine milieu, and uterine implantation. Not a single dollar is shown as spent on the barrier methods of birth control (see Fig. 1). Close analysis of the research areas of the individual grants and contracts, however, indicates that the HEW categories have been artificially broken down to give the erroneous impression that funding for the categories of male fertility and female fertility are approximately equal. They are not, because most of the research in the categories "reproductive endocrinology" and "zygote transport/preimplantation development/implantation" also pertains to female fertility.

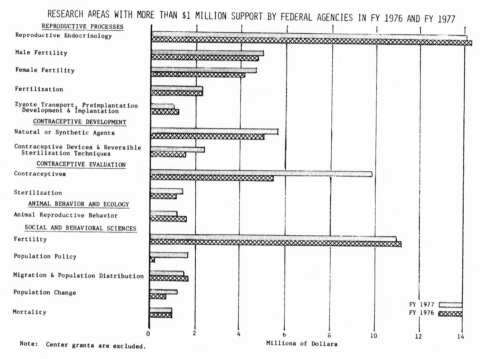

FIG. 1

In reviewing each project, the Network found that, of the 82 projects in the "Contraceptive Development" section totaling $14.6 million, only six dealt solely with male contraception. Of these, five were for the development of an agent to suppress production of sperm, whereas one was for the development of a hormone to reverse the suppression. In the "Steroid Hormones" section of Reproductive Endocrinology, only nine out of 55 projects focused on the male (human or animal), and in the "General or Multiple Section" of Reproductive Endocrinology, the only study that included males also included females.

Although the number of studies listed under the categories "Male Fertility" and "Female Fertility" was approximately equal (80 and 83, respectively), it appears that the "Male Fertility" category may have been expanded with the inclusion of studies that really belonged in the "Social and Behavioral Sciences" category. The "sex equity" balance in research conveyed by the *Inventory* is highly misleading. For example, there are three studies on the effects of alcohol on male sexual performance. No comparable studies on the effects of alcohol in female sexual behavior were undertaken, although the National Women's

Health Network did find two projects funded in 1977 that looked at the effect of alcohol on menstruation. In the category "Human Infertility" there were only six projects in total. Of these, two were geared to the male only—"Treatment of Physiological Impotency" and "Androgen Metabolism in Massive Obesity." There were no projects geared solely to the female, nor were there studies on female sexual functioning and infertility.

With regard to female contraceptives, HEW admits that "the safety of current contraceptive drugs for female fertility regulation has been seriously questioned..." But HEW's answer appears to be that, "Research should be directed toward seeking further improvements in intrauterine devices." The data indicate that it may be decades before American men have more than the condom in the contraceptive repertoire. Lack of government support for male contraceptive development is a major stumbling block. The little interest there is in male contraceptives, moreover, shows a heavy emphasis on *safety*. In fact, "safety" appears to be more important than efficacy; hence the preoccupation with animal studies.

Therefore in all the categories of government research shown in Fig. 1, the National Women's Health Newtork found that the *female* is overwhelmingly the "object of study" in the development of experimental drugs and devices. Furthermore, not once was there mention of the diaphragm, jelly, cream, foam, cervical cap, or vaginal sponge as a barrier method of birth control for women. The condom— one of the safest and least expensive contraceptives available—with its added benefit of preventing venereal disease, is totally ignored by HEW. It seems that the government's equation is as follows: $CD = W(D_r + D_e)$.

Contraceptive Development $=$ Drugs for Women $+$
Devices for Women

The *Inventory* states, "The major emphasis of studies of intrauterine devices has been on the more common minor (sic) adverse effects. Data is required comparing major health risks associated with various devices that are currently in use."

What HEW fails to acknowledge is that American women assume that data on major health hazards have been collected *prior* to the release of a new IUD. Even with the deaths associated with the Dalkon Shield and the unnecessary hysterectomies resulting from the Majzlin spring IUD, the tendency of the American public is to believe that if the government approves a pill or device then it must be safe. The *Inventory* correctly admits the large gaps in knowledge about the safety of contraceptive pills and devices for women. This admission, however, does not seem to deter HEW from funding the development of even more drugs and devices that have not been adequately tested for safety in women.

In its review of the 979 grants and contracts, the National Women's Health Network found several projects whose purpose was to study the incidence and history of genital tract abnormalities and cancer in the offspring of mothers who were given diethylstilbestrol (DES) and other estrogens in pregnancy. Another five projects attempted to determine a dose relationship between DES and carcinogenicity.[2] At the same time that HEW was awarding grants and contracts to study the cancers caused by DES and other estrogens, HEW also was giving contracts to Planned Parenthood League (New Haven, Conn.), Baylor Medical School (Houston), Magee Women's Hospital (Pittsburgh), and the University of Florida (Gainesville) for experiments using various estrogens as a "morning-after pill" (postcoital contraceptive) with human subjects. Of the four projects (totaling $532,615), at least one was conducted primarily on college students through their student health center. The estrogens used were ethinyl estradiol and Premarin (a brand name estrogen manufactured by Ayerst Labs). Yet the FDA has never approved the use of estrogens as a "morning-after pill." Ironically, Baylor Medical School was holding two of HEW's contracts on DES-and-cancer *at the same time* as it was dispensing the "morning-after pill" under a third HEW contract.

It is unclear whether the women in these contraceptive experiments were aware that they were taking a drug that FDA had never approved for use as a contraceptive. Previous "morning-after pill" studies on college students at the University of Michigan, the University of Pennsylvania, and Yale University reported failures to prevent pregnancy and inability to follow up all subjects in the experiments.

In 1975, I presented the results of a survey research project I directed on the use of DES as a "morning-after" pill with students at the University of Michigan (1968–1974). I testified before Senator Edward Kennedy's Subcommittee about an unethical experiment where 1000 women students were given DES, many of whom were unaware that they were participating in an experiment. I had interviewed 65 of those women (see Table 1). Half stated that they were unaware they were part of a contraceptive drug experiment. Two-thirds stated that they received no followup.[3]

It appears that scientists, federal officials, doctors, and the drug

Table 1
Survey of 65 Women Who Took the Morning-After Pill at The
University of Michigan Student Health Service 1968–1974

How many times did you take DES?	Once	Twice	3 times	More
	70.8%	20.0%	7.7%	1.5%
Are you a DES daughter?	Yes	No	Don't know	
	6.2%	75.4%	18.4%	
Did the doctor take a personal and family medical history?	Yes	No	On file[a]	
	26.2%	44.6%	29.2%	
Were you given a pelvic and breast exam?	Yes	No	Only pelvic exam	
	20.0%	46.2%	33.8%	
Were you told you were taking an experimental drug?	Yes	No	Not sure	
	43.0%	41.5%	15.5%	
Did you take all 10 pills?	Yes (all)	Not all	Uncertain	
	75.4%	4.6%	24.0%	
Did you experience nausea?	Yes	No		
	81.5%	18.5%		
Did you experience vomiting?	Yes	No		
	33.8%	66.2%		
Was there a followup to see if you had a period?	Yes	No	Uncertain	
	26.2%	61.5%	12.3%	
Would you take the morning-after pill today if you were in the same situation?	Yes	No	Uncertain	
	7.7%	64.6%	27.7%	

[a]Personal, but not family, medical history was already on file.

companies, besides changing the definition of "safe," have also
changed the definition of "ethical." We are accustomed to thinking
that "ethical" refers to high moral standards of behavior or
professional conduct. We're finding, in the field of contraceptive

research at any rate, that "ethical" seems to mean "whatever a researcher can get away with." In the HEW publication "Women and Their Health: Research Implications for a New Era," male experts in the field of contraception say that about "ethics" in a section entitled "The Ethics of Pregnancy" (which describes a double-blind birth control experiment on unsuspecting people):

> By now everyone is familiar with the San Antonio study of the side effects of birth control pills in which 11 poor, mostly Mexican–American women became pregnant while taking a placebo. The ethics of that study are not faulty since the placebo-taking women were given a back-up contraceptive (which some failed to use effectively). Moreover, it could be argued that no net harm was done since in all probability many more would have become pregnant had it not been for the study. Under the principle of "less severity," it might seem that none of the women was worse off than if she had not been a participant, and many were probably better off... And, in fact, some of the women, believing themselves protected against pregnancy, might have increased their level of sexual activity...[4]

Several of the women on placebos who got pregnant sued the investigator—Joseph Goldzieher—for child support. They lost.

A 1974 article by three doctors from Downstate Medical Center (New York) describes a study of the long-term effects of medroxyprogesterone acetate (Depo-Provera) on the adrenal glands of ten women who came to the medical center seeking birth control. The women received injections every 90 days for a year.[5] The study illustrates violations of two different ethical standards: (1) harm by design; (2) lack of informed consent. The authors cited animal studies in 1961, 1964, and 1969 that showed Depo-Provera to be "a potent suppressor of adrenal function" that "when administered for a two-week period, results in adrenal atrophy."[6] In normal practice, doctors avoid suppression of the adrenals. This experiment "proved" what everyone already knew. What gives the medical community the right to legitimize this "protocol?" The ethics of conducting such experiments on women remains a critical question apparently ignored by male policymakers.

By analyzing the *Inventory and Analysis of Federal Population Research,* the National Women's Health Network has found that significant numbers of American women are subjects, perhaps unknowingly, in contraceptive research studies. HEW needs to monitor closely its grantees and contractors for proof of informed consent among women who participate in the testing of contraceptives. Women incarcerated in prisons or mental institutions may be especially vulnerable to abuse. HEW has seen in the last decade increasing evidence of sterilization abuse among women, primarily minority and poor women. The spectre of abuse in contraceptive experiments looms large. It seems clear that the only "ethical" answer is for women to make the policies and to control the research spending for female contraceptive development. What the Women's Health Movement has learned over the last decade is that it is we who must force the male scientists to examine their unethical conduct. But often this occurs only after a tragedy—for the men will not listen to us each step along the way. We continue to be denied our rightful entitlement to determine these questions for ourselves.

I'd like to conclude by saying that, although I'm delighted to be here to discuss these issues with you, I hold no illusions that academic conferences (where some of us have scholarly exchanges about "ethics") can change anything. There is no reason to believe that unethical contraceptive experiments on women will cease once the proceedings of this conference are published. Those of us fighting on the front lines for women's health rights know that neither the scientists, academics, researchers, doctors, drug companies, nor government officials are going to change unless we force them to. In the past decade, we have succeeded in a few instances:

DES. The first published report in the media on DES-related cancers in female offspring was in 1972 in the feminist newspaper *her-self*. Since then, DES Action groups—education and support groups—have been formed for women, by women, to alert the public to the need for screening and followup, and to pressure for DES legislation (now in New York State, Oregon, Maine, and Michigan; pending in Illinois, Maryland, and California.)

The Pill. The publication of Barbara Seaman's book *The Doctor's Case Against the Pill* prompted Senator Gaylord Nelson to hold hearings on the pill's safety. All the witnesses were men. A group of women health activists disrupted the hearings to demand patient warning labeling for the oral contraceptive—a shockingly radical demand in 1970.

Cervical Cap. Although drug companies in the US are not testing the cap because of its potentially low profit margin, feminist women's health centers and clinics have begun to test the cap in clinical trials where the subjects themselves design and control the studies.[7]

Depo-Provera. A national Stop Depo-Provera campaign initiated by the National Women's Health Network has thus far helped to keep FDA from approving the drug. The Network recently established a national Depo-Provera Registry to assist Depo-Provera victims. [8,9]

Treatment of Rape Victims. A network of rape crisis centers in the nation's largest cities has forced local hospitals to follow standard treatment protocols; patient advocates at these centers counsel against the use of DES for rape victims.

Sterilization Abuse. A coalition of minority women's groups, and health and civil rights groups, pressured HEW for strict regulations to curb coerced sterilizations among Medicaid recipients.

Abortion. Although the Supreme Court ruled that abortion was not "illegal," it did not guarantee a woman's right to choose this option. We are only now beginning to fight for this choice as a health right.

Menopausal Estrogens. A public interest law group (representing the Network and three other consumer groups) successfully argued in federal district court that FDA had the regulatory authority to require patient labeling for menopausal estrogen replacement therapy and other estrogen drugs.

Elective Induction of Labor. Network pressure on FDA resulted in FDA's withdrawal of approval of labor-inducing oxytocic drugs (Pitocin) for the practice of electively-inducing labor in pregnant women.

All of these changes were initiated by women.

Through the years, we have developed a good sense of what is, and what is not, "ethical" in the contraceptive development arena. It is "unethical" to expect or require a healthy person to risk her life or her health for the purpose of remaining not pregnant.

However, I feel that, ultimately, the question of contraceptive research technology is not a question of ethics, but more a question of "control," for when women have control over reproductive choices as well as reproductive technology, medical "ethics" will no longer be an academic issue to be debated in the nation's medical schools; rather, it will become a focus for determining how best to serve women's health and reproductive needs. We have come to learn, in a very painful way, that men think of us as statistics, that their risk/benefit ratios often ignore our health needs and our concern for safety as well as efficacy. To the male scientists working on contraceptive development, I say, try explaining your "ethics" to a 23-year old who has been paralyzed by a pill-related stroke—try talking about the so-called "population explosion" to a middle-aged couple whose only child, a 20-year-old college student, is sterile because of an IUD infection. When it happens to *you,* the incidence is 100%. To the extent that birth control is still primarily the responsibility of women, and that women are the ones who bear the major consequences of childbirth, as well as the risks and serious complications of contraception, women should have the major voice in determining which contraceptive research priorities best meet our needs.

Value Conflicts in Biomedical Research into Future Contraceptives

Carol C. Korenbrot

Techniques for contraception are not the invention of recent biomedical research. Contraception has been sought and used by people for ages, and for a long time has been primarily an issue of politics, and not of technology.[1] However, the politics of contraception changed dramatically with the shift in technological base from products developed by lay men and women (condoms, diaphragms, and pessaries) to products emerging from biomedical laboratories, from medical surgery, and from the drug industry (the "Pill," IUDs, and laparoscopic tubal ligations). In fact, what is new about contraception in the last thirty years is the promotion of the development of new biomedical contraceptives by scientists and physicians, national governments, private groups concerned with the rate of population growth, and the drug industry. Because of this, the research and development of new contraceptives has become entwined in politics, both national and international. Furthermore, in the last ten years, these politics of contraceptive research have changed dramatically, largely out of the growing awareness of the question of safety of biomedical technological contraceptives. What has been realized is that there are two critical considerations in the evaluation of safety: one is "risk" and the other is "safety." Although "risk" can be restricted to the likelihood of the occurrence of an adverse effect, "safety" is the judgment of the acceptability of risks.[2] Risks may be measured largely by scientific techniques and by scientists, but judgments of the acceptability of those risks are social decisions made by individuals or groups.

In the 1950s and 1960s, the safety of biomedical technological development was assessed by those who, it was believed, could best "understand" the risks, that is, by scientists and physicians. The limitations of the abilities of scientists and physicians evaluating risks

47

to understand safety became painfully obvious with events surrounding the Pill. As information grew about the risks associated with the use of the Pill, it became clearer to women that scientists and physicians who determine risks are not selectively endowed with abilities to evaluate safety. The acceptability of risks is a function of the desirability of benefits, and that is a matter of judgment and not of scientific expertise. To make such a decision involves the application of values to facts. Scientists and physicians enter realms of judgment as all other people, shrouded in their personal values.[3] The change in the politics of contraception in the last ten years reflects an underlying change in the values to be applied to decisions on the safety of new contraceptive techniques.

On the one hand are advocates interested in decreasing population growth, who desire to increase research and development funds for the drug industry to develop more biomedical drugs and devices, and faster. The aim is to provide new contraceptives that are highly effective and easily distributed, contraceptives that are widely accepted and used because of their convenience. On the other hand, advocates of the women's and consumer's health movements desire to increase research and development funds specifically to develop methods that represent a lower health risk, even though they may be less effective, less easily mass-distributed, and less convenient to use.

In his recent book, Djerassi[4] articulately expresses many of the concerns of the population groups and drug industry. The FDA regulations for toxicological testing and the greater difficulties in obtaining informed consent from research subjects are described as having slowed down the process of developing new contraceptives and as having at the same time increased the price. The process of research and development of contraceptive drugs that took four to five years in the case of oral contraceptives in 1955, now takes ten to twenty years for any of the contraceptives currently being researched. The process has become costly in money as well. If the FDA approves the drug or device, the chances of the drug companies reaping sufficient profits before the patent expires are small. Therefore it is argued by contraceptive advocates in the drug industry and population groups that the government ought to provide further incentives if there are to be new contraceptives, either by reducing regulations on testing, or by providing economic subsidies to research and development, or both.

The women's health movement is not opposed to development of contraceptive drugs and devices as long as the health risks associated with their use are continuously investigated and publicized. But they advocate that, at the same time, more money should be available to develop programs to increase the effectiveness of the safer nonpharmaceutical methods.[5] They are particularly interested in user education to attempt to enhance effectiveness of barrier methods. Further, they advocate that human support systems (like self-help groups) should be financed to develop the human dimensions of contraception along with the use of technological approaches.

The clash of these two groups of contraceptive research advocates is largely over which is more important: the social welfare from an anticipated decrease in population growth, or the social welfare from an increased reproductive control of women and men over their own bodies. Thus, which of the technologies are to be favored in research reflects the differing values of the two groups in their judgments of the acceptability of risks of contraception. I shall describe the clash in values surrounding the current development of three potential contraceptives: prostaglandins, the collagen sponge, and gossypol.

Prostaglandins, like the steroids estradiol and progesterone, are a group of physiological compounds that can be synthesized and chemically modified to make synthetic compounds. Such a synthetic modified prostaglandin, F_2-alpha, developed by a United States drug company, is currently undergoing clinical trials in Sweden to determine whether it is effective and safe enough for women less than 50 days pregnant to be used at home as an abortifacient.[6]

Such a product offers a large degree of "user control" of application, although the drug itself would presumably be medically prescribed. To those interested in population problems, user control is important because it does not require medical personnel, who are sorely lacking in many developing countries. This increases the likelihood of its wide distribution. To the women's health movement, user control is valued because the woman herself is administering the agent that affects her body. It represents her decision, her involvement, and her taking charge of herself. It avoids medicalization of her abortion, which would be a transfer of much of the control to a system she cannot control.

The safety of prostaglandin use for early abortion is considered differently by the two groups. Although the patients in the clinical trials who tested prostaglandins were admitted to the hospital and stayed eight hours, to allow observation of side effects and start of bleeding, and to monitor the use of the pain killers and drugs to reduce vomiting and diarrhea, this procedure is intended for eventual home use. A woman having a pregnancy determined to be of sufficiently short duration could receive prescriptions for the vaginal suppository prostaglandin, for pain killers, and for drugs to counteract vomiting and diarrhea, and could administer the drugs to herself and wait for the expulsion of the uterine contents. The acute side effects apparently have not yet been reported in the literature. Vaginal bleeding normally follows the procedure and continues for several days. Risks in this procedure at the high dose level were estimated at: less than a 1% risk of continued pregnancy, about a 5–6% chance of an incomplete abortion (which can require dilatation and curettage), and less than 1% incidence of endometritis (inflammation of the uterine lining). Although the high dose produced the most effective contraceptive protection for the single suppository trial, the high dose is associated with the greater degree of acute side effects. It is important to note that side effects and risks for prostaglandin use increase as the length of pregnancy increases. Theoretically, if this drug were the only contraceptive being used by a fertile couple having intercourse four times a week, the drugs would be required three times a year for the expected three pregnancies.

With the development of prostaglandins the safety issue that population programs and the drug industry must confront is: what risks are acceptable to women to assure that the product is used? The issue facing contraceptive advocates in the women's health movement is: would women choose these risks if safer alternative early abortion techniques were made as convenient for them to control and use at home?

The problem with contraceptive safety in general is that the more effective a contraceptive is, the more risky it is to health. Women's reproductive freedom is compromised if we do not have highly effective contraceptives and abortions. But in general, effectiveness must be paid for in risks—or is this always so?

Let us take a look at another example of current contraceptive research, the intravaginal collagen sponge. This promising barrier method appears to offer significant advantages to many women over previous barrier methods. The collagen sponge maintains the inhospitable acidity of the vagina over the cervix and immobilizes sperm reaching the cervical area. The sponge is prepared from cowskin that is impregnated with a salt solution buffered to an acidity of pH 4.5–5.5.[7] It is inserted with a cylindrical applicator, and can be removed with an attached tape. Since the buffer is very stable it can be inserted long before intercourse (unlike diaphragm jellies, which lose spermicidal potency within hours), and it can absorb multiple ejaculates. If a way is found to prevent the development of offensive odors—current attempts are with zinc salts, which are also spermicidal and so far do not seem to have risky side effects[8]—the sponge can be left in place for days. The sponge can be washed, retreated with the simple buffer salt solution, and reused. Although similar to the diaphragm, the collagen sponge does not have to be fitted or placed over the cervix with as much care to be effective. Problems with the current design of the collagen sponge appear to be expulsion (usually during bowel movements) in about 2–3% of women trying them in small clinical trials conducted to date, and the development of odors after intercourse or menstruation. But how effective can it ultimately be? Much further research is needed.

To the contraceptive advocate interested in a drug and a decrease in population growth, such a device is not highly valued because it is not as effective as alternative methods. One reason its effectiveness is reduced in family planning programs is that there are many cultural inhibitions about handling genitals. One can develop technologies that are effective when used and do not depend on overcoming this human problem with support groups. Although the Agency for International Development (AID) has funded research into the intravaginal collagen sponge, they have not done so to the same degree that they have sponsored contraceptive drug research.

Contraceptive advocates in the women's health movement see in the greater variety of available barrier methods the chance that individual women can choose the method that suits them best, and not take the higher risks associated with contraceptive drugs. Indeed, cultural inhibitions can change through mutual education in women's self-help groups. However, such a process is very expensive to set up and adapt, and is still experimental. Little research money is being directed that way.

The question of applying values to the conduct of research becomes particularly complex where male contraceptives are concerned. Safety is a vital issue in male contraceptive research as well. Although the particular example I discuss here is the male contraceptive, gossypol, that has been developed in China, parallel situations and problems have been recognized with certain male contraceptives being investigated in the United States. (See the discussion of alpha-chlorohydrin and 1,2-dibromo-3-chloropropane analogs.[9]) Gossypol was discovered after a 1979 visit of officials sent by the Chinese Academy of Sciences to the Hopei Province to investigate the outbreak of a disease in men and women characterized by fever, general malaise, and burning sensations. It was eventually found that the long-term consumption of cottonseed oil in the daily diet[10] affected cardiac muscles and reproductive organs, resulting in infertility. In 1971, experiments conducted in rats demonstrated that gossypol was the active material responsible for the antifertility effect. A great deal of biological and toxicological work has now been done on gossypol and a wide variety of side effects in experimental animals has been reported, predominantly loss of appetite, reduction in growth rate, diarrhea, vomiting, anemia, and when high doses are given, cardiac irregularity, which can cause death. At doses used for contraception, gossypol apparently has not produced these effects. However, effects after long-term consumption of low doses have not been sufficiently studied yet. Infertility (as judged by semen analysis) is achieved within two months of daily pill-taking, implying that it inhibits male sperm production, since it takes two months to deplete a male's sperm reserve. Thereafter, the dosage to maintain infertility is reduced to one-fourth the starting dose. After discontinuation of gossypol treatment, sperm production is gradually resumed and within three months both the physical appearance and the number of sperm appear to be normal. By now more than 4000 men have been on gossypol for more than six months, over 2000 of those for two years and some as long as four years. Offspring of those discontinuing gossypol were reported as "normal in every respect." Men, however, were reported to be "not too enthusiastic to take the pill."

To the drug industry and population groups, male contraceptives are not as effective as female contraceptives because men are not as easily motivated to take responsibility for contraception as women. Men are likely to accept only far lower risks in contraceptives than women both because the risks of pregnancy are more remote and because masculinity is socioculturally connected to maintaining full reproductive potential. The women's health movement is concerned about the need to depend on men to take responsibility for contraception. But it is also committed to research seeking to develop male contraceptives that will provide women more alternatives, so that they need not be taking all the risks and responsibility of contraception at all times.

The value conflicts in the development of the new contraceptives described above are essentially about the extent of freedom in contraception: freedom to make a choice among the broadest possible variety of contraceptives, including the user freedom to detemine the acceptability of the risks of contraceptives. To exercise such freedom, there must be alternatives and there must be information on the effectiveness, the risks, and the benefits of all methods. The choices are often made for the users by the drug industry and by population groups. They do so through their selection of specific types of contraceptives to research and develop, and through their selection of the type of information they will distribute about these methods. The women's health movement is asserting that what is needed is greater involvement on the part of users in deciding what type of contraceptives should be researched and developed, what types of information about the methods should be sought, and how the information should be shared.

Status of Contraceptive Technology Development

Linda E. Atkinson and Jacki Ans

As interested consumers, it is necessary for us to have a greater understanding of the system in which contraceptive development takes place. To this end, this article will provide information on (1) the contraceptive development effort—who is doing it, where, and with what resources; (2) the complexity of risk and benefit issues being addressed; and (3) the consumer inputs needed in the contraceptive development system.

In 1960, fundamental research in the reproductive sciences had low level support from private foundations and agencies because governments were concerned that the subject was not appropriate for public funding. Applied research and contraceptive product development were done within the pharmaceutical industry, which was soon to turn out a plethora of pills and intrauterine devices.[1]

But, since 1971, an increasingly larger portion of contraceptive development has become the task of public sector organizations. This largely owed to the changing perceptions of the public and governments about population growth pressures both at home and abroad and to concerns that contraceptive methods, including highly effective pills and IUDs, had some serious health risks and did not seem appropriate for use in the developing world. It was also apparent that the pharmaceutical industry had maximized profits from contraceptives on the market at that time. Faced with ever increasing US Food and Drug Administration regulations and requirements, the industry was losing interest in the development of new methods.[2] Indeed, only one new method, an IUD, has been marketed in the 1970s. Thus, both basic research in reproduction, which is the source of our knowledge of the reproductive processes and new possibilities for fertility control, and applied research, which tests promising ideas from existing knowledge for their potential as fertility control agents, are now largely funded by public monies through government agencies.[1]

Contraceptive research is done primarily through the Special Programme in Human Reproduction of the World Health Organization, the International Committee for Contraception Research (ICCR), the Contraceptive Development Branch of the National Institutes of Health (NIH), the International Fertility Research Program (IFRP), and the Program for Applied Research in Fertility Regulation (PARFR). These organizations are sustained by contributions from governments and private agencies.

The activities of these organizations are carried on in the US, Europe, and the developing world. All the organizations have the mandate to develop safe, effective, acceptable, and inexpensive methods. The Contraceptive Development Branch of the NIH focuses on US needs, while the others focus on the needs of the developing world. The former utilizes a contract mechanism for research, while the others operate through grants and their own clinical research networks. All the organizations have advisory committees, variously constituted of scientists and clinicians (men and women) and an occasional lay person.

According to a Ford Foundation survey, in 1976 an estimated $125 million was being spent worldwide on research in the reproductive sciences and contraceptive development. About 20 percent, or $25 million, could be attributed to contraceptive research. Of that $25 million, about $11 million was spent by public sector organizations. Partial information from US industry indicated that at least $14 million is expended for contraceptive research and development. Public sector estimates of development costs in 1980 are about $20 million for moderate progress in product development.[3]

The issues of safety, effectiveness, acceptability, and cost, singly and together undergo constant evaluation in today's contraceptive development environment. Serious concern for the health and comfort of the user has, for the most part, replaced the naivete that surrounded the introduction of oral contraceptives in the early 1960s. With today's drug regulations and increased knowledge about the side effects, most potential drugs, devices, and procedures for suppression of fertility will be eliminated early on by animal toxicology tests. The remaining candidates will be carefully examined in well-controlled clinical trials for those side effects for which animal models are insufficient or inappropriate.

The issue of "safety" becomes more complex and open to debate with side effects that occur with relative infrequence. This is illustrated by the association that has been observed between oral contraceptive use and morbidity from heart attacks. This association was totally unpredictable at the time pills were introduced and was not noticed or confirmed until several years of use had passed. Only recently have possible biological explanations for this association been discovered. The hindsight of this experience raises the question of how to weigh the potential usefulness of an apparently safe and effective contraceptive agent against the potential, but as yet unmeasurable, serious side effect. The debate is further complicated by the "risks" of pregnancy that noncontraceptors undergo in settings where health and nutrition are substandard.

The issue of safety of non-invasive and/or natural methods of fertility control is often difficult to evaluate in view of the higher risk of pregnancy and its consequences even though other side effects are minimal. Improving spermicides and barrier methods is important and holds some promise, but safety issues are of concern here because the vaginal epithelium absorbs most substances quite effectively. Presently used spermicides are not without side effects; some people are sensitive to certain formulations, but systemic side effects have not been observed as yet. An example of a desired attribute in spermicides is better taste. Since there is the possibility that spermicides will be ingested, they would also undergo oral toxicity tests. Research on barrier methods, such as the collagen sponge, have been disappointing so far. This device has not proven to be effective in its present form and now has returned to the drawing board. Other problems with materials to be held in the vagina for long periods of time are those of irritation and vaginal infection. Cervical caps likewise will need a thorough testing of design and materials to eliminate the risks of infection.

The issue of acceptability is also not simple. Alternative non-invasive methods of fertility regulation are already available to us, but fewer than 15 percent of contracepting couples use the less effective methods of abstinence, spermicides, and barrier methods. Improvement of these methods so that they are more effective or easier to use will undoubtedly require high technology. We cannot consider the elimination of technology, but must pay closer attention to see that it is applied in ways that are acceptable and appropriate. The majority of contracepting couples are using those methods that have the highest efficacy: sterilization, oral contraceptives, and IUDs. These are also the methods that have a greater incidence of side effects. The couples who choose these methods are balancing the known risks with their life-style and their level of desire to prevent conception. It is not yet clear to what extent consumers are willing to trade high efficacy for risks.

Korenbrot divides those interested in contraceptive development into two camps, one interested in high technology methods and population control, and the other in the use of "safer" methods and control of their bodies. This dichotomy may be artificial. In fact, improvements of nonsystemic methods, in terms of effectiveness and ease of use, will require high technology with specialized materials and new chemical formulations.

Questions of safety and toxicological requirements will not disappear either. If population control were the only issue at hand, there would be little rationale to continue contraceptive development because highly effective methods are available to reduce fertility. Over the past decade as adverse side effects became known, the concern has been growing that current methods, both systemic and nonsystemic, are inadequate to meet the needs of the users in either industrial or developing societies.

Since most contraceptive research today is not undertaken with profit as the objective, more humanistic values can be developed and are developing. Adaptation of methods for self-use are being sought; for example, a contraceptive ring that is inserted by the woman.[4] The practical problem that is constantly faced in the search for safe and effective methods is the paucity of knowledge about the reproductive processes that would allow interference with specific events, e.g., very early pregnancy, but not have wide-spread side effects as, for example, the prostaglandins do. It is probably true that if a glimmer of the ideal contraceptive method arose, it would be developed immediately.

Several inputs from contraceptive users are necessary to the contraceptive development process. One is how to evaluate the trade-offs of effectiveness, ease of use, and risks, particularly those that are unknown or infrequent. It is not useful to cut off the dialog by simply demanding an end to research on methods that may have side effects and promoting a wholesale return to barrier and local methods that may be inappropriate for many individuals and cultures. Further, the issues are much too complex to be decided by researchers alone.

A second input stems from the recognition of the diversity of contraceptive methods that are needed. The method of choice may vary according to frequency of exposure to pregnancy, stability of personal relationships, health problems, whether childbearing is completed or not, and life-style. No one method will be appealing or appropriate for all, but the acceptable range of methods needs exploring.

The possibility of government supported research on early abortifacients is nonexistent in the current political atmosphere. If this kind of method is appropriate for US women, their desires should be made known.

Descriptions from contraceptive users regarding the characteristics of barrier method improvements would be useful. How should the present methods be modified to increase their use?

Education, information, and self-help approaches for contraceptive users are extremely important to safe, effective, and satisfying use of fertility control methods. These efforts are more within the sphere of private organizations and governmental agencies that provide contraceptive services than within the sphere of the contraceptive research community. Demands to these agencies for more appropriate educational services on all methods are needed.

Newer methods of contraception will only be as good as our understanding of the reproductive processes. Method risks are predictable only to the extent of our knowledge of molecular interactions. Yet, research in reproductive biology and contraceptive development is not thought to be important by our elected government officials. To some, the research is synonymous with the abortion issue, or is less pressing because US birth rates have fallen. Others have said, "No one ever dies of a reproductive disease." Perhaps contraceptive users have something to tell their Congressmen—something about reproductive health.

Women-Controlled Research

Laura Punnett

Medicine claims to be based upon "objective" science; yet its content is biased to uphold certain ideologies and research priorities. The questions—both asked and unasked—reflect the interests of the technical experts, the white, affluent men who control both medicine and research science.

Medical investigators frequently fail to ask questions that are relevant to women's experiences and needs, while women healthworkers have defined many such areas in need of attention. Women's real problems are frequently dismissed as neurotic behavior. It has been demonstrated that women are more likely than men to be "diagnosed" as having "psychosomatic" complaints, especially when these are problems exclusive to women, such as menstrual cramps, premenstrual depression, or hot flashes.[1] Women who suffer from dysmenorrhea may be labeled "childish," "hysterical," or rejecting their role as women.[2] Those with chest pain or migraine headaches are less likely than men to be thoroughly examined for possible physiological causes.[3] These prejudices are exaggerated even further when racism and class bias are involved.

Medical ethics parallels medicine in addressing questions that reflect interests other than women's. In 1975, the Department of Health, Education, and Welfare instructed its National Commission for the Protection of Human Subjects to investigate the "nature and extent of research involving living (sic) fetuses." The Commission's deliberations and conclusions on fetal research engendered substantial discussion among ethicists concerned with safeguarding the "dignity" and "well-being" of the fetus, while the dignity or even the physical safety of a woman pregnant with such a fetus was completely ignored.[4]

This is a consistent attitude among academic disciplines that have also ignored irresponsible experimentation on women in contraceptive research,[5] such as the Puerto Rican birth control pill trials, the Goldzieher study of 1970, or the Karman supercoil abortions on raped Bangladesh women.[6] Ethical discussions of informed consent and free will in decision-making are popular. Yet consideration of "special subjects in human experimentation," those who might in some way be coerced, manipulated, or exploited in medical research, includes fetuses, children, students, prisoners, dying patients, the poor, and the mentally ill—but never women.[7]

An examination of the program of this workshop shows that here, too, where women are to speak about our concerns, the issues we are invited to address are limited, excluding numerous priorities as defined by women in our lives. What about the special occupational hazards of typical women's work, inside and outside the home, for women who wish to bear children as well as those who do not? What are the specific health needs of lesbians, such as easy access to artificial insemination and health services that do not assume that every woman is heterosexual? What is the difference, if any, between menopause and the normal aging of the human body: would appropriate birth control methods for menopausal women be any different from those used by younger women?

Professional medicine and medical ethics are *not* objective; they are inadequate and ineffective in addressing women's concerns and health needs, which are either ignored or used as a means to increase control over our lives. In contrast, a feminist approach to health care for women is marked by respect for and reliance on each woman's experience and knowledge of her own body. Feminism is an ideology that mandates that women have full and active control over all conditions affecting our lives in order to achieve total well-being.

The process through which women have developed our own empirical information base, through caring for our health needs and each others' in a cooperative, respectful way, has existed among women of all times, cultures, classes, and races. We of the second wave of American feminism call this process "Self-Help." The women's self-help health movement translates the demand for self-determination into specifics: control over medical information and technology, active participation in health care, and research programs developed and controlled by those most directly affected, with priorities reflecting the real, experiential needs of women. These goals actually result in demonstrably improved health conditions and medical procedures. This is my thesis: that women-controlled health care and research is both ethically and medically preferable for women.

Unfortunately, there are few documented examples available to demonstrate what women have been able to accomplish when we control our own health care, and so I will look to the nineteenth century for my first case. I use nineteenth-century birthing practices to discuss women-controlled settings because in the late 1800s birth control was a household rather than a medical issue, and thus was rarely, if ever, addressed at medical institutions. Meanwhile, childbirth was becoming medicalized as contraception is now. Therefore childbirth is historically comparable in examining women's role, especially in an area of changing practices.

The New England Hospital for Women and Children, founded in Boston in 1862 by Marie Elizabeth Zakrzewska, a midwife from Berlin, was staffed exclusively by women physicians until the 1950s. This was the first hospital in the country to have an all-female staff, the second to admit medical women to hospital internships, and the first formally organized nurse-training school in the United States. Thus it was an example of women who were not only practitioners, but in control of their own working situation. Furthermore, their practice originated in European midwifery, a women's tradition, as much as in American medicine. A rare opportunity for medical training for women, the New England Hospital pioneered certain practices and offered generally superior medical care, of which respect and caring for other women were integral components.

From its founding the medical staff enforced strict regulations for cleanliness for physicians, interns, and nurses, especially on the maternity ward. Whether reflecting the traditions of midwifery practice or standards of household cleanliness, these regulations appear to have been based on women's empirical information. Before general acceptance of the germ theory of disease these women washed their hands, sterilized instruments and cloths, bathed patients, and aired the wards regularly. Students on obstetrics call were prohibited from attending autopsies, contagious diseases, or infected wounds on pain of being discharged from the hospital immediately. The maternity ward was housed in a building separate from the rest of the hospital, in order to minimize the spread of infection. (This fact was a source of public pride for the hospital staff for many years.) As a direct result of these precautions, in an era when most male physicians resisted even considering themselves as possible agents of disease and when lying-in wards were frequently closed altogether by epidemics of puerperal sepsis, the New England Hospital was never closed and rarely lost more than one or two women a year to this infection.[8] Concurrently, in the medical campaign against midwives at the turn of this century, midwives were blamed for high rates of maternal and child deaths, while the evidence suggests that doctors were in fact more responsible for infant morality, puerperal sepsis, and other complications than midwives were.[9]

There is often no clear distinction between medical research and medical practice, which is illustrated by the examples of DES and Depo-Provera as experimental drugs that have been marketed and used widely and carelessly. At the New England Hospital, the medical staff firmly upheld policies that had been demonstrated empirically to be sound, although they were in fact experimental in a conservative direction. I maintain that women-controlled health care is characterized by just such careful attention to and responsibility for specific practices and their actual consequences for individual women, and their right to take or avoid predictable risks.

Women originally active in the struggle for abortion access and legalization developed, in the early 1970s, the most recent version of the self-help process in this country. As these women monitored refinements in abortion technology, it became clear to them that a nontraumatic abortion procedure would always be superior in protecting the health of the women undergoing the procedure. By 1971 they developed standards for techniques that are now used in feminist, women-controlled abortion clinics. Since this procedure is more demanding of the practitioner, it is still not available at many medical facilities. Although most physicians continue to use large, often rigid, cannulae along with sharp metal curettes, the Center for Disease Control has confirmed the self-help experience and judgment: that safe abortions result from the skill of the abortionist, minimal dilation and anesthesia, and use of suction with a flexible cannula only, rather than with back-up curettage.[10] As these same early self-help activists observed that abortion techniques were becoming safer and could be used earlier in pregnancy with less trauma, they also discussed the possibility of women gaining more direct control over this procedure. The result of this discussion was the development of menstrual extraction (ME).

Menstrual extraction is the term correctly used only to describe the procedure in which women in advanced self-help groups use a narrow, flexible, plastic cannula and mild suction to remove the uterine lining for a member of the group, either on or about the first day of her menstrual period. The extraction of a normal menstrual period can eliminate the menses, relieve cramps or backache, and be a means of gaining and sharing with other women information about menstruation. The extraction of a late period can also serve as a method of birth control. Many women consider this to be an ideal contraceptive technique because it is used only when needed, separately from the act of intercourse; it does not appear to change the body chemistry; it is highly effective; and it is easily accessible, being under the control of the woman using it, who is not dependent on a physician for its use. A recent issue of *Quest* contains a thorough description of the procedure.[11]

Menstrual extraction is still experimental; that is to say, the self-help movement has not yet been able to collect data on large numbers of women using ME over long periods of time, and therefore we do not yet have complete information on its safety. However, women who have full control over the conditions of the research would not perform an experimental procedure on themselves that they had reason to believe was unsafe. Menstrual extraction is women-controlled research, in that each woman formulates her own criteria for deciding whether she wishes to experiment on her own body, aware that there may be risks involved in the procedure. It is not a technique to be merchandised or marketed, as so many birth control methods have been. Research within a self-help model insures that a woman who is a subject has control over the project and immediate access to information on the purpose and method of the study, as well as access to all current raw data and conclusions, for her own evaluation or even reconsideration of her participation. Another way to state this is that all investigators participate in the study and that all participants are investigators—so that there is no opposition of interests between researcher and subjects.

Women-controlled research should be seriously considered as an ethically superior design for development of new contraceptive methods and of other technology to be used on women's bodies. The goal at which "informed consent" hints is fully realized in this model, because it gives women the complete information necessary to make an informed decision.

The practice of menstrual extraction by lay women in the United States, whether as research or for birth control, has been condemned by the medical profession, ostensibly for safety considerations. Yet no significant complications have been detected in nine years of menstrual extraction research in self-help groups. Medical objections in the past have included a supposed greater danger inherent in the practice by lay women, and inadequacies in the procedure and equipment used. These criticisms are unsubstantiated, and furthermore arise from a misunderstanding of the menstrual extraction procedure, assuming it to be similar to abortion techniques that include dilators, large rigid cannulae, and curettes. In fact, menstrual extraction uses carefully designed equipment and is a very safe procedure, in part exactly because it is done by lay women. The woman undergoing the procedure is in total control and works with the extractor(s) as an active participant; any discomfort is generally regarded as an indication for caution and re-evaluation. Women do not have to be told to be gentle with each other. Participants are knowledgeable regarding symptoms of complications such as infection or perforation and measures to prevent as well as treat them, however low the risk. The same concern for safety that motivated the development of a safe abortion procedure and of safe equipment for menstrual extraction makes the risk of an ME procedure truly negligible.

This attention to safety, along with mutual identification among the women in a group, should not be underestimated in importance as a factor in the safety of ME. Physicians are trained to perform procedures that cause discomfort, and so do not necessarily consider pain as an indication to discontinue the procedure. But in an ME, an awake and aware woman can distinguish the heavy cramp that occurs when the tip of the cannula touches the back wall of her uterus from the sensation of the cannula passing through her internal os. Since the woman directs the procedure according to her understanding and interpretation with the other women in the group, perforation of the uterine wall can thus be easily avoided. The risk of infection is minimized in part because the woman herself, again in consultation with her group, decides what precautions are appropriate for her to take rather than receiving instructions from a practitioner. Similar active and informed participation enables a woman effectively to monitor a possible incomplete procedure or other sequellae.

Since menstrual extraction has been increasingly recognized as safe, it has also increasingly been co-opted by population controllers. In this country, the term "menstrual extraction" is often incorrectly used to refer to an aspiration performed by a physician on a patient as an early or pre-emptive abortion. The same procedure, properly called "menstrual regulation" (among other names), is also being exported to Third World countries. Yet the very use of this procedure as a professional service or a population control tool, rather than in the self-help context, completely changes its purpose, its safety, its ethical validity, and its political ramifications. With appropriate equipment in the context of a women's self-help group, menstrual extraction is far safer and far more responsibly undertaken than menstrual regulation.

It is an obvious contradiction that medical and population interests should oppose the former while they support the latter. Clearly the male-dominated profession will never support self-help menstrual extraction because their real objection is not to its medical hazards but to control by lay women and the challenge to medical domination that it poses. They are threatened by "the independence that menstrual extraction in particular and self-help in general gives women rather than [concerned about] the dangers of either."They see, "quite correctly, that menstrual extraction was developed precisely to give women autonomy over their own bodies and that it is inseparable from the concept of self-help."[12] In fact, one has only to look at the vehement reaction to something as simple as cervical self-examination to realize that any procedure used by the self-help movement will be attacked because of the political implications of self-help, regardless of the technique itself.[13]

Population control is "a large scale social policy of (either encouraging or) limiting births throughout a whole society or in certain social groups for the purpose of changing economic, political, and/or ecological conditions."[14] It is an ideology with a strong backing; the population control establishment currently spends enormous amounts of money and other resources to develop techniques for limiting births. Birth control pills, diethylstilbestrol, prostaglandin abortions, Depo-Provera, and sterilization abuse are only a partial list of what women have been subjected to as a result.

Menstrual regulation, either as a backup to other contraceptives or as an early abortion procedure in its own right, is one more procedure that has been offered as a potential solution to the problem of finding an "ideal" population control method that can be used on all women. All the advantages for which feminists advocate menstrual extraction for our own use, such as safety, lack of discomfort, economy, simplicity, and accessibility to lay women, have been used in the literature on menstrual regulation to recommend it in population control. Physicians in Third World countries are encouraged to consider means for introducing menstrual regulation into their own countries so as to give it an image of respectability and safety that will not "generate rumors" or "embarrass politicians."[15] (In other words, if they avoid calling it "abortion," they can sidestep both the objections of individuals to whom abortion is not acceptable as well as the need to defend abortion as an *option* for all women.) One scheme discussed at the International Menstrual Regulation Conference in Hawaii in 1973 carried the use of the technique far beyond concerns of informed consent, to outright coercion: it would have required a woman to "turn in" her menstrual period in order to pick up her monthly welfare check.[16] Nor, in any of these settings, is there any proposal for careful monitoring of side effects or other acknowledgment that this use of the technique would be experimentation on women. The distinction between research and delivery becomes theoretical when delivery systems employ a major proportion of experimental methods, usually without informed consent, in population control.

Furthermore, the ideology of population control sacrifices women's self-determination to male-defined goals; an increase or decrease in the growth of a population has a higher priority than advancing the freedom, life options, or responsibilities of individuals. These latter considerations, called "beyond family-planning policies," are held to be of dubious value, with high costs and uncertain effects on the birthrate. They are given weight in planning policies only if it appears that they will aid in manipulating the population growth rate, not because of their own moral validity. For example, population researchers use the concept of "role incompatibility" to plan their policies:

> According to this theory, female employment would reduce fertility most effectively when birth planning is widely practiced and when the roles of worker and mother are most incompatible, that is, when (a) the place of work is away from the home, which may pose practical problems relating to child care; (b) the prevailing belief is that a woman with children should devote all her time to them, in which case the woman feels she must choose between work and children; and (c) a woman's employment provides her with significant social, psychological, or economic rewards, which she may be unwilling to forego in order to have another child.[17]

In contrast, feminists are concerned with solving problems and contradictions in women's lives and with broadening our options, which would include making the roles of worker and mother *more* compatible for those women who wish to bear children and also to work outside the home. Those aiming to control "fertility" contradict feminists' efforts, manipulating the social and economic factors affecting *all* women's ability to thrive, e.g., making child care less accessible, and increasing the social pressure on mothers not to work outside the home or on working women not to have children. Women's oppression is to be intensified and deepened in order better to achieve a male-defined goal, whether it be more or fewer children. Women's needs will be considered only when it is expedient to do so, and our desires to bear children or not are irrelevant altogether. From a feminist perspective "the provision of family planning services is no substitute for radical social, economic or political reform."[18] From the viewpoint of the population controllers it is exactly that—a substitute—intended to co-opt women's demands and to perpetuate women's oppression, just as withholding birth control options did previously and still does in some groups.[19]

As the Federal government begins to require the "natural family planning" method to be included in all federally-funded contraceptive services, what appears to be an expansion of choice of methods may in fact become a further reduction of women's options. In addition to the limitations discussed by the Women's Community Health Center, the government is supporting a Church-based program, accepting its criteria for teacher certification ("a happy marriage *with* children"), and thereby creating a new mini-profession of natural family planning teachers. This institutionalizes the Church's anti-abortion and anti-contraception dogma into the teaching of the method. Professionalization of teachers along these lines could totally exclude the feminists who teach Fertility Consciousness as woman-controlled birth control, which supports women's total self-determination and self-definition.

In summary, the fact that women have been largely excluded from setting medical policy or controlling the direct delivery of services has profound implications for women's health care in general and specifically for women's control of reproduction and reproductive technology. The historical and contemporary cases show us that women's control of our own health care delivery and of work in experimental areas results in significantly better care and conditions for all women. Self-determination mandates self-help research and feminist control of technology. These in turn require that women have full information about choices (rather than having to fight an information monopoly by the technocrats); access to decision-making power for all women, not just tokens; and resources with which to put decisions into effect. Conferences and workshops should be organized on a grass-roots level, to include large numbers of women: young, old, poor and working-class, lesbians, ethnic women and women of color, in the setting of policies that affect our lives so intimately.

We must redefine the ethical issues in reproductive technology. Debates on full access to abortion services on demand, including financial access, are unacceptable altogether, since any limitation on abortion availability directly limits the right of all women to choose whether or not to bear children.

In general, controversies over the ethics of reproductive control are not merely traditional debates among academic philosophers, but rather are political struggles between women who assert the right to control our lives and values, and institutions such as male domination of women, corporate profit, medical professional dominance, racist, imperialist control over other peoples, or obedience to a masculine, Church-defined "morality." In these arenas, white male-dominated medicine claims to practice "objective" science, which, because it does not acknowledge its own biases and interests, can be used to obscure the deeply political significance of any ideology or system that attempts to exploit or limit any woman's control of her own reproductive options.

Woman-Controlled Birth Control

A Feminist Analysis of
Natural Birth Control

Fertility Consciousness Group,
Women's Community Health Center

We have written this paper not as individuals, but as members of the Fertility Consciousness program at Women's Community Health Center, a feminist self-help center in Cambridge, Mass. The Center was founded in 1974 by women who were struggling to gain control of their own bodies.

The Center is owned and operated by those of us who work there. We are not professionals, and we do not see ourselves as "professional nonprofessionals" or "nonprofessional professionals." Those concepts deny the fact that women—ordinary women—are able to take control of our health care if we can get access to the resources to do so. We are not talking about merely replacing male professionals with female professionals.

Our work is motivated by our needs to control our own lives and our recognition that this cannot become a reality for us unless all women gain that control. We do not see ourselves as victims or as advocates for victims, although women certainly have been victimized. The strength of our work comes through working cooperatively in groups, rather than individually, so two of us presented this work at the conference.

INTRODUCTION

Information regarding our fertility is self-knowledge basic to all women and is every woman's right. It is information that has been lost through the isolation of women from one another and the medicalization of women's reproductive functions.

71

There are a number of methods that have been used to determine a woman's fertile and infertile times. These techniques can be applied to prevent or to facilitate conception; the present discussion considers only contraceptive aspects. Techniques range from the rhythm method to the recording of basal body temperature and of cervical and other body changes, from observation of cervical mucus to measurement of the physical and chemical properties of that mucus by machines. The rhythm method is based on calendar calculations of a woman's menstrual cycle lengths over a period of time and entails guessing that future cycles will be similar to the past. It has been shown that for birth control purposes the past is not an accurate predictor of the future, which explains why the rhythm method is not effective.

There are three methods of effective natural birth control in common use: basal (resting) body temperature, ovulation method, and sympto-thermal methods. Basal body temperature can indicate that ovulation has occurred, but gives no information about fertility until after ovulation. Basal body temperature is often altered by time of day, amount of sleep, alcohol consumption, illness, or other factors, and basal thermometers are impractical in many situations. Many women have temperature patterns that are difficult or impossible to interpret.[1] Therefore this method has limited usefulness.

The ovulation method is based entirely on observations of cervical mucus. This mucus is the only sign that can be used to assess a woman's potential fertility each day. Mucus is affected by very few factors other than hormonal events, and mucus changes accurately signal ovulation. Unlike any other sign, cervical mucus also indicates infertile days in the absence of ovulation; for example, cycles without ovulation are common in women who are breastfeeding or approaching menopause. Since accurate observation and interpretation of mucus depend only on the woman herself, she can completely demedicalize the birth control process, keeping it out of the control of the medical profession.

Sympto-thermal methods combine basal body temperature with observation of mucus, cervical changes associated with ovulation, and sometimes even calendar rhythm. These indicators are used to confirm each other in defining times of potential fertility. However, they do not always coincide exactly, and a woman must not consider herself infertile until all signs are in agreement. Sympto-thermal methods are unnecessarily complicated, and not as widely applicable as the ovulation method.

We represent a group of feminists who formed a self-help group to study natural birth control 2-½ years ago. Proceeding from the scientific literature and our ongoing research on our own bodies, we have chosen to provide detailed information on the ovulation method as a primary tool for woman-controlled natural birth control. We chose the name "fertility consciousness" to indicate that this information has broader applications than birth control.

THE OVULATION METHOD

The fact that cervical mucus is related to fertility was known well before modern times. The Bantu people in East Africa passed this information from grandmother to granddaughter at puberty. Each woman used a smooth stone to wipe the outer lips of the vagina to collect the mucus. We also know that the Native American Cherokee people passed similar information from mother to daughter. Imperialist disruption of these and other cultures broke down these traditional communication networks and their values; profitable medical birth control devices and procedures were then imported.

Modern cervical mucus birth control research began in the 1950s in Australia. Drs. Lyn and John Billings were looking for a method of child spacing that was both acceptable to the Catholic Church and effective in preventing pregnancy. The Billingses measured women's hormone levels by blood and urine tests while at the same time asking the women to observe their vaginal discharge and note their sensations of wetness or dryness at the vaginal lips. They found that women were able to identify the time of ovulation as accurately as the laboratory measurements of hormone levels! Women did not need to follow their basal body temperature in order to do this.[2] The Billingses continued their work, devising rules for preventing or facilitating pregnancy, based solely on mucus observations. They chose the name ovulation method or Billings Ovulation Method.

To use this method for birth control a woman pays attention to whether she feels a sensation of wetness or lubrication at her vulva, and notices the characteristics of any vaginal discharge present on the external vaginal lips. She keeps track of these observations by writing them down every day. Women learn how to interpret the significance of different kinds of discharge. With this information and an understanding of the menstrual cycle, a woman can tell on a day-to-day basis whether she is potentially fertile. The rules for determining potential fertility are based on the survival time of an egg cell after ovulation and the survival time of sperm cells in a woman's reproductive tract in the presence or absence of favorable cervical mucus.

The ovulation method provides a way to recognize the approach of ovulation. The cells lining the cervix respond to ovarian hormone changes by secreting different types of mucus. Very simplisticly, estrogen dominates the preovulatory part of the menstrual cycle, and progesterone the postovulatory phase. Estrogen-dominated mucus is necessary for fertility. Among other functions, this type of mucus nourishes and transports sperm, protecting them from lethal vaginal acidity. Mucus that is fluid enough to flow from the cervix to the external vaginal lips may contain enough estrogenic mucus to support sperm life. Thus, checking for the presence of mucus that has flowed out to the vaginal opening is an accurate gauge of hormonal activity. All days on which external mucus is found before ovulation, plus an interval following, are presumed to be potentially fertile.

A woman learns to recognize her mucus pattern over the course of one or more cycles. She describes her mucus in her own words, records the description each day, and applies the rules to determine whether she might be fertile on that day. Despite the uniform descriptions in books attempting to teach natural birth control techniques, mucus characteristics do vary quite a bit from woman to woman, so that it is difficult or impossible for many women to learn adequately from books. The most effective teachers are women who themselves practice mucus observation, have worked with a wide range of other women, and have learned how to share their knowledge responsibly.

The fact that different measures are used to assess effectiveness of birth control methods makes it difficult to compare some studies. A number of factors influence effectiveness rates, including the way the method is taught or provided, the motivation of people using the method, and the way that pregnancies that occur during the study are categorized and reported. Some studies of the ovulation method use women teachers, while others use couples, men, or even correspondence courses. A study by Rice, Lanctot, and Garcia-Devesa found "a 3½ times higher pregnancy rate for those who have not reached their desired family size over those who equal or exceed their desired family size."[3] It is also important to distinguish between different factors resulting in pregnancies. Pregnancies can result from failure of any method; that is, women who understand and apply the method correctly occasionally become pregnant. Teaching-related failures result when women do not understand and therefore apply the method incorrectly. Total pregnancy rates also include women who correctly identified a day of potential fertility and chose not to follow the rule of avoiding heterosexual genital contact. Some studies distinguish between these factors and others lump them all together.

The effectiveness of the ovulation method compares favorably to other highly effective birth control methods (condom and foam, diaphragm and cream or jelly, IUD, pills, sterilization, and abortion).

Recent World Health Organization (WHO) studies in 5 countries demonstrated a 98.5% method effectiveness rate, yet concluded that this method was relatively ineffective because overall pregnancy rates ranged from 10.4 to 33.7 pregnancies per 100 woman years. WHO reported that 97% of women were able to interpret their mucus pattern correctly, and that the high pregnancy rates resulted from "couples knowingly taking a chance during the fertile phase."[4] In our opinion this shows that the method is highly effective and that motivation is a critical factor.

POLITICAL IMPACT

Birth control methods have the potential to allow women to control our reproductive lives; they can also be used as a tool of political and social repression. Many dangerous and experimental birth control methods have been widely spread throughout the world in a coercive manner for the purposes of population control. Women of color are among the special targets. These methods are promoted to women without giving full explanations of the risks, without giving adequate information about and access to the full range of methods to choose from, and without increasing a woman's knowledge of her own body. For example, many poor and third world women are injected with Depo-Provera or sterilized without their understanding or consent.

Keeping women ignorant about our bodies is another way to control women, to decrease our ability to make choices, and to create dependence on the medical establishment. This can be countered by learning to examine and understand our own bodies; by learning that there is a range of variation, rather than one standard norm; by validating our experiences through sharing them; by exploring what we all have in common as women. The name we give this process is self-help. Self-help challenges the existing power of the medical establishment over women's lives. As we know more about our bodies and health care, we can make stronger demands for changes in the medical system and reclaim control of women's health care. Learning about mucus observation and the ovulation method in a self-help group is an empowering experience and provides tools for fertility consciousness as well as for woman-controlled birth control.

Most nonfeminist natural birth control programs present the information in ways that do not necessarily improve the quality of women's lives. For instance, the vast majority of these programs throughout the world reinforce stereotyped roles of women. They are aimed at promoting and strengthening traditional marriage rather than increasing the range of choices open to women. Motherhood within the nuclear family is defined as woman's ultimate fulfillment. A recent publication directs natural birth control users as follows:

> Among the contraceptive populations of the West, I believe that the message ought to be 'get having babies!—you are going to ruin your country and often your personal future, by regarding, say, two as quite enough, when you have no great excuse.[sic][5]

These groups actively oppose a woman's right to control her body. They reject other methods of birth control as undesirable or immoral, often refusing to refer clients to birth control clinics. They also deny the right to choose abortion.

Transmitting these stereotyped values is a fundamental part of the ways that natural birth control methods are usually taught. There may be more concern that a teacher propagate this value system than that she know and teach the method accurately.

> The teacher will inevitably communicate her own hierarchy of values to the clients. Her attitudes towards married love, towards the place of the physical sexual act in married life . . . will be sensed by the client, and will hopefully influence them [sic] to their advantage.[6]

In order to ensure that women learn this value system, the teaching is usually done on an individual basis or in classes including men, so that women remain isolated from freely sharing experiences with one another. The stated goal is to give each woman only the bare minimum of information necessary for her to use the method without broadening any of the implications of the information. This oversimplification, also found in books, is summarized by the term KISS (keep it simple, stupid!), a shorthand term to remind teachers that they should share as little factual information as possible.

The Catholic terminology has for the most part been adopted directly by other groups teaching natural birth control, often without examining the assumptions inherent in the use of these terms. Roman Catholic morals consider penile/vaginal intercourse with ejaculation directly into the vagina as the only approved form of sexual activity. "Abstinence" therefore is used in Catholic natural birth control literature to mean both not having intercourse and not having sexual contact of any kind. For people whose sexual expression includes activities other than penile/vaginal intercourse, the meaning of the word abstinence may become unclear. Also, the word abstinence perpetuates sexist assumptions that penile/vaginal penetration is the most desirable sexual activity and anything else must be somehow inferior. As women talk more about sexual experiences and feelings, the oppressive nature of these assumptions becomes more clearly understood. In an analysis of women's descriptions of ways they do and do not experience sexual satisfaction, Shere Hite reports:

> Insisting that women should have orgasms during intercourse, from intercourse, is to force women to adapt their bodies to inadequate stimulation, and the difficulty of doing this and the frequent failure that is built into the attempt breeds [sic] recurring feelings of insecurity and anger.... Sex is defined as a certain pattern—foreplay, penetration, intercourse, and ejaculation—... indeed, intercourse *is* the pattern.... This pattern is what oppresses women.[7]

FERTILITY CONSCIOUSNESS AND WOMAN-CONTROLLED BIRTH CONTROL

Women's Community Health Center has developed a self-help format for sharing natural birth control information with groups of women. We use the term "fertility consciousness" to indicate that this information has a broader applicability than birth control. Fertility consciousness self-help groups include basic body information about anatomy and physiology, including cervical self-examination, as well as detailed information about the ovulation method. The group process creates a setting in which women can explore issues generated by learning this information. For many women it is revolutionary to discover that discharges that they had assumed were unclean or abnormal are in fact a universal, informative sign of healthy body functions. Women considering relying on a natural birth control method confront issues of who defines what form their sexual expression takes and how such decisions are reached. Groups meet for several consecutive weeks with regular followup sessions open to all women who have been in a group. Everyone is encouraged to be an active participant, sharing her experiences. Rather than a teacher-to-class dynamic, women support each other in developing confidence in mucus observations and taking responsibility for our reproductive lives.

Our goal is not only to provide a birth control method, but also a process that women can choose to use in a variety of ways. Lesbians and celibate women, as well as heterosexually active women without interest in birth control, find fertility consciousness groups relevant and empowering. Women in menopause self-help groups are also excited to gain access to this way of monitoring estrogen levels in their bodies.

Since the ovulation method was developed to promote Catholic values, it is steeped in restrictive assumptions about sexuality, morality, and women. In fertility consciousness groups we work actively against making assumptions about how women will use the information. We recognize and value sexuality as separate from reproduction. As feminists, we are working to expand the choices available to women. Therefore, the use of barrier methods of contraception is discussed as an option. Women share their experiences learning whether they can distinguish mucus in the presence of spermicidal chemicals. Women who choose to use barrier methods along with fertility consciousness take responsibility for knowing that there is the potential for higher pregnancy rates. There are no studies of the effectiveness of mucus observation combined with barrier methods.

Understanding of the scientific basis of the ovulation method, of the research process that determined the rules for preventing conception, and of the philosophy that determined the research process, allows women to make informed decisions about using this information in their lives in a way that best fits their needs.

If natural birth control information is presented along with a restrictive set of values about women's biological functions, such as sexuality or pregnancy, and about women's role in society and the family, natural birth control will reinforce the repression of women. Alternatively, this information can be presented only as a birth control method free from physical side effects and medical interference. However, failure to challenge the oppressive assumptions built in during the development of these methods thereby perpetuates them. Or this information can be used as a self-help tool to expand the choices available to women, and to expand our ability to control our own bodies and our reproductive lives. Being able to choose whether and when to have children is an integral part of that control. These decisions, however, are difficult to make if the means to carry them through are not readily available. We must have safe and effective birth control, access to abortion regardless of economic status, and freedom from forced sterilization and medical experimentation. Every woman must have a decent income, high quality health care, childcare as needed, and the freedom to define her own sexuality. Seen in this light, natural birth control, like other technologies, can be used to control women or to free women.

Response

Rosa Cuéllar

While I've been sitting here, I've been trying to assess what I wanted to say to you. One thing is that I haven't understood everything everybody has said. I come from south Texas, but I've also worked in the South. Just as I didn't understand these terms, many of the women I work with don't understand what these drugs are or what their effects are.

Not only do we never hear about much of the research, but even the programs funded to reach people do not reach them. One example is in housing—we have houses with no bathrooms and no running water. The program people say, "We're going to put your plumbing in, but the house has to be in a certain condition before you can qualify for this program." Well how are we going to remedy these problems if the people who are most in need of the programs don't qualify financially?

I also think we need to look further than what we've so far discussed. For instance, we know that sterilization is happening all over, especially with minority women. *Why* is it being done? And why aren't certain types of birth control available to women and put in every drug store? One reason is that there's no profit in them. Those are the sorts of connections we should be looking for.

We have to look at the whole labor situation—not only for farm workers, but for others. What is happening right now is that the cost of living is going up while wages are going down. And if it's affecting us right now, it's going to affect you in the urban areas sooner or later. In fact it already is affecting you because mechanization doesn't benefit the workers—or any of us.

Through this conference I hope I—and many of you too—will get past a sense of isolation. The everyday work of many women out there is a life and death struggle for a decent wage. They are fighting for their own particular needs as women, but also for their children's education, day care, and so on. I think we should try, when we leave here, to see how we can work with each other's struggles.

Response

Kristin Luker

A variety of questions and themes have emerged from the papers and the responses. Some of these are only implicit, and I'd like to make them more explicit for us to consider.

One critical question being asked is: "What is choice?" That question was touched on at the very beginning. One of the working definitions of choice is that people are allowed a range of options, and they're allowed to assess the risks in line with what they see as the benefits. I feel that the people who run those risks ought to be the people deciding whether the benefits are worth the risks. But it's also important to point out that how risks and benefits get defined is culturally, historically, and ultimately, personally determined.

I spent the early '70s telling people in the US government that effectiveness wasn't everything. I may spend the '80s telling people that maybe safety isn't everything. There is a strong trend—particularly in the Women's Movement—that safety is the single most important thing; but perhaps our lives are really much more diverse than that.

Additionally, the argument about physical safety in contraception implicitly assumes that there is an open and risk-free alternative of abortion but we have to look at *that* presupposition pretty carefully, too. First of all, it's at least possible that abortion as a political alternative may disappear. Moreover, as people try to move away from the stigma that was associated with abortion in the 1930s, '40s, and '50s, I think there's been a tendency to downplay it as a social and psychological event. For many women, having an abortion is not a trivial event. I believe it's perfectly rational—and a responsible choice I can respect—for people to tolerate the higher risk of the pill because they really don't want to have an abortion. Yet I feel that that's been invalidated as a legitimate choice at times.

It's not clear that abortion—even suction abortion—is an entirely safe method of fertility control over the long run. I see the potential for another pill scandal. When the pill first came out, for example, we thought it was safe, effective, without problems, and the most thoroughly tested drug that had ever been released to the American

81

public. And I think we may be running the risk of doing that with abortion, too.

One of the problems in assessing the risks of abortion is that suction abortion hasn't been around that long. You can hear a whole range of statistics for everything from the "fact" that abortion will seriously compromise your future fertility, cause cervical incompetence, etc., to the "fact" that it has no consequences whatsoever. The truth probably lies somewhere in between, so I think we have to be a little careful about casually saying, "Oh, well there's always a back-up abortion," until we've looked at the long-term statistical and historical kinds of risks.

There seems to be a tendency—now particularly—to look back at the "good old days" with a sort of warm glow. I think that we have to be skeptical about that. My research suggests that most of the folk abortifacients used historically were, on the whole, quite safe, but they were also relatively ineffective. Mostly they were things like laxatives. And it's true that if you drank black cohosh tea or tansy or things like that, if you poisoned yourself to within an inch of your life in the 19th century, you could probably get yourself an abortion—sometimes. But probably in large numbers of cases people were having miscarriages anyway, after they drank their black cohosh tea, and thought it was efficacious.

It is probably the case that one of the reasons for abortion laws in this country—and you don't get them until about 1860–1880—was that all of a sudden surgical abortion became more common, and while effective, it was also relatively dangerous. Even in the 1930s, before you had antibiotics, it was not a trivial matter to enter the uterus and empty it. So, again, I think we have to be a little careful about easy assumptions that somehow women had control over fertility and reproduction, that we had effective folk methods that have somehow been lost.

Another theme that I hear emerging here, and a very encouraging one, is a resistance to quick technological fixes. There is a feeling that perhaps the answers to some of these questions lie in the political, the social, and the personal realms, as opposed to the laboratory. Maybe we can find answers to such things as more effective diaphragm use by having support groups or peer counseling rather than by inventing a better diaphragm.

Women are very diverse; we live in a variety of life-styles and in different classes; we're different races; we have a whole variety of life agendas. And I think we have to be tolerant of a range of personal decisions. In fact, I'd like to see the range of alternatives broaden and I'd like to see us validate a range of personal assessments of costs and benefits.

The problem with this perspective is: where do we reach the point where we think that people don't have the right to make their own decisions? Let me give you an example that will come close to home: I feel very uncomfortable with seventeen-year-old women deciding to be surgically sterilized. It's a lifetime decision, not easily reversible. And yet because I do believe in choice and in having the widest range of choices available, I feel very uncomfortable about rules that seventeen-year-old women may not be sterilized. It echoes some of those old days of the "one-hundred and twenty rule," where your children times your age had to equal one-hundred and twenty. Although we should validate a range of choices, some choices may not be acceptable, and we have to think about that.

Given that we have our values, and given that we have these diversities, where do we get the power to implement them? What's the power base that we have? What's the organizing strategy? What kinds of resources can we call on? What kinds of tactics can we use? These are all questions that we will be exploring, and should be exploring. Although I don't think the answers are easy, at least we can hope to be better informed by the end of the conference.

Response

Judy Norsigian

One of the most basic issues we're discussing here is control: who's making the decisions about what kinds of contraceptive research gets done, what kind of options or other services are offered; what kind of information actually reaches women about contraceptive options. At this point I don't think women have much control. And I doubt that we are gaining ground in this area.

I was really struck when Laura Punnett said something like "women wouldn't do things to themselves that are unsafe." I'm not sure this is always true. I am reminded of a recent survey by a professor of pharmacology and toxicology at the University of Rochester.[1] One hundred and sixty four women who were post-partum and had decided not to breastfeed their infants were given patient package inserts for estrogen products (to dry up their milk). Half of them decided that the risks were greater than the benefits after reading the package inserts. But after discussing the estrogen products with their physicians, only six of them refused the drug.

Why would so many women decide that something is unsafe and then take it anyway? To answer this we have to consider many other factors like subtle and not-so-subtle pressures from physicians, family, and friends, or a lack of confidence in our ability to make good decisions for ourselves once offered information to absorb and assess. However, in women-controlled health care settings, such obstacles are less likely to interfere with a woman's decision-making process. Instead, a woman more likely would receive support, often in a self-help group, to absorb information at her own pace and to come to a decision that is truly her own.

Many of us are calling for more women-controlled research and women-controlled services. It is only ethical, I think, that women have major control over the research and services that affect us primarily. Some might argue that the efficacy of women-controlled research or women-controlled facilities must first be "proven" (by whose standards, one might ask) before their widespread existence can be justified. However, this position fails to acknowledge the primary importance of women-controlled research and services, as well as the fact that the evaluation criteria used in women-controlled settings might be quite different from conventional criteria.

Carol Korenbrot suggested that in this current era of contraceptive research we're seeing a resurgent interest in safety. Yes, there may be more rigid protocols, and yes, the FDA is requiring much more extensive research on drugs. But basically I don't think that safety is of much current concern among researchers and policy makers. In fact, I think it's of much less concern than efficacy.

For instance, when the Central Medical Committee of the International Planned Parenthood Federation (IPPF) met in March of this year to review the new data on Depo-Provera, even though the physicians present were supposedly all reputable scientists and practitioners, they didn't even read the data themselves. Instead, they read a short, several page summary prepared by a staff person at IPPF. The summary concluded that IPPF should not change its policy vis-à-vis Depo-Provera, but should continue providing 60 to 70 countries around the world with it.[2] Their policy continues as is.

Yet the word is getting out to other countries. Sometimes we can have unexpected allies. Even the Colombia Society of Obstetrics (which is practically all men) discourages the use of Depo-Provera, as indicated in the following memo sent from Colombia, South America:

> Much caution. The injection that is safe for a sexual life without risk of pregnancy for...three months might cause sterility or tumors. A measure of security for three months, not to be subjected to the routine of taking a drug daily, and it is 99.9% effective [which isn't even true, JN]—what woman would not have a feeling of attraction for the apparent benefits of this contraceptive? However, this product, which is a source of pleasure of great popularity with the peasant class because its use doesn't involve the necessity of periodic travel to town to acquire contraceptives, is dangerous. Depo-Provera is a drug whose license is under a freeze in the U.S.

Further on, it says,

> In October, 1974, many doubts arose about the effects of the drug, causing its licensing to be frozen in the US. Then the manufacturer decided to export the product to developing countries. Meanwhile the drug continued in Colombia at a price of eight pesos and is sold liberally in all drug stores in the country [eight pesos is about twenty cents], with a notice that the literature on the drug meets the requirements of the medical community. Nothing is said about its dangerous effects.
>
> Up to now, the health authorities have not formulated any contraindications or recommendations regarding the effects of

this contraceptive or its unpredictable consequences. But now the woman must be forewarned. She should avoid the use of this drug and consider the opinions of organizations like the Colombian Society of Obstetrics, which discourages its use.

I might add that a reputable scientist in the field of drug research, Bruce Schearer, also has come to the conclusion that Depo-Provera should not be on the market at this point, given the findings of recent studies. He says,

> Dogs and monkeys appear to have developed cancers of their reproductive systems while receiving Depo-Provera. Other contraceptives tested in a similar manner in animals have not produced this effect. Based on these facts, it is my view that Depo-Provera should not be given to women as a contraceptive until and unless convincing new evidence is gathered to show either that these animal data are wrong or that Depo-Provera does *not* cause cancer in humans.[3]

So there can be unlikely allies. As unpleasant as it may seem at times, women health activists have to make whatever allies we can. Already drug companies and population control advocates have identified many common interests. Drug companies want to get their products onto the market, and population control advocates are always after new, more "acceptable" products. The power these two forces represent can quite effectively counter anything that we might do. I don't thing that co-optation is necessarily inevitable whenever women's health activists and feminists work with establishment groups, individuals from government agencies, or even population control groups. Sometimes we can avoid being co-opted.

In addition, I hope we will all look carefully at natural family planning programs now emerging in many of our communities. Currently, most of these programs are run either directly or indirectly by Catholic groups that usually are anti-abortion. In fact, "natural family planning" is really a Catholic term. As government funding becomes available for natural birth control programs, it is important that nonreligious, nondogmatic, women-controlled programs also receive Federal support. If Catholic groups succeed in obtaining the major portion of Federal monies earmarked for natural birth control programs, as it appears they well might, anti-abortion forces will have obtained a new, possibly more insidious, foothold in their campaign against the reproductive rights of women.

Contraceptives Discussion

Moderated by Margaret A. Kohn and Michael Gross

Joan Holtzman: Have more women recently become involved either in high technology research into new contraceptives or in barrier method research, since more women are going to medical school or becoming scientists?

Belita Cowan: The National Women's Health Network analyzed all of the federally and privately funded contraceptive research projects in fiscal 1977. We found that approximately 10.5% of 900 researchers were female; in the private sector it was a little lower.

Helen Rodriguez: Although I basically agree with Kristin Luker that we need to demand some kind of prospective monitoring of new modalities introduced—including methods of abortion—it seems to me that a large part of the story was left out. Illegal abortions and their mortality and morbidity weren't talked about at all.

Kristin Luker: It's very hard to get any data, but after World War II most illegal abortions seem to have been done by family doctors. The back alley abortionists certainly existed, of course, and were disproportionately used by women of color and poor women. If you were middle-class, you would just come in after the office closed; you probably would have a D&C; they would "forget" to do a pregnancy test beforehand and pathology work-up afterwards. With mostly physicians doing these illegal abortions you have antibiotics, and some degree of followup. I think that is a real dividing line. So while I'm not arguing for illegal abortion, its current risks, although higher than those of legal abortion, aren't as high as they were in the 19th and early 20th centuries.

Terry Courtney: As a women's health activist, I'm particularly sensitive to the abortion issue right now because of the increasing difficulty that women are facing in gaining access to abortion. Abortion has been here since the beginning of time. Until the 1900s, abortions were done by nonmedical abortionists, and women who performed those services for other women provided good care. The lack of separation of church and state and a political swing to the right

89

are clouding the abortion issue for many people in this country. It's important to acknowledge that abortion has been a positive choice for many women to make. Women have died, and are dying now, because of lack of access to safe abortion, and we have to recognize the vital importance of keeping this option available. Abortion is a cornerstone of women's reproductive rights. There must be an ongoing struggle by all women to retain this right.

Kristin Luker: We wouldn't want to go back to 19th century medicine anywhere, even though 19th century abortions were much better than 19th century amputations or some other surgical interventions. It's not something that is trivial or without meaning for lots of women, and it may not be an operation without risk. It's also not necessarily a dangerous, life-threatening, wrong, "immoral" thing to do. But before we choose it we ought to think about the social and psychological implications.

Joyce Berkman: Actually historical statistics on infanticide record a substantial drop in the early 19th century, as abortion became more widely practiced. I think we need to be wary of historical overstatements. In recognizing the dangers of abortion, we don't want to paint too bleak an image of the irregular folk healing methods often offered by skilled female abortionists of the 19th century.

Laura Punnett: Concerning Judy Norsigian's remarks, I want to clarify that I am promoting women-controlled research not only because it is safer. I take a starting position that it's ethically preferable because the research is being controlled and evaluated by the people who are the subjects. Women-controlled research isn't just a theoretical concept or fantasy. There are concrete examples that are valuable to look at to inspire us and to suggest ways to explore it further.

Emily Culpepper: I have two concerns: I don't feel we're really developing the context that women are in. We've talked about personal values, religious values, class, race, etc. But consider the absence of male agitation for male birth control side-by-side with the growing women's agitation for control of information about ourselves, and with the male predominance in current research technology. The whole context becomes almost overwhelming.

Also, I have an uneasy feeling when talking about women as "them." I'm not trying to be accusatory, but it's especially important when we talk about who will understand and employ which method. For example, I'm really fascinated by natural birth control methods and observing the vaginal mucus as one form of birth control. But relying on that can be discussed in a way that sounds like women who are not going to inspect their vaginal mucus every day are somehow leading less responsible lives, or that, in an ideal world, all women should be responsible in that way. I'd like to see other models. I'm interested in birth control technologies that will work *now* for women in a diversity of situations.

Tabitha Powledge: I certainly view informed consent regulations and patient package inserts as an improvement over the situation ten or fifteen years ago, but there's a big danger in relying too heavily on those documents. They are being written essentially to protect the researchers from being sued, rather than to impart information. The aim of providing information to the patient really conflicts with the aim of protecting the scientist from legal liability.

Do the other speakers see the methods they talked about as complementary to more technological methods, or as more desirable, something that we ought to work towards exclusively?

Laura Punnett: I was speaking about options—about the need to increase the number of options that are directly under women's control. I'm not sure there will ever be one ideal method and I don't advocate any particular method for every woman.

One of the reasons I speak about menstrual extraction is that there has been legal harassment of women experimenting with that method. I think it's important for us all to know about that, and to be prepared to defend our right to participate in women-controlled research.

Jill Wolhandler: The self-help philosophy about birth control is that women should have access to all information about the full range of options and make their own choices. I don't think there's ever going to be one method that's desirable to everyone who wants to use birth control. The work of our health center demonstrates that very clearly. A lot of our birth control work is done in groups where women talk to each other about their experiences with different methods of birth control, and where health workers make sure that all the different effective methods are summarized so that women know what they are, including the risks and complications. It's important to know that some natural birth control methods *are* effective, and that you don't have to have an advanced education or a religious background to use your own basic body information for effective birth control. At this point we provide pills, IUDs, diaphragms, and abortions, as well as woman-controlled natural birth control. We have women doing research into the cervical cap, and we're very strongly involved in the abortion struggle.

Judy Norsigian: Women may choose not to use all the information they get. That's not a reason to withhold it. Many people *don't get* the information, though they still have a right to it.

Emily Culpepper: Belita, the Health Study of the American

Male, costing millions of dollars, is meant to study the long term effects of vasectomy. What is being done to study the long-term effects of sterilization procedures in women?

Belita Cowan: In our inventory, there were fifteen projects under the category of "sterilization." All fifteen concern men, and the bulk of them were evaluating the health effects—short and long term—of vasectomy. I didn't find any similar studies for women.

Renée Jenkins: I take care of teenagers for family planning care as well as for general health. The difficulty in prescribing is just immense because many times the methods available are not safe or appropriate for young women; it's not just that they aren't interested. I have never fully considered natural family planning. Have younger women been involved in this and, if so, what's been your experience?

Jill Wolhandler: There have been only a few teenaged women in our groups. We do know of younger women who use natural birth control successfully. Again we run into the problem that almost all of the natural birth control studies have been done by Catholics who teach and study married couples.

Elizabeth Kutter: I think that these methods are being developed more on the West Coast. I had two students working quite successfully with the ovulation method. One was teaching the method at The Evergreen State College Health Services. Another has been working with teenagers and others for two years through Planned Parenthood in Portland, Oregon. With 300 women there was only one "failure" out of the first 12 months; that individual knew she was fertile at the time she was having intercourse, so that was a so-called "patient failure" rather than a "system failure." This student's work shows, I think, the importance of making a variety of alliances with all sorts of groups.

In all these areas we need to carefully train ourselves to collect and analyze data on effectiveness and consequences. The student in Portland is examining in detail variations in cyclic patterns. She finds, for instance, that cycles almost always are abnormal for a number of months after going off the pill; this has many implications for pill-users in general, and particularly for those trying to switch to the ovulation method. The main reason for her general success, I think, is that she insists on careful followup in the first few months after the initial class. It's a very different approach from the self-help group's, but it's reaching a different and equally important group of people and it's also not being done in a specific religious context.

Judy Norsigian: The Population Council estimated that in 1976 about $50,000 out of $70,000,000 spent worldwide on population research went to barrier methods of contraception. Two years ago, the *Inventory Analysis of Federal Population Research* didn't mention barrier method research. Last year, a short paragraph in it called for more research into barrier methods. That paragraph was inserted in large part because of pressure from groups like the National Women's Health Network. Hopefully the Center for Population Research soon will call for proposals on research into barrrier methods such as the cervical cap. [In the fall of 1979 an RFP (request for proposals) *was* released by the Center for Population Research for a comparative cervical cap/diaphragm study. Awards are to be granted in 1980.]

Margaret Kohn: I have a couple of comments on informed consent and how it gets corrupted and used for the benefit of the researchers. On the one hand, if you overdo informed consent, then you're being protective and people aren't making their own decisions— and of course we think that people should make their own decisions. On the other hand, we know from research that people will agree to do things that are clearly bad for their health because they are presented by people who, they believe, know better. Or they are convinced that, because it's offered by a physician, it can't hurt them—even though the physician himself says it could be dangerous. That dilemma and that problem make all the more important the involvement of feminist women on human subject review panels that review research protocols, determine what must go into informed consent, structure the research so that it isn't damaging to those subjects, and draw the line against some research because it's not appropriate.

The development of contraceptives of any kind is going to involve research on women. We need to assess how to balance our need for new methods against the injuries that will happen to people in the course of that development. Basically we had a huge experiment in the United States when the pill went on the market. At present the FDA conducts inadequate post-market surveillance. A new food and drug bill now on the floor of the Congress proposes a better system for post-market reviewability. I think we should all take an interest in that legislation.

The other critical thing is patient package inserts and information on prescription—as well as nonprescription—drugs. In the United States only three or four prescription drugs have a package insert that goes to the patient when that drug is prescribed: IUDs, oral contraceptives, estrogens, and a nasal spray for asthmatics. For all other prescription drugs written information is given the patient only when the providers themselves—usually clinics and rarely private physicians—volunteer to provide that information in written form. Requiring such an information sheet is another issue in the drug bill. You can be sure that organized medicine and the drug companies are not very eager—though from time to time they say they are—to require patient package inserts on a wide variety of drugs and devices.

Norma Swenson: I also know that physicians are on the committees that are writing those inserts, and we've just heard that the lawyers are too. But as far as I know we have not established the right for women to get on those committees to help state the information in a way that is meaningful and relevant to women consumers, the majority. I don't know what sort of act or agitation is required to get that right, but I think that's something else we ought to be pressing for—and certainly the National Women's Health Network is one of the groups that's pushing for that possibility.

Byllye Avery: Poor and minority women are the first to know when there's something to be experimented with to gather data from, and they can't even translate or get the information about the outcome. How can we talk about contraceptive research when the very subjects practiced on are absent? I, for one, would love it if this group could hear what it's like to be a poor woman overburdened with financial and social pressures who goes in to seek health care. You don't want to have any more kids. My god, you can barely make it yourself. You are handed something that might have certain risks, but then you look at the other side and say, "What is life worth anyway?" I don't feel any link between the discussion here and what we in direct services say that is meaningful to those people back home.

Depo-Provera and Sterilization Abuse

Organized by

Marie M. Cassidy

Depo-Provera and Sterilization Abuse Overview

Marie M. Cassidy

Depo-Provera is a progestogen, a synthetic compound with the effects of the natural hormone progesterone. Like oral contraceptives, it prevents pregnancy largely by inhibiting ovulation. It also increases the viscosity of cervical mucus, thus creating a sticky barrier to spermatozoa. The drug appears to make the endometrium (the lining of the uterus) less suitable for implantation. It is a long-lasting contraceptive administered by injection every three months that is almost 100 percent effective.

Papers and discussion on Depo-Provera and sterilization abuse— by a panel diverse in ethnic background, work activity, and volunteer interests—raise themes that emerge again and again in discussions of other aspects of reproductive technology. It does appear that women share some new and alternative applicable social values. This is evident regardless of the specific topic considered, and across the categories of women, whether they be consumers (or the "consumed"), medical researchers, advocates, philosophers, or medical practitioners. The health care system and the closely allied biomedical research activities of this society are undoubtedly dominated by a patriarchal, white male view of societal needs. (This has recently been documented with impressive thoroughness by Naomi Naierman.[1]) We share the belief that there has to be a better approach to policy development and to the utilization of our planetary resources in the resolution of the very real ethical conflicts confronting us in a free society.

Five themes emerge from the contributions and comments to follow. They are:

1. The genocidal aspects of certain policy developments and actual practices.
2. The quality of medical care in American society as it relates to a corporate capitalistic, extractive, and technological view of human needs.

3. The principles and, more important, the desirable practices associated with free choice, informed consent, and participation of users in the structure and detailed operation of the medical care mechanisms.

4. The overwhelming importance, in the closing decades of the 20th century, of the American medical model to other people and older civilizations, whether that be a "hands-off" neglect or "hands-on" manipulation attitude.

5. Finally, perhaps the most difficult and challenging problem of all, namely: the concepts of equality versus true equity; the conflict between the moral good or ethical characteristics of a human act and the selfhood or "rights" orientation that has been well articulated in the past two decades in this century.

The linkage between the issues of Depo-Provera and sterilization abuse are clearly brought forth in Sandy Serrano-Sewell's and Gena Corea's papers. Two policy objectives strongly correlate: the extraordinarily large number of Puerto Rican women who have been sterilized, and the utilization by or provision of Depo-Provera to Third World populations. In both milieux, uncontrolled fertility is seen to pose a threat to mainstream American life-styles and to continued consumption economics. As pointed out by Helen Rodriguez and several discussants, abuse per se happens and is occurring whenever choices are arbitrarily limited by those with power, whether the limiting factor be social, political, or economic. Poor women and Third World women do know what they want[2] and can express it very eloquently indeed.

Concerning the quality and operative procedures common in the medical care system, Helen Barnes suggests that consumer education and the exercise of options by patients could be a faster route to improvement than planning a reconstruction of the system from the top down. This view was hotly contested by participants who believe that removal of the profit motive, removal of the focus on high-intensity extractive technology, and elimination of an elitist patriarchal approach would be more effective pathways for improvement.

The third issue is broader and difficult: how much regulation is good, and how much is demeaning to the idea of free choice. Democratic processes require participation by those who understand not only complex technical matters but, in addition, other human beings. Most medical practitioners have had little exposure to such tedious and time-consuming interchanges. An important clarification that emerges here is that "informed consent" should include a provision whereby the patient must reflect back to the medical practitioner her or his understanding of the explanation offered. Practicing medicine in this way requires both linguistic and psychosocial interpretive skills and services.

A large portion of the responsibility for drug safety in this society currently resides in government agencies. Carol Levine's appraisal of the Depo-Provera decision-making process and its implications, and Joyce Lashof's stimulating remarks during the discussion demonstrate that making the right decision about these matters is beset as much by a lack of knowledge of the probable outcome as it is by malign intent on the part of people with power.

Corporate investments propel the development and then inevitably the mass marketing of drugs and devices that may prove unsafe, but also overwhelmingly profitable. The medical scientific world currently has no way of predicting the "nuisance" side-effects that a woman may experience *or* the life-threatening consequences that might develop in the long-term. Should there be a "cafeteria?" What and how much should it contain? It is certainly clear that risk/benefit ratios are appropriate tools to use in grappling with this problem. Although it is certainly not a new idea it would be a new *approach* to assessing values and determining policy to include significantly more women and especially Third World women in the debate. Even our knowledge of overseas medical-care systems as they relate to women is rudimentary[3]; we are highly suspicious of what little we do know. Participants express the need to strengthen our bonds with all other women everywhere in identifying and formulating some answers to our common and very real concerns.

The most intriguing concept to arise, especially in a feminist gathering, derives from feminist thought at the frontiers of philosophy. Should we view health-care practices and priorities in the context of asserting our rights and needs (and naturally those of others)? The demand for our rights in any situation may be monopolistic and manipulative rather than communal and caring. As expressed by Helen Rodriguez, providing education and "supportive" help in a given situation may be preferable to the delivery of questionable high technology. This particular perspective certainly would broaden the policy debate on reproductive issues, but it has not yet received important public expression.

Depo-Provera

Some Ethical Questions About
A Controversial Contraceptive

Carol Levine

INTRODUCTION

Depo-Provera is convenient to use, and simple to administer. No deaths directly attributable to the drug have been reported. It does not require the male partner's cooperation. Its use is not related to the timing of sexual intercourse.

Depo-Provera sounds too good to be true. And, not surprisingly, Depo-Provera turns out to be less than the ideal contraceptive. It has many serious risks and side effects. Among the major side effects are disturbed menstrual patterns and a delayed return to fertility once the drug usage is stopped. Suspicions have been raised that it causes permanent sterility and birth defects. Perhaps most worrisome, it has been linked to increased risk of cancer.

For twelve years the FDA has vacillated about Upjohn's application for approval of Depo-Provera as a contraceptive. It is approved for use as a palliative in endometrial cancer. It is being used under an FDA Investigative Drug Permit in an experimental program for male sex offenders as a form of chemical castration. The FDA will probably grant Upjohn's request for a hearing before a special Board of Inquiry—the first in FDA's history. That board will be made up of scientists who will discuss the scientific evidence about Depo-Provera.

What they probably will not discuss are the ethical issues:

- Informed consent and access to information.
- The ethics of placing special populations—with special contraceptive needs—at special risk.
- The ethics of establishing a double standard for American women and Third World women.
- The conflict of values between autonomy and birth control.
- The overriding issue: Who will decide these questions?

My position is essentially a conservative one: I believe that the present FDA disapproval of Depo-Provera as a contraceptive should stand, both to protect American women from unnecessary risk and to prevent further American involvement in the distribution of this drug abroad.

RISKS AND "LIMITED USE"

Perhaps the most accurate conclusion that can be drawn from all the claims and counterclaims about risks and benefits is that Depo-Provera, definitely effective and convenient as a contraceptive, does present a certain degree of risk—in some respects higher, and in many respects unknown—in comparison with other contraceptive methods. The presence of some risk is not really at issue; most proponents are not arguing that Depo-Provera ought to be added to the list of contraceptive methods that are offered to the average middle-class woman visiting a private physician. Nor, on the other hand, is it argued that a contraceptive or any drug must be risk-free before it is approved. Many drugs—for example, chemotherapeutic agents—carry substantial risks, yet are approved for use in treating serious diseases such as cancer. The benefits—prolonging life, inhibiting the spread of cancer—here outweigh the risks and the very unpleasant side effects.

Is there a comparable benefit to be attained through the use of Depo-Provera? The purpose of this drug is not to treat disease, but to prevent pregnancy. Is that goal so crucial to the lives of those patients for whom Depo-Provera might be recommended that the risks ought to be discounted? This is an arguable point; however, those who are arguing that contraception is paramount are not the women themselves, but those who claim to speak for them—family planners, medical professionals, and program administrators.

Although Upjohn vehemently denies the allegations that Depo-Provera is intended for poor women or for "second-class citizens," it is difficult to avoid the conclusion that the drug's target population in the United States would be those or other similarly vulnerable groups, such as institutionalized mentally ill women and the mentally retarded. The FDA's Advisory Committee in 1975 described the list of potential users:

> Patients who have been made aware and accept the possibility that they may not be able to become pregnant again after discontinuing Depo-Provera and *refuse* or *are unable to accept the responsibility* demanded by other contraceptive methods; or *are incapable or unwilling* to tolerate the side effects of conventional oral contraceptives; or patients in whom other methods of

contraception are contraindicated or have repeatedly *failed* (italics added).

One can feel in these words the frustration of medical professionals and family planners in dealing with women who will not or cannot do what is considered by others to be in their best interests!

In a letter to FDA Commissioner Donald Kennedy, included in Upjohn's response to the FDA's letter of rejection of its application, Richard Brookman, M.D., of the Children's Hospital Medical Center in Cincinnati, cites, in addition to the retarded, another group in need of Depo-Provera: adolescent girls with sickle cell disease (who are likely to be black). There are a small number of these girls, Brookman claims, for whom pregnancy imposes serious health risks, sexual activity does not appear to be preventable, and methods of contraception are inappropriate. He outlines some of the medical reasons oral contraceptives and IUDs may be poor choices; however, the key seems to be that "... like most adolescents, young women with sickle cell disease have great difficulty in employing mechanical methods of contraception consistently, correctly, and hence effectively." This claim is certainly open to question, but it is a social argument, not strictly a medical one, that is being used to support the drug.

Even if one were to concede that for some very limited groups Depo-Provera might be the only contraceptive choice, how will they and others be protected against abuse? The FDA had proposed as a condition for its earlier approval that an information sheet outlining the drug's risks and benefits be given to the patient (or parent or guardian) before the drug was administered and another brochure given to the patient (or parent or guardian) afterwards. Physicians who prescribed the drug would have been required to register with the FDA, so that patients could be contacted later on for followup if evidence of risk appeared. The protection that would have been provided by these mechanisms is grossly inadequate. No enforcement procedures were mandated; reliance on the physician's good will would surely seem to be a misplaced trust in this sensitive area.

Because of their age, intellectual capabilities, or environmental circumstances the capacity of these special populations to consent is diminished. Yet precisely because of those prior limitations, they (or their guardians) must consent to even greater risks. If these patients were capable of asking all the right questions about risk, understanding the answers, and making competent decisions for themselves, they would almost certainly be able to use other contraceptive methods. That they cannot is surely cause for concern— for education, further research, more individual attention—but not necessarily grounds for administering a risky contraceptive.

DOUBLE STANDARDS FOR THE THIRD WORLD

One might conclude that Depo-Provera ought not be licensed for American use, but still ought be made available to the Third World. This was the position of many foreign witnesses at the US Select Committee on Population hearings last summer. Dr. Frederick Sai of Ghana, speaking on behalf of International Planned Parenthood Foundation, said, "The maternal mortality rates in the less developed countries, particularly Africa, range from one to ten per thousand births. This is 100 to over 200 times the comparable rate for the US." Any risk comparison of Depo-Provera, he said, "would have to be comparison not only with other contraceptives, but also with pregnancy itself."

FDA Commissioner Donald Kennedy held open the door for a new policy on Depo-Provera.

> Quite obviously, a drug that may not be suitable for approval here could well have a favorable benefit/risk ratio in a less developed nation.... The Administration in cooperation with Congress is presently involved in a total rewrite of the drug laws. The new proposals will address the export of drugs which have not been approved for marketing in the United States. An approach we are exploring is the desirability of authorizing the Secretary to grant a permit for the export of such a drug if, among other conditions, evidence is provided that the drug meets the specifications of the foreign purchaser, and that the Government of the country of destination has approved the importation and distribution of the drug.

Fertility control is a very real problem in the Third World. Still, serious ethical problems remain if such a legislative shift were to be carried out. The capabilities for screening high-risk users from the general family planning program population are likely to be very limited, particularly in rural areas. The information about risks is likely to be under-presented given the program planners' commitment to the drug. Medical followup is also likely to be restricted to the most severe side effects. If Depo-Provera is to be used at all, in very special circumstances, it seems to require the most careful kind of individual medical attention, a situation that is very rare in poor countries.

The best results in birth control do not depend on family planning programs alone, and certainly not on the availability of one contraceptive, but on a whole range of measures that improve income distribution, raise the educational level of women, provide better maternal and infant health care and sanitation, and create more jobs, and more opportunities for meaningful choices in life. Given that range of social and economic measures, women will seek on their own to control fertility and, thus motivated, will choose methods that are best suited to their medical and other needs. Under these circumstances, the simplicity and convenience of Depo-Provera will probably not weigh so heavily in the risk/benefit equation.

Still, the decision about the use of Depo-Provera properly belongs to the citizens of each country, not the United States. It would be a continuation of the kind of paternalism that has plagued the United States' presence in poor countries to try to establish an outright ban on the drug. In the final analysis, perhaps the best policy is to continue the current practice of prohibiting American sales of Depo-Provera overseas, unless it is approved for domestic use, not because it would be wrong for those nations to use the drug, but because it would be wrong for this country to provide it. Depo-Provera will still be available through other sources, and this country will not have assumed the responsibility of providing a drug that may in the long run turn out to be detrimental to the health of millions of women.

The Depo-Provera Weapon

Gena Corea

Experts testifying on contraceptives before the Senate last year occasionally sounded like army generals giving Congressmen a briefing on new weapons systems. For example, in a paper he co-authored and submitted for the hearing record, one witness used such terms as "the vaginal delivery system," "target organ," "subject compliance," "delivery platform," and "the target population."

At these hearings, Dr. Stephen D. Mumford argued that world population growth is a national security issue, and that responsibility for slowing that growth should be handed over to the US Department of Defense.[1]

Dr. R. T. Ravenholt, director of US Agency for International Development's Office for Population, also sees the teeming masses of the Third World as a potential threat to US security. In an interview with the *St. Louis Post-Dispatch,* he explained why the United States should lead world population control efforts. Continuation of the population explosion, he said, would result in such terrible socioeconomic conditions abroad that revolutions would result and these revolutions could harm the US. In a conversation with me, Ravenholt amplified: An increase in population results in extreme poverty and "where people are poor and intensely dissatisfied with their lot in life, they are sooner or later engaged in trying, even through violent methods, to change it."[2]

I bring all this up because at those Senate hearings I've referred to, experts also discussed the synthetic progesterone-like hormone, Depo-Provera. With all its side-effects—minor and major, suspected or known—it is difficult to imagine how such a drug could even be considered as a contraceptive for free citizens. But if we look on Depo-Provera, not as an aid developed to help women control their reproductive lives, but as a particularly efficient weapon in a war against female fertility, then much confusing information becomes comprehensible.

In March, 1978, the US Food and Drug Administration (FDA) declined to approve Depo-Provera as a contraceptive because of the

107

drug's potentially serious risks to women. (Upjohn, the drug's manufacturer, wants this decision reversed. FDA will grant the company a Board of Public Inquiry hearing on the matter.) Despite its non-approved status, the drug is administered as a contraceptive in this country—largely, but not exclusively, to minority and institutionalized women.[3]

Men aim the Depo-Provera weapon at the powerless. As witnesses testified before the House Select Committee on Population last August, the drug's "target population" includes the poor, the illiterate or semiliterate woman, the "unmotivated"—i.e., women who might choose not to use contraception were they allowed that choice— and women in developing countries.

"...A long-acting contraceptive would have nearly ideal advantages...in populations with low socioeconomic status and low educational attainment...," Dr. Juan Zanartu of the University of Chile Medical School stated.

A long-acting injectable is considered desirable for "a certain population" because its use requires a minimum of intelligence and initiative in recipients. Like the eugenicists, their ideological forefathers, many population controllers tend to view the poor as ignorant and irresponsible.[4] (Eugenicists, active in America from 1900 until the 1930s, often advocated sterilization of the "unfit"—i.e., the immigrant, the poor and people of color—in order to improve the "stock" of the human race.) The great advantage of Depo-Provera to population control advocates is that they can inject the women, send them on their way, and not have to see them again for another three to six months. The program is designed without a provision for followup. As Dr. Philip Corfman, director of the Center for Population Research, testified at Congressional hearings in August 1978: "We estimate that from 3 to 5 million women presently use this drug as a contraceptive worldwide, but unfortunately very little effort has been made to follow these women to monitor long-term safety." By its very nature then, the injection of women with Depo-Provera is human experimentation on a massive scale.

Let me describe the effects this drug weapon has on the bodies of women.

Depo-Provera does successfully prevent conception. It may do so by dealing a substantial shock to the hypothalamus resulting in suppression of ovulation.[5] The long-term effects (or "fall-out") of Depo-Provera, it is generally agreed, are unknown. Animal and clinical studies, however, suggest that risks of the drug include: a lowered life expectancy; temporary or permanent infertility; anemia;

diabetes; uterine disease; permanent damage to the pituitary gland; lowered resistance to infection; deformities in offspring; and cervical, endometrial, and breast cancer.

Among Depo-Provera's immediate possible side-effects are: abdominal discomfort; substantial weight gain or loss; depression; loss or diminution of libido and/or orgasm; headache, dizziness; loss of hair; spotty darkening of facial skin; elevated levels of sugar and fatty substances in the blood; nausea; limb pain; vaginal discharge; breast discomfort, and disruption of the menstrual cycle.

These are the *minor* side-effects. Medical experts usually run through this list hurriedly as though such effects were of little consequence. They move on to the more worrisome question of Depo-Provera-induced cancer. Before I follow suit, I must make these points:

1. Depression is a minor side-effect that merely destroys the entire quality of a woman's life.

2. It is distressing to see your hair fall out and dark blotches appear on your face.

3. As many women lose weight on Depo-Provera as gain it. To thin, undernourished women in the Third World, weight loss can be an extremely serious health threat.

4. It is doubtful that a male contraceptive that entailed such a "side-effect" as "loss of libido and/or orgasm" would be acceptable to men. Neither is it appropriate for women. Without sexual arousal, intercourse is a distasteful ordeal—an ordeal women should not be expected to endure routinely.[6]

Another immediate side-effect of Depo-Provera is the almost total disruption of the woman's menstrual cycle. At first, the bleeding is highly irregular and sometimes very heavy. This can produce severe anemia in well-nourished women. In women who are marginally nourished, the dangers are much greater.

With continued administration, 40–95 percent of women become amenorrheic; that is, they lose their periods. Dr. Mokhtar Toppozada of Alexandria University, a proponent of the drug, noted at Congressional hearings: "Very little is known about the possible risks induced by cycle alterations caused by Depo-Provera."[7]

The potential long-term consequences of drug usage affect the children of Depo-Provera targets. The breast-feeding infant and the fetus *in utero* may both be at risk. In Africa, in promotional literature distributed by Upjohn and in many family planning materials, Depo-Provera is recommended for the lactating mother because, according to some medical studies, it does not decrease milk production. But

Depo-Provera is found in very high concentrations in breast milk and its safety for the infant has not been established and is not being studied.

The newborn is physiologically immature. She has a poorly developed capacity for metabolizing and eliminating drugs.[8] As one investigator has noted, this increases the risk that the exogenous steroids the infant sucks in with her milk will adversely affect her.[9] There is some concern that the steroids may impair the infant pituitary and, years later, affect the onset of puberty.[10] Studies in nursing mice, which have shown that Depo-Provera significantly delays the reproductive development of females, heighten this concern.[11]

There is reason to fear for the welfare, not only of the nursing child, but of the fetus exposed to Depo-Provera *in utero.* Depo-Provera is a synthetic progestin. Because of evidence that progestins pose an increased risk of congenital anomalies (teratogenic effects) to the fetuses exposed to them, the FDA has recently revised the labeling of all progestin drugs to include a warning against their use during pregnancy.

If a woman is already pregnant when she is injected with Depo-Provera, there is no way to remove the drug from her body. The fetus will be exposed to the drug—not for one day, as with other progestins—but for up to six months. In one study, two percent of the women injected with Depo-Provera were already pregnant and another two percent became pregnant while on the drug.[12] FDA Commissioner Kennedy stated before Congress: "In the Bureau's view, this could result in an increased number of infants born with serious congenital malformations."

Although all these effects are disturbing, most discussions of Depo-Provera focus on the cancer issue. The results of studies dealing with the drug's carcinogenic potential are often inconclusive, partly because studies commissioned by Upjohn were sloppy, used questionable protocols, and produced data that investigators have difficulty interpreting.

In 1972, studies conducted by FDA and Upjohn found that Depo-Provera and several other progestins caused malignant breast tumors in the beagle dog. Some of the malignant tumors spread to other organs.[13] As a result of the studies, oral contraceptives containing chemicals identical to or similar to Depo-Provera were removed from the US market.

When the beagle studies were publicized, proponents of injectable Depo-Provera quickly moved to discount the significance of the findings, arguing that dogs are uniquely sensitive to progestins generally, and that beagle dogs are more susceptible to breast tumors than humans are. In March, 1976, the Human Reproduction Unit of the World Health Organization convened an international committee to evaluate the arguments. It concluded that the beagle dog is an appropriate animal for testing the long-term effects of sex hormones on the human breast.[14]

While the beagle studies raised the question of Depo-Provera-induced breast cancer, studies on women raised concern about cervical cancer. Suggestive, but not conclusive, evidence indicated that Depo-Provera may increase a woman's chances of developing cervical cancer by up to 9.1 times the national rate.[15]

Until now, the debate on Depo-Provera has focused largely on these studies. But the National Women's Health Network has recently obtained documents on the drug that suggest the possibility that Depo-Provera may also cause fatal endometrial disease.

Upjohn began seven-year beagle and ten-year monkey safety studies on Depo-Provera in 1968. Within four years, 18 of the 20 dogs in the first study were dead. Depo-Provera's action on the uterus had killed them. The two remaining dogs had been saved by hysterectomies. In the control group, only one dog died, the cause attributed to pneumonia.

In Upjohn's subsequent study, researchers removed the uteri from all dogs *before* injecting the animals with Depo-Provera. FDA approved this protocol.[16] "Why the FDA would agree to the routine removal of a large part of the reproductive tract in contraceptive studies needs to be further explained,"[17] commented Stephen Minkin, health policy analyst for the National Women's Health Network and author of "Depo-Provera: A Critical Analysis."

Upjohn and FDA offered me this explanation: The hysterectomies were a valid scientific procedure. Researchers undertook the beagle studies to learn whether Depo-Provera would cause breast tumors, not to see whether it would harm the uterus. The uterus of the dog is especially susceptible to progestational agents, including Depo-Provera. Therefore, the dogs would have died of endometrial disease before they had had time to develop breast cancer. The hysterectomies then had to be done to save the dogs' lives so they could have the opportunity to develop breast tumors.

Although the question is still open, I am not persuaded at this point by the argument that the canine uterus is especially susceptible to progestins.[18]

Another objection to the reasoning of Upjohn and FDA is this: The major concern about Depo-Provera was not breast cancer, but uterine cancer. Other Upjohn studies had shown a very dramatic increase in cervical cancer—not in any controversial animal studies—but in human beings. The FDA had known of this potential problem since 1971, when it discontinued all Depo-Provera studies in humans. If such a problem is seen in human populations, it is most important to make careful observations of that organ in animals.[19]

The unanswered question remains: Why did FDA not mandate tests for uterine cancer *as well as* tests for breast cancer?[20]

While attention was focused on the breast cancer issue (". . . at that time, FDA was principally concerned with mammary effects," FDA's Dr. Victor Berliner told me), observers tended to ignore what are probably the most important data from that first dog study: Depo-Provera kills animals.

"The second beagle study served to divert attention," Minkin contends. "They didn't come out and say, 'The drug killed dogs.' They just started getting into esoteric discussions about beagle responses to progesterones and so on."

Even when the uteri were removed, 30 percent of the high dose Depo-Provera dogs were dead in three and a half years.

Evidence Upjohn reported to FDA in 1979 confirmed the fear that Depo-Provera had an adverse effect on the uterus. At least two animals out of ten in Upjohn's monkey study developed endometrial cancer.[21]

In rhesus monkeys, endometrial cancer is very rare.

Commenting on the study, Dr. Rhonda Einhorn, a staff member of the recently disbanded House Select Committee on Population, told *Newsday* that the discovery of cancer in the monkeys was "astounding." She added: "When we talked with researchers at the National Institutes of Health, they had never heard of a case of uterine cancer in the 20 years they have experimented with rhesus monkeys."[22]

"What happened to the monkeys was no surprise," Minkin observed. "After the endometrial findings in the beagles, researchers should have been watching the endometrium in the monkeys."

They claim that they were not. According to the monkey study protocol, the breast was examined each month, but there were no plans to examine the uterus regularly.

Upjohn asserts that researchers did not notice the endometrial cancer until the 10-year study was completed and the monkeys were sacrificed in late 1978. The development of endometrial cancer was allegedly unexpected.

But Dr. Berliner found evidence against the claim that the cancers appeared only in the 10th year of treatment. In a report dated May 11, 1979, he wrote that one monkey with uterine cancer was reported to have had a palpable uterine enlargement for the last two and a half years of the study.

"This upsets the claim by the sponsor that endometrial tumors were not found before the final sacrifice," Dr. Berliner wrote.

This time, Upjohn's response to the bad news on its drug was not that the monkey was especially susceptible to endometrial cancer. This time, reaffirming its belief in Depo-Provera, it stated: "We feel that it's dose-related. It was two of them (the monkeys) in the 50+ human-use group. Again, we do not feel that in the normal contraceptive dosages, it would pose a problem."[23]

Dr. Einhorn disputes that contention: "The reason we give such high doses (in animals) is that we can't afford to wait 50 years until they (cancers) develop."[24]

Cancer was not Upjohn's only finding in the Depo-Provera studies. All the dogs treated with the drug developed anemia. Researchers attributed it to the drug. No control dogs developed the condition.[25]

In the second beagle study, the deaths of several dogs were attributed to "drug induced diabetes."[26] Hyperglycemia was found in two of these dogs. Both treated and untreated dogs developed lumps and other abnormalities in the breast. But, in the Depo-Provera dogs, the incidence, size, and severity of such abnormalities were substantially greater.[27]

Depo-Provera-treated dogs also showed evidence of lowered host resistance to infection. It is suspected (and Upjohn president Dr. William N. Hubbard, Jr. confirmed this in testimony before the House Select Committee on Population) that Depo-Provera may suppress the immunological mechanism. This may make those treated with the drug more susceptible to illness.[28]

If this is true, then the Depo-Provera weapon does not simply attack fertility; in weakening natural female defense mechanisms against disease, it represents the ultimate in suppressing a people's ability to fight back.[29] *Lowered resistance to infection may be the most devastating effect of Depo-Provera,* an effect more significant than any possible induction of cancer. I must emphasize this point: Animals given Depo-Provera die much sooner than animals not exposed to the drug. Proponents argue that the use of Depo-Provera is partly designed to lower the maternal mortality rate in developing countries where that rate is high. But by increasing the susceptibility of child-bearing women to fatal disease, Depo-Provera may, in fact, be raising the death rate among these women.

I suspect that all experts on Depo-Provera are not fully conversant with Upjohn's animal studies. I'll explain how my suspicion arose. Upjohn conducted the dog studies partly to test its claim that natural progesterones, and not just the synthetic progesterone Depo-Provera, can lead to mammary cancer. There were three groups in the study: one control group; one group that received Depo-Provera; and a third that received natural progesterone. But the dogs treated with natural progesterone were given larger doses of the hormone at more frequent intervals than were the dogs who were administered Depo-Provera. Researchers compared the progesterone-treated dogs, which were receiving 1140 mg *every week,* with the Depo-Provera-treated dogs, which were receiving 690 mg only *every 90 days.*

Stephen Minkin and I recently talked with a leading expert on Depo-Provera, and he did not know this. He thought the two groups of dogs were given comparable doses of progesterone and Depo-Provera. Neither was he aware of the fact that three monkeys in the high-dose Depo-Provera group who had died during the study were replaced by fresh animals a year and a half into the study, and that four animals in the control group had been killed by the researchers.

When researchers are removing animals from the study and adding fresh animals to replace corpses in the Depo-Provera group, it is very difficult to compare, in any meaningful way, the survival rates of control, Depo-Provera, and progesterone-treated monkeys.

It appears that medical experts may be making judgments on Depo-Provera's safety based on mere summaries of the data—summaries that can be misleading.

In one version of the Drug Regulation Reform Act of 1979 (S-1075) now pending before Congress, a provision allows the public access to only such summaries of data submitted with new drug applications. Senator Edward M. Kennedy, backing down on the public disclosure issue, now supports this weakened provision. Whether citizen or expert, summaries provide one with grossly inadequate data for judging the safety of a drug. When there is no public access to the studies, FDA and drug companies can orchestrate the kind of data that will come out, and mislead the public on the degree of danger a drug presents.

The Drug Regulation Reform Act also allows pharmaceuticals judged too dangerous for US citizens to be exported for use abroad provided that certain conditions, including the request of foreign governments for these drugs, are met. Depo-Provera is always mentioned as a drug that could be exported under the new act.

Proponents of this provision argue that other countries have different risk/benefit ratios for drugs and they have a sovereign right to weigh these risks and benefits for themselves without being subjected to the paternalistic protection of the United States.

The sovereignty argument ignores the neocolonial reality in much of the Third World. When Third World countries are negotiating for badly needed funds with a 21-nation consortium led by the World Bank, they are pressured to prove that they are dealing with "the population problem." If they do not show that they have an effective population control program—one with long continuation rates for contraceptives—they jeopardize the whole aid budget. Sterilization and Depo-Provera programs are pushed because their continuation rates—unlike rates for the Pill or condom—are long-term and automatic.

Furthermore, it is rarely "the people" of a Third World country who will decide that the benefits of Depo-Provera outweigh the risks. Those making the decision may well be government officials bribed by drug companies. In papers filed with the US Securities and Exchange Commission (SEC), Upjohn admitted that, in order to secure sales, it made payments of more than $4 million to employees of, or intermediaries for, foreign governments and to numerous hospital employees from 1971 to 1975. Gerard Thomas, the vice-president, secretary, and general counsel of Upjohn, informed SEC that small amounts paid to minor government officials were not included in the total.[30]

Male officials of foreign governments may take money from male officials of Upjohn, loudly proclaiming that they have a sovereign right to import Depo-Provera, and women, with their bodies, will pay the price for that deal between men.

I want to raise a final issue about the validity of any "ethical" conclusions we, at this Workshop, come to on Depo-Provera when the women most vulnerable to these shots are not here to speak for themselves.

It bothers me that in the papers we college-educated people deliver, we tend to find an issue like Depo-Provera usage merely an intriguing ethical question. We are so removed from the battlefield, so busy being "objective," "fair," and scholarly, that the whole matter seems to be nothing more than a stimulating intellectual game.

We can write papers on the issue, publish them, add the titles to our increasingly impressive curriculum vitae, and use such papers to gain promotions and further invitations to prestigious workshops held at charmingly situated colleges.

Yet while we talk, somewhere off the campus of Hampshire College, Depo-Provera is maiming women. It is right that we acknowledge that, feel that.

Somehow a conviction seems to have been loosed among female

professionals that if we feel passionately about such maimings, that invalidates our judgments. We are not being objective.

But it is possible to feel passionately and think very clearly indeed, both at the very same time. The belief that reasoning and feeling are mutually exclusive functions and that the former is far more valuable than the latter, is one of the serious handicaps under which men labor. We do not have to impose this male handicap on ourselves and mislabel it "reality."

One more point related to the validity of our ethical conclusions: In discussing Depo-Provera at this workshop, the professionals among us should speak with some humility, realizing that it was and is our kind—physicians, university professors, and authors—who spearheaded the racist eugenics and population control movements. Here we are talking about ethical "problems" when, in fact, *we* may be the problem. Most of us participating in this workshop come from the very socioeconomic class that judges the poor to be stupid and irresponsible, and therefore, fit subjects for injections of life-shortening drugs.

Those women most vulnerable to Depo-Provera attacks—women trying to survive in a world that perceives their wombs as "target organs"—are those women least skilled in writing grant proposals for workshops on ethical issues in reproductive technology.

They are not here today. At some point during this workshop, we must discuss why they are not here. But this we must acknowledge: They are the experts on their own lives. We are not. We never can be. We should not pretend to be.

Response

Helen Barnes

The two ladies preceding me have said all there needs to be said about the scientific data as it pertains to Depo-Provera. They have told you in succinct fashion the risks, side-effects, possible and probable complications. I can do no better. What I can do is to tell you what I think family planning is all about. Having defined that, I would like to tell you, philosophically, the difference between the person who walks into my office asking for a contraceptive device and the person who walks in with a "disease"—and then to explain to you as best I can how I think that person makes the choice of what contraceptive method she wants. I would like to impress upon you that I think that each of you has the right to make the decision concerning what method of contraception you want to use, but also to impress upon you that I am not bound by that decision, either *professionally* or *personally*.

Now first, what is family planning? What is contraception? If you had been one of the individuals ten years ago, along with Joyce Lashof and myself, to establish criteria for the federally funded family planning programs, you would know that the intent was to provide all of the medical, social, and economic information that was necessary—that they deemed necessary—to help individuals to make a decision how many children they wanted and how to space the arrival of those children. In a very orderly fashion, all the methods of contraception that we had at our disposal, whether they be pills, IUDs, or barrier methods were to be presented. And when we talk about barrier methods, we talk about a whole armamentarium of foams, condoms, jellies, whether they fizz or whether they don't fizz, whether you put them in the vagina a half hour before intercourse or three hours before intercourse. The patient was allowed to know that she had available a whole series of contraceptive methods, including an injectable method of contraception.

What is the difference between the healthy patient who walks into your office and requests contraceptive advice and the person who walks in with a temperature of 102, whom you have to treat for a disease? Philosophically, contraceptive drugs and devices are used

117

primarily by young healthy people to prevent an unwanted pregnancy. They just don't have information on how to use birth control methods, or why they should use them. These drugs may be used for relatively long periods of time, off and on. They may be used for spacing. Intermittently, they may take them for two, four, six, eight, ten, or twelve years. We are not treating a disease. I had to sort out the dangerous, ineffective, and unsafe methods from those that were safe and effective.

As health providers we have to make sure the patient understands. If you can't speak the language, it is your responsibility to provide somebody who can speak it: make sure that the patient understands how her or his selected method works. Why does it work? What are the risks? What are the side-effects? Are they life-threatening? Can one live with them? What about a partner? Does the birth control method affect him or her? Your responsibility is to provide accurate information on how the contraceptive works. Occasionally, we try to interpret what we read and put it in context with our clinical practice. It is extremely difficult to do that. If you've ever worked with guinea pigs, rats, or rhesus monkeys, you find yourself trying to interpret those data in terms of that lady you see in front of you—Susan, Dorothy, Betty, whomever. Most poor people will understand things if you take the time to explain it to them. There's not one person in our clinic who doesn't know what she wants. There's not a person in Mississippi who doesn't know what kind of medical care they want and need.

What else is my responsibility? All patients who walk into our clinic are not healthy. We do a complete physical examination on each patient and decide whether or not this lady has pathology before we help her select a method of birth control. Doe she have an abnormal Pap smear? Does she have a breast mass or a nipple discharge? Does she have any medical contraindications? Having examined her and talked with her about what method she wants to use, we discuss with her how this might affect her sexuality.

If the patient decides, in this exchange of information, that she wants to use the birth-control pill, I prescribe them. If the individual returns and says that she made a mistake—that this has made her sick, or she's got headaches all the time, or that she's bleeding all the time, you do not coerce her into continuing a method that is unacceptable to her. Try another method.

My preference in presenting methods of contraception is cafeteria style. All the methods of birth-control are discussed—including risks, benefits, complications, reversibility, irreversibility, side effects, safety, and effectiveness. Now, I used Depo-Provera, in the manner in which I have just told you. If a patient did select Depo-Provera, then I explained to her again what the medical risks are, and had her come back for a check-up to follow up what is going on. We have not used Depo-Provera in this country on a sufficient number of patients to know whether or not we have a substantial amount of post-injection or post-Depo-Provera infertility.

Unfortunately, we did not know 20 years ago that a group of women would be infertile when they stopped taking birth-control pills. From 50–70 percent of pill users take 90–120 days to get pregnant after they stop the pills. A very small percent—10 to 15 percent—do not get pregnant for a year or more. That sounds like a very small number to us here. But you take the individual who has delayed her fertility to get her husband out of school and put her grandparents in a long-term care facility. She's thirty years old now, and she's getting a little edgy because she doesn't know whether or not the kids that she's going to have are going to be mentally retarded.

Patients have the right to decide with information on what method of contraception they want to use. They also have the right to change their mind. And that's why we're improving the procedure of tubal reanastomosis. When life-styles change, couples may want another child after tubal ligation.

Get excited about patient counseling and good health care. But, keep it in proper perspective.

Sterilization Abuse and Hispanic Women

Sandra Serrano Sewell

Women health care consumers have a unique relationship to the health care delivery system. Hispanic women share that unique relationship, with other factors added. As women we relate to male gynecologists, surgeons, obstetricians, and pediatricians as 75 percent of the entire health system labor force, but as only 7 percent of the physicians. As Hispanic women we are confronted with discrimination and ignorance on the part of medical personnel regarding our health needs. Hispanic women, as a group, are the victims of unsafe health care, poor quality health care, and physical, social, and psychological stress.

Historically we have had few options in determining our reproductive health. Many forces have acted to deprive us of this basic choice. Poverty, racism, religion, elements of our culture, political powerlessness, and our own constraints as individuals have made it very difficult to exercise any choice. These forces have been used to keep us in the home and outside of social and institutional decision-making regarding our reproductive lives. Nonetheless, we have taken some very significant steps that have changed our consciousness. Gains in employment, educational opportunities, and growing access to birth control technology have all helped. However, Hispanic women must, as in other aspects of our lives, become our own advocates. We will soon be one half of the largest minority in the United States.

We must begin to educate our communities further on reproductive health issues in order that we can make choices to fit the needs of our own lives. This is essential so that we will control our bodies, whether we choose to bear ten children or no children.

To understand our right of choice is the key to changing the present situation. With this understanding we would not have great numbers of forced sterilizations. Two million sterilization procedures that render people permanently incapable of having children are performed each year in the United States. These two million sterilization procedures include 200,000 sterilizations financed by the Federal Government yearly for low income people through various Federal programs.[1] Sterilization abuse occurs when the decision to undergo a sterilization is made under circumstances that are not free from duress and coercion.

Sterilizations are pushed by teaching hospitals in order to train new physicians. Deceptive labels such as "tying the tubes" and "bandaid surgery" are used and these mislead people into consenting without understanding the true nature of the procedure; consent forms are presented during times of great stress, such as during labor or prior to an abortion; racist medical and social services staff push sterilization on poor people as a means of reducing the number of persons on welfare. English-speaking staff approach non- and limited-English-speaking persons who do not understand the nature of the procedure. Poverty persons seek sterilization as a means of relieving their economic burden, and government makes it easier for persons to obtain a sterilization than to obtain adequate pre- and post natal care and other services required to raise healthy children. Female sterilization presents unique opportunities for abuse because women can be subject to coercive pressures merely by virtue of the fact that they must come to a hospital for childbirth or abortion. Much of the abuse occurs during these reproductive events.

Sterilization abuse impacts on minority and poor women. Racism, poverty, lack of information, and absence of government-sponsored measures to regulate abusive medical practices all play a part. The race and class nature of the abuse is demonstrated in various studies of the attitudes of medical professionals. One study polled doctors on their attitudes toward contraceptive methods for private versus public patients. Only six percent said they would recommend sterilization as the method of choice to their private patients, while 14 percent would recommend sterilization for public patients.[2]

Raza women are being sterilized. One survey showed that 37.6 percent of Spanish speaking women who responded and were classified "at risk of unwanted conceptions" have been sterilized. One women's health group has reported that Raza women represented 21.7 percent of the women of childbearing age in the United States who have been sterilized.[3] Over 35 percent of the women in Puerto Rico of childbearing age have been sterilized.[4] The lawsuits that have been filed, principally in California and New York, are yet another indicator of the extent of the abuse. In addition, personal statements provided by victims of abuse add still more documentation.

Some people say that sterilization abuse is only one more example of how our health care system mistreats its clients. But sterilization abuse, the loss of fertility without an informed and voluntary choice, cannot be treated as only another problem. The loss of fertility means much more within the context of Raza feminism. We have yet to explore the psychosocial complications resulting from coercive sterilization of Raza women.

Perhaps the greatest source of sterilization abuse is the economic duress under which Raza women must make reproductive decisions. This duress is fostered by government and nongovernment programs that make it far easier for poor women to get sterilization services than to get prenatal care and financial assistance to have a healthy child. These programs act to make sterilization a reasonable alternative for poor women faced with economic survival in extremely difficult circumstances.

One lawsuit must be mentioned because it tells us how both the medical and legal systems view our reproductive health rights. *Madrigal vs Quilligan*[5] was filed in 1975 on behalf of eleven Raza women in Los Angeles, California. Ten of the Raza women had been sterilized at the Los Angeles County University of Southern California Medical Center under circumstances that, they said, precluded their informed consent. These women are low-income Mexican women, most of whom do not speak English. Their medical histories indicate that they underwent severe depression following their sterilizations.[6] Some of the women reported severe mental tensions soon after sterilization and some separated from their husbands. All except one of the nine signed consent forms only after admission to the hospital while pregnant and bleeding, or while in intense labor.[7] One of the sterilized women had signed no consent form at all. Whether consent was truly informed is extemely doubtful, since not all were provided interpreters and time was not allowed for adequate instruction, reflection, and feedback. Many of these women did not realize that what they had signed were consent forms for sterilization. The trial on the damages issue was held in July 1978. The question addressed was the monetary value of losing your fertility without your consent and against your will. The court answered that the women would not be allowed to collect even one penny for the harm done to them. The court said that:

> There is no doubt but that these women have suffered severe emotional and physical stress because of these operations. One can sympathize with them for their inability to communicate clearly, but one can hardly blame the doctors... [8]

The women appealed the decision and were back in the courts in July 1979. Their appeal was denied.

Concluding Remarks

Helen Rodriguez

There's been a tremendous amount of information shared here. Although the points of view do not coincide, there is, I believe, a common thread going through all of the presentations which question present practices.

Carol primarily addressed the question of Depo-Provera as a drug fraught with risks at this point in time. From her own viewpoint, there are no grounds for recommending it as a contraceptive. Export to the less developed nations is particularly questionable. (That practice is also exemplified by the export of DES and chloramphenicol, an antibiotic that is not currently in use in the US.) Her question is: "Is this an ethical practice?" Is the US perpetuating the usage of drugs in other countries, in particular drugs that are too toxic for its own citizenry?

Gena, I think, makes a very strong case for opposing Depo-Provera. Her analysis and analogy of it to an attack on women's fertility is very graphic and thoughtful. The questions that she raises must be thought about, particularly the fallibility of experimental methods, and especially those experimental methods used by manufacturers. It's obvious that a great deal of research in this country is being carried out not by independent researchers—if there are any such people around—but by drug companies themselves, by the manufacturers of the substances that are being researched. We must question that as well as the controls that FDA or anyone places on premature marketing. A particularly heavy burden is upon us, who are often responsible for dispensing some of this medication, to be practically reviewers or researchers ourselves. You may know that many providers do not take the time to read or analyze the literature. All too often the informants of providers on the contraindications or indications of drugs are the drug salesmen themselves. These practices may therefore create a dangerous cyclical process of misinformation. In regard to contraceptives, we must ask ourselves to what extent do we, certainly without intent, fall into the practices of population controllers as we carry out our professional work?

Helen Barnes talked to us about her definition of family planning

125

and particularly the very basic differences between people seeking family planning services and those seeking health care of another sort. For me, it was very valuable to hear her clear statement that although often women come into the health care system through their needs for contraception, they still need and have a right to *total health care.* All of us who meet people who have had very little health care know that many unmet needs can be identified during that first history and thorough physical examination. The performance of a thorough examination is extremely important to underline as the responsibility of providers.

She also emphasized that the language—and this was also said by Rosa Cuéllar and others—has to be a language that is understood by people. There are many levels of language. Whether it's Spanish or English or one of the Native American languages or whatever, is one level. Another is the level of people's understanding—whether it is pictorial, emotional, vernacular, or whether it's at grade school, high school, or whatever educational level. The judge's opinion in the Madrigal case certainly is a perversion of our responsibility to gain understanding: actually it is a negation of our responsibility.

The judge's statement to the effect that doctors could not be expected to explain the full meaning of a procedure to their patients placed the onus for understanding on the patients. The precedent set by his opinion—that the burden of understanding *is on the patient*—is very dangerous. An even more disturbing element in the court case itself is an opinion that, since the doctor specified it was not his usual practice to perform sterilization procedures without an adequate explanation to the patient, he must therefore have *given* an adequate explanation. This becomes a retrospective justification of the doctor's actions. Thus Sandra illustrates, through the Madrigal case, that redress through the courts is nothing but an illusion, and that the cost to the people who are involved in this kind of attempt at redress of grievances is incalculable.

The professionals' arrogance was also confronted by Helen Barnes when she said that understanding *must be corroborated.* By the way, the guidelines on sterilization that are promulgated by HEW, which were modeled on the *law* for New York City, specifically require feedback in the consent form. That is, the person must express in his or her own language what he or she understands the operation to entail. To me, feedback is a basic element, in the informed consent process.

Helen Barnes ended by saying that there ought to be, strictly from the contraceptive method point of view, as many options as possible available to people. People should have clear explanations of what the risks and benefits are of each option and should be able to make choices. She also stated that she has used Depo-Provera in certain circumstances, and had no problems with it, and that we should have a broad overall perspective of people's needs.

Sandra's paper on sterilization abuse illustrates clearly the relationship between the pushing of Depo-Provera on certain populations outside of the United States and the sterilization of certain groups within the US. There is one other difference that I would like to have people think about: sterilization in the United States today is being pushed as the most important modality of ending fertility, and that's for all groups. There's been a great deal of propaganda in favor of sterilization in media—all media—beginning with *Good Housekeeping* and ending with *Sexual Medicine Today.*

There was a cover illustration in *Sexual Medicine Today* showing a sterilization machine processing masses of couples walking into it and coming out of it—sort of being imprinted by it. Although it *is* happening to Hispanic women, and it *is* happening to Black women, and it *is* happening to Native American women, in large numbers, and it *is* happening to women on welfare and to other poor women, it is also happening to middle-class people and even to upper-class people. I think we get a more cogent picture if we look at this. There was a survey performed by the CDC in 1975 by Dr. Carl Tyler that showed that 80 percent of the departments of urology were remiss in explaining to their patients who were undergoing vasectomies what the procedure entailed and what the risks were. The study also revealed that 56 percent of the departments of gynecology were remiss in explaining sterilization procedures to the women. That kind of information makes me see abuse in a much larger context. We're saying that abuse occurs whenever people have no choices either because sterilization is being offered and/or pushed by the available services, or because they are lied to about what sterilization entails. An example of the lying is what happened in Puerto Rico; women were told that "la operación" was reversible, that sutures would dissolve in five or six years, or that a simple operation would reestablish their fertility. The opportunities for abuse at the level where people are giving consent are many. I think that's very important for us to recognize that it's happening to other people besides the poor of the land.

An anecdote by Barbara Seaman tells of two writers she met who had read Jane Brody's glowing account of her own sterilization, in the *New York Times.* She was delighted with it, since she didn't trust condoms, hated the pill, etc., and was so happy after she got sterilized, that she went out and bought three pairs of shoes and has been happy ever since. The misfortune was that the two fellow writers who had been thinking of sterilization and got the final push from the article, were really completely destroyed by the operations. One, who had never had menstrual difficulties, developed extremely painful menstrual periods following sterilization and became incapacitated for several days each month. The other, who had quite regular periods, had become very irregular and had heavy bleeding. Needless to say, both were very upset. Maybe they should have been told that data we have so far indeed suggest that the laparoscopic method, and particularly the one involving cautery—which may to some extent, compromise the blood supply to the ovaries—is giving rise to a greater incidence of menstrual difficulties. So far, it also seems that there is an increased incidence of hysterectomy in women who have undergone it. These data are preliminary, because the incidence of complications has not been surveyed to the extent that one would wish for greater certainty.

At any rate, we can see that the hazards of misinformation exist for *all* women, not just women from minority groups or women who receive welfare.

Let me summarize the issues addressed by this panel. We have to take a serious look at the health care system and the role it plays, because women have very specific positions vis-à-vis the health care system. We cannot talk about modalities of care without looking at the deliverers of these modalities and the nature of their relationships with women. We must look at the role of class and the role of ethnicity in terms of what is happening. We must examine the social factors, the economic climate, that surround our choices and options.

One of the social and health care delivery factors is the acceptance of hysterectomy, its high incidence in the United States as compared to other countries. A recent study that's being carried out by the Center for Disease Control suggests to date that perhaps as many as 20 percent of hysterectomies are really done for sterilization purposes. We must also analyze the effect of propaganda on us. The hysterical propaganda on overpopulation has convinced us all to some extent. Some of us may come from a healthy viewpoint, say from an environmentalist one and as a result, fall in with the arguments that too many people litter the environment. We must look critically at that tendency because it slides us into the position of the population controllers who justify population limitation by rather extreme means. I would like us to discuss some of our notions about who ought to be sterilized and who ought not to be, if among us there is the belief that there are some people who ought to be, whether they want it or not.

Depo-Provera and Sterilization Abuse Discussion

Moderated by Renée Rosiland Jenkins

Katsi Cook: This issue always burns me. There's something even deeper that goes beyond its medical and social aspects. The American way of life is based on technology and the poor are trying to buy into that way of life, too. At the same time, technology is used against poor people. We Native Americans are poor, too, but our complaint is not that we're poor. Our complaint is that the way of life that works against our way of life is dominant.

I just want to read you a quote from our paper,

> The scope of the U.S. government and corporate interests in sterilization becomes even more ominous when considered on a global scale. Puerto Rico has the highest incidence of sterilization in the world. At least 35% of Puerto Rican women of childbearing age have been sterilized through programs largely funded by the U.S. government. In Columbia, between 1963 and 1965, Rockefeller Foundation-funded programs sterilized 40,000 women who were coaxed by gifts of lipstick, artificial pearls, small payments of money, and by false promises of free medical care. In many foreign countries, the U.S. government finances population control projects through the Agency for International Development. The money is being used for the testing of often dangerous sterilization techniques for use at home and for use by repressive governments against troublesome ethnic groups.
>
> While AID has increased money for training police in counterinsurgency tactics and medical personnel in sterilization techniques, it has reduced money given for education, health, and agricultural development. [In Mass, B., *Population Target: The Political Economy of Population Control in Latin America,* Charters Publ., Brampton, Ontario 1976]

Our women look at this issue from three levels: local, national, and international. No government such as the United States or Belgium is in control: it's the corporations and the Tri-Lateral Commission. And our belief is that this sterilization is just one aspect of that greater disease. What's happening to people in Thailand or South America right now is what was going on in this land about 300 years ago: mass genocide. That's what it is—nothing less. It's genocide.

Jeanne Hubbuch: To say we will "allow" third world countries to decide for themselves about Depo-Provera really ignores the fact that often the demand that these countries control their population is originated in the United States. Importing birth control methods is not really a free choice for third world countries to make, if, for example, it is linked to foreign aid.

Gena Corea: Also, the officials who make those decisions may have been bribed by the drug companies. We do have evidence of this. In papers filed with the Securities and Exchange Commission, Upjohn admitted giving more than four million dollars in payments to government officials in foreign countries' and to the employees of foreign health care services in order to secure sales. The decision is not made by the people, but possibly by government officials who've been bribed.

Julie Melrose: Carol Levine spoke of the need to eliminate control by the white worldwide minority over the worldwide majority, which is people of color. But I think there's something else to be looked at. In a world in which violence against women varies in form from country to country but remains a constant worldwide, an end to concern as well as control can be seen as leaving the women of individual patriarchal nations at the mercy of the men in those nations—who are probably committing crimes of violence against women in their own countries, just as men in the United States commit crimes of violence against women here. If we are truly committed to ending global violence against women, we can't afford to say that what happens to women in other countries is none of our business. We have to start creating nonimperialistic ways of going beyond artificially created national boundaries and allying ourselves with a global community of women.

Elizabeth Kutter: When we talk in general about violence by "the men" in these patriarchal societies against "the women," we are short-sighted when we assume that all men are being violent against all women. There clearly is a hierarchy that is violent and there clearly are patterns that lead to its being easier to be violent. But I think we really need to distinguish between the serious imperialistic problems we're discussing and things that automatically set "the men" against "the women."

We're dealing with challenging political and social problems, and we need all the support we can get. For instance, at this conference the key roles are clearly being played by women, but I am pleased to have some men here, as well. Many of the issues raised deal with men as well as women—such as the use of Depo-Provera with male sex offenders to cause chemical castration. I would really like us to be careful not to use sexist language, in general, when we talk.

Caroline Whitbeck: I want to point out what happened in the literature on vasectomies, because it shows significant differences in the way in which men and women are harmed and constrained by recent biases in medicine. When vasectomies were becoming common, in the '50s, the first wave of studies of vasectomies, written almost entirely by men, tended to argue that there *must* be something wrong with a man who would have a vasectomy; he must want to be castrated. Then other researchers began to question the biases of these studies. They did some better-designed studies that found that the men who elected vasectomies were actually very stable and secure. What we see is that the biases of physicians and researchers have been very different regarding the sterilization of women and the sterilization of men. Male doctors have often been reluctant to vasectomize a male patient (usually white or middle class) when that patient wanted a vasectomy, because the operation raised the physician's own castration anxieties, but physicians have often been willing to sterilize women, especially, but not only, women of other classes and races, without their consent.

Joyce Berkman: Are there no limits to the cafeteria? Helen Barnes and Carol Levine said they were in favor of keeping Depo-Provera a possible option, with informed consent.

I have serious qualms about that. What is the purpose of the FDA? Are there no ethical limits? A Catholic doctor will not, as a matter of conscience, prescribe certain kinds of contraceptives. What stops other doctors from saying, "I will not—due to certain values and judgments that I have reached as to risks and benefits—prescribe certain contraceptives." We need to think about setting limits to the notion of absolute reproductive choice and a completely free cafeteria situation.

Emily Culpepper: Joyce, I welcome your question of, "Are there no limits to the cafeteria?" I think it's very easy to get into a pseudo-liberal position and say, "Everybody has a choice about everything." This kind of "liberal" stance leaves out serious questions of context. It's not easy to define where one's limits are set, but it is or should be *the point* of a conference on ethics. The "cafeteria" is supplied by males and in a very biased way.

Renée Jenkins: It is the responsibility of the physician prescribing contraceptives to eliminate those contraceptives that are deemed unsafe and injurious to that person. At different times, different types of information become available and you may reassess what you want to put in your cafeteria.

Carol Levine: I am in favor of keeping the legal status the way it is now. The proposal is to *change* the law so that Depo-Provera could be legally exported, and I am *not* in favor of that. I would hesitate to say to another country, "You cannot buy it somewhere else." In other words, we should not export it at all, but we should not say, "You can't buy it anywhere."

Helen Barnes: There are several students at the University of Mississippi who, for moral, religious, and cultural reasons, will not provide contraception of any kind to teenagers. That is their belief. I say to them, "That's your decision. You have to decide how you're going to practice medicine *and,* more importantly, how you're going to live with it." On the other hand, there are those who say, "I *can* prescribe a method of birth control because I'm tired of aborting twelve-year-olds, or I'm tired of treating toxemia, and seeing fetal wastage, and higher prematurity rates in teenagers." It depends greatly upon individual attitudes, mores, philosophies, religion, and communication skills of doctor and patient.

Marie Cassidy: There is one aspect of this issue that has surfaced repeatedly, i.e., if you are not willing to provide something within your cafeteria, then you must be scrupulous about referring people to another cafeteria. That is a critical issue in medical education right now. Providers of care should recognize their own biases and recognize when to refer people to other providers who do not share their biases. That's a very difficult thing to do.

Leslie Laurie: I think that may be fine in an urban area where you don't have to travel fifty miles with no gas. It may be wonderful to discuss ideal referral systems in a medical school setting, but I'm not sure of its applicability to the community or if it really helps consumers to get their needed services.

Joyce Lashof: The whole question of the role of the regulatory agency, and what we allow, and what is the government's responsibility, is undoubtedly one of the hottest issues this country is facing. There's no question in my mind that there is a very strong movement that wishes to abolish all regulation and, under the cloak of liberalism and individual liberty, is saying, "We will leave everything to the freedom of the individual and freedom of choice, and remove the responsibility to protect the people from the government." It's come full circle. It's a very "far left" approach to a very rightist position. How to draw the line between the government's protection of the people and interference with the liberty of the people is not easy. One can get caught up in rhetoric on either side. It's a very serious, very difficult issue to which there are no simple answers. Further, with Depo-Provera there is the international scope and thus the added complexity of whether we have the right to decide for other people or to make judgments about whether their governments are being fair to them. The evidence on Depo-Provera is obviously growing, and, if we accept it, there will be no question that Depo-Provera should not be easily available. Helen Barnes has not yet discussed what data would convince her.

Helen Barnes: In our family planning clinic, we have about 9000 patients. Depo-Provera has been offered, up until two years ago, along with all the rest of the contraceptives. Only twelve people of the 9000 accepted it. That demonstrates that if you do a fairly decent job of telling people what is available they can decide for themselves. Of the twelve people that agreed to use Depo-Provera, three of them are between the ages of fifteen and twenty-five, and are mentally retarded. I elected, along with the mother or guardian, to assume the "medical responsibility" with the mother or guardian's understanding that if this youngster came back for a three-month injection and had not had a period, then I would ask the mother or guardian to choose another contraceptive, because I would not give the patient another injection. There are six who are at the other end of their reproductive lives, who do not want more children, and who just cannot tolerate the idea of being put to sleep for surgical sterilization. Two ladies believe that if they go to sleep, they'll never wake up. We discussed Depo-Provera and the side effects. They have been on it less than six years, having Pap smears and periods regularly. One of those ladies will be forty in January. She will have to decide to use another method of contraception, because of the concern about the serious life-threatening medical side effects of Depo-Provera.

Elizabeth Kutter: There appear to be two kinds of side effects of Depo-Provera. One kind is immediately obvious, e.g., loss of libido, weight gain, depression, splotches on your face. Women experience pain from the IUD and nausea and depression with the Pill, and those individual women have the right to stop at that point. The second set of effects, e.g., cervical cancer, are long-term and more difficult to control. We really need to think about educating women about the nature of both kinds of risks. And we need to ask the further question: How many women are thus affected? If the risks are primarily of the first kind, is it appropriate to deprive 95% of the people of something potentially very useful because 5% of the population has such side effects? I would like to know, specifically: what are the probabilities of the *long-term* problems, where it is *harder* for people to respond individually?

Helen Barnes: I was on the ob/gyn committee of the FDA during the time that we discussed Depo-Provera. There were twenty people on the panel. Three of those people were clinicians. That was a time we "agonized over" much of the animal data. It looked as though there was beginning to be an increase in the incidence of dysplasia—which is abnormal cells—and then in the next 6–18 months, more cervical carcinoma *in situ*. Then we looked at some statistics from New York City. Patients taking birth-control pills had the same results. But there were no controls. Both studies are inconclusive without controls. What about the ladies who had multiple sex partners? What about the women who begin having intercourse when they're in their teens? Are there multiple factors that cause change in the pathophysiology of the cervix other than the birth-control pill? Or Depo-Provera? The problem again with the Depo-Provera was that we in the United States had very small numbers of people using the drug. We began to look at Dr. McDaniel's report from Ching-Mai, Thailand. However, in that study they did not require the women to have Pap smears initially and routinely every 6 months. We do not have cytology or controls even though we have large numbers of women on Depo-Provera. Clinicians working in the field have one idea as to what's going on. Researchers are trying to give us the kind of statistics that we need, but control studies are just not available.

Upjohn had the rhesus monkey experiment going over ten years without realizing until recently that accumulating data might ultimately be detrimental to marketing of Depo-Provera. Presently Depo-Provera is used for treatment of endometrial cancer in patients that are poor surgical candidates.

Gene Corea: In clinical studies conducted by Upjohn between 1965 and 1968, 36% of the women reported one or more side-effects. That is an incredibly high figure when you understand the conditions under which those studies were conducted and the conditions under which the women were obliged to report those side-effects. The investigators were specifically instructed not to ask about side-effects. The only side-effects recorded were the ones women voluntarily reported without the encouragement of questioning. In most cases, those physicians were white and male. Eighty-eight percent were clinic patients and almost half of the clinic patients were nonwhite. We suspect that the Hispanic women may have been classified as white, which would have made the proportion of minority women even larger. So, a very large percentage of these people were minority women dealing with white males. Even when you're a white woman going to a white male doctor, you're hurried through and intimidated and made to feel as though people are dying out in the waiting room while you are wasting this doctor's precious time—time he could be spending salvaging the people in the waiting room. It's very hard to say, "I have this question about these headaches I've been having..."

And very few women are going to feel comfortable enough to say, "Listen, I've had no sexual desire ever since I started taking this shot."

So despite the fact that conditions militated against the women reporting side-effects, 36% of the women nonetheless did so. How many women did not overcome these barriers? Also, in many of the studies conducted on Depo-Provera, there was no followup. When Depo-Provera advocates say things like, "No woman is known to have died from Depo-Provera," they can, because no one bothered to find out what happened to the women after they were injected.

Helen Rodriguez: I can think of an analogy in the sterilization abuse struggle. In grappling with the question, "What regulations are good regulations?" we got into all kinds of issues. To this day, mind you, there are even people who are members of the same organization such as the Committee for Abortion Rights and Against Sterilization Abuse (CARASA) who may not see eye-to-eye with other members on the question of regulations. For instance, some said, "If you tell women that they may have adhesions of organs in the pelvis secondary to sterilization, or that there might be accidental discharges of the laparoscope causing burns of the intestine, or that menstrual irregularities may occur, nobody would ever choose to have a sterilization." And our response to that was, "So what? It's their right to choose not to have it." But Joyce is right. There are serious problems about how much regulation, where does the regulation originate, who is being barred from immediate access because there's a thirty-day waiting period, or who is under twenty-one and is therefore being denied rights because the legislation says, "No one under twenty-one may be sterilized." I think all these things have to be weighed. My contention is that every process is questionable unless there is full involvement of the affected people. You cannot, in any way, make those far-reaching decisions for others without their full participation. The question is what does informed consent mean to *you,* the one who is going to give the consent?

Joyce Lashof: I agree with you that we have to look at the process, but that does not mean we can leave it up to each individual.

Helen Rodriguez: No. But we can come in with guidelines that respond to the needs expressed by individuals.

Joyce Lashof: We must weigh when we are willing to allow risks—when the benefits outweigh the risks. Certainly, where there are no benefits we should allow no risks, and when the risks are god-awful and the benefits are very small, you don't allow it. But somewhere in between, we continue to face a dilemma. In that process of looking at the benefits and the risks, one must look at the social, cultural, and economic situation of the area. If we have the ability to produce something of value to another country, where the benefits to the people of that country, at that time, far outweigh the risks, then we cannot morally prevent them from having that benefit. Depo-Provera may not be it, because the risks of Depo-Provera may be so great that they outweigh the benefits. But other drugs? How you protect the people is important, but the answer is not the simplistic one that we won't let anything be done somewhere else that we won't allow here. The benefit/risk ratio may be quite different here from what it is somewhere else, and we may deprive people of something that would be of great benefit to them if we use our ratio and impose it on other people.

Diana Axelsen: We can't deal with any of these medical issues without looking at the socioeconomic and political frameworks, especially our foreign policy toward developing countries. The United States has too often decided for developing countries what drugs and medical technology will be available. One example concerns Tanzania, which has made much progress in its approach to population. Both women and men helped develop and implement a program of child spacing. The concept of child spacing, unlike population or birth control, recognizes the traditional values of the people; but it also involves recognition of the country's commitment to see that education, housing, and health care keep pace with population growth. But we caused trouble with the child spacing program by exporting Depo-Provera and other contraceptives. If we responded to Third World demands for fairness in international trade, if we paid Tanzania, for instance, a decent amount of money for its exports, these countries would have the money to make their own decisions. The issues raised by Depo-Provera and other medical exports cannot be understood outside the framework of international economics.

Judy Norsigian: One of the biggest problems that we're constantly coming up against is the question of who's making that decision about risk/benefit ratios. You'll constantly hear from population control advocates, "Those women suffer from malnutrition, they have baby after baby, and anything's better than ten pregnancies. So even if we have to manipulate their lives, sterilizing them or giving them a birth-control agent whether they want it or not, it's better for them in the end."

Even if, in retrospect, many of the women so manipulated might say, "I'm glad it happened," this is unethical in my view. This manipulation eliminates an essential autonomy that ought to be guaranteed.

In many Third World countries, women do not want to have as many kids as they've got. They do not have access to adequate birth-control, either because of their macho husbands or for the lack of contraceptive options. But the fact that they may not be able to control their fertility as they want does not justify manipulating their lives in order to reduce population growth. Offering sterilization and/or hazardous contraceptives to women who don't understand the risks and consequences involved is unethical, I think. If it takes years and years of education before we get to the point where people are making informed decisions, then I think we have to take those years and years.

There is something about Depo-Provera that has always disturbed me. I like what you said, Helen, about your interaction with patients, but what about most physicians? I don't think most physicians practice medicine the way you do. The incidence of women taking Depo-Provera without any information is very high, and once a woman gets the shot, she can't turn around and stop taking it as with the Pill. Plenty of people say, "Well, we can give you an estrogen shot to counteract some of the effects," but some people take Depo-Provera precisely because estrogen is contraindicated. How do you deal with that?

Helen Barnes: I tell all my patients who come to the family planning clinic that they have the right to leave any doctor's office if they are not satisfied. That's the only way you're going to *make him change what he does.* Get up and walk out. *Don't pay him. Go where you know you can get the service you want.* Ask your friends.

Judy Norsigian: But you know most women would be far too intimidated to do that.

Helen Barnes: You need a cause! It's your job to teach them.

Anne Davis: That puts the burden on the individual woman to clean up the physician's act.

Helen Barnes: Right! How else do you plan to do it? You are the one that's accepting the service. We train them. That's true. I've been at the University of Mississippi Medical Center for ten years, and maybe I teach one medical student a year to practice medicine the way I do. The economics of medicine usually has priority. Our competitive society makes it necessary to pay off previous indebtedness, and to own a boat, to own a new house, to go on vacation every year, etc. It's just not the way things are done. You have the solution in your hands. You have the money or fee for service. If you don't like the service or the way he or she practices medicine, get up, walk out of the office, don't pay him, tell him why, find someone else. We will change. Medicine is a business, ladies, and you can treat it like any other business.

Hilary Salk: The obvious answer is not what you gave, but that we have to take the profit motive out of medicine. There are so many women who have become the victims of this profitable medical system that now we're spending more energy trying to *protect* ourselves from the damages done by the system than we are trying to ensure that every woman has equal access to medical care.

Helen Barnes: But how do you do that? Don't you educate; don't you *reeducate;* don't you change what people have done in the past?

Renée Jenkins: But if you talk to people who have socialized medicine, that isn't the answer, either—because it becomes so impersonal. I think those of us who are in our system look to another system to solve some of our problems. But if you talk to people who have other types of systems, they have equal dissatisfactions for another set of reasons.

Elizabeth Kutter: In trying to change the system, one way is to take out the profit motive—fine, but rather unrealistic. Another is what a lot of us do, which is to develop viable alternatives and to educate women about those alternatives to purely allopathic medicine. That means doctors who've been properly trained, and easily available information for women about specific doctors and self-help.

Helen Rodriguez: Betty, I don't think we can abstract ourselves from the reality of medical care in this country, because the masses of people in this country are those I see lined up in the emergency room of King's County, Metropolitan, Harlem, Lincoln hospitals—you name it. Alternative care, which is beautiful, provides models, provides food for thought and for enjoyment and for writing about, impacts in some minor ways on what gets into the literature or what is done in education. For instance, a particular institution may try to teach its students physical diagnosis of the pelvic organs at the self-help clinic instead of on the anesthetized patients in its operating room. But the fact remains, we must address the health care system as a whole, because people are getting care in large institutions and that's where people are getting *bad* care. As long as it's structured as it is, we are going to have difficulty with rights or with responsibility, accountability or justice—however you want to say it.

I, myself, am active in the struggle for a national health service in this country—and I am not alone. I'm convinced that although it isn't going to come tomorrow—since we *are* talking about the third largest industry in this country—the education must begin now. We must understand that talking about nationalizing health care is almost like talking about nationalizing US Steel. It is not a joke. People get killed for attempting that kind of thing. But the very fact of organizing around nationalization, of exposing the nature of the present health care system, of carrying out the kind of education that occurs in this process, is an essential prerequisite of progress on any level of health care.

Diana Axelsen: To me, the bottom line of the doctor/patient relationship is mutual trust and respect. These make it unnecessary to argue about rights, and they create a climate in which honest mistakes can be forgiven. Such relationships may be hard to find, but they should be encouraged in and out of conventional medical settings.

Susan Peterson: There is a problem in all the discussion thus far, namely that every single issue has been framed in terms of individual rights. I know that women's rights have been stomped on, en masse, in this country, by capitalism and by patriarchy. But I wonder whether people are really aware of how masculinistic and capitalistic a concept "rights" is. There was no such concept until capitalism began. Aristotle did not have that concept. It is a male concept that is property-related, protective, and adversarial in stance. Rights are negative—they are limiting factors beyond which others cannot go. It's not a very productive approach, since for every right someone has, there is bound to be someone else's that may conflict with it. In many rights conflicts it is not possible to decide what to do. I wonder if we can't change our ethical language a bit, become more feminist, and think of things more positively. An example of an alternative conception would be that of a communal society. The concept of rights would be unnecessary in a communal group of persons who share. Another concept we can use is the plain old moral concept of "the good." Is Depo-Provera morally good? Another is, what duties, what responsibilities do we have to our friends, lovers, children? Not what rights do they have. Also, there is "justice." I haven't heard that word much here. We can ask what is fair. It may be that I have a right to do something that would be unfair for me to do.

Please don't misunderstand. I fight for rights, too, and my first published paper is on the right of women to be free to go out at night and drink if they want, to emphasize the fact that now if they have a drink and get raped, they cannot get a conviction. But that paper was in the context of liberal, bourgeois, democratic theory. Although that is perhaps not the best theory, it *is* the one our country's running on right now, so it's realistic. The liberal form of feminism that says, "As long as we get our rights taken care of, everything will be fine morally," is naive.

It is also not true that for every right there is another side to the coin. Animals have rights, but do not have duties in return. Sometimes rights language is appropriate, for instance, when Sandy said that in her ethnic group women don't have a right to reproductive freedom (contraception) that other American women have had. She's absolutely correct that they should have that right. But when every single point is made that way, it is confusing. We might as a group decide to use duty, loyalty, friendship, responsibility, goodness, and justice as moral criteria besides rights.

Childbirth

Section 1
Childbirth Technologies

Organized by

Norma Swenson

Childbirth Overview

Norma Swenson

Each generation of women and men, in every culture, creates images and fantasies about childbirth for itself, from the spoken words of women who have given birth, from experts who may or may not ever have given birth, and from mythology, literature, and media. Some have also been informed by domestic animals. Childbirth is always a highly charged subject for every person, and especially so for women. Like sexuality, birth calls up strong and individually patterned responses, often inaccessible to rational analysis. Birth, death, and mating produce the most ritual-laden events in all societies. As paradigm or metaphor, birth can be an incredibly rich, multifaceted teacher about what really matters in a culture, about what the values are, about what the importance of and the roles of women and children are within that society.

It has been women's unique and irreplaceable function in the species to give birth to new human beings, at least until now, and perhaps for just a little while longer. Such power as women have had in the past derived primarily from that potentiality, whether or not they actually performed that function. The primary imperative was to express rather than to control fertility, and to realize the capacity for nurturance through childbearing. Yet women have always sought, and found, ways to control their fertility. At the same time, for most women, during most of recorded history, the *in*ability to bear a child, or children, when desired was considered a personal and social problem ranging from moderate to severe. In many parts of the world, even today, bearing children—sometimes bearing only male children—is still a woman's only justification for existence. In all societies, most women still feel that children and families represent their major life work, whatever else they may do or wish to do. Birth for them is mainly a means to that end, hopefully, but not certainly, a safe one.

For feminists in the industrialized world, childbearing has been problematic because the struggle to empower women to participate fully in society has always had to begin with the struggle to control, rather than to express, our fertility. Because we are still so often reduced to and defined by our unique capacities as childbearers, we have sometimes been taught to resent the function as well as the institution of motherhood. In this post-industrial, post-contraceptive age, many women now feel that to conceive, to give birth, and to nurture a new child is an incredible luxury, an indulgence that they and the world can ill afford; or that the world's unclaimed children should have first priority on our commitments. Others feel grateful to be able to choose not to bear a child, without giving up their uniquely expressed sexuality. Some would gladly transfer the function of childbearing altogether—to other women, or to machines—as part of a rightful claim on liberation or deliverance from what we perceive as unnecessary suffering.[1]

In non-industrialized communities, the issues are quite different. Women have always worked in and outside the home for survival, and not often by choice. Neither they nor their menfolk have ever had much to say about public policies, and the rules inside the community are frequently distinct from, and more cohesive than, the rules outside it in the dominant culture. Controlling fertility has been a vital necessity for many women, and not always a choice. To be able to create a new life in some communities can be like a miracle, a symbol of renewal for adults who are threatened with extinction by the dominant, hostile culture around them.

What is different about us, in our time and place, what is unique about us, might be useful to keep in mind as we examine the rich material on childbirth assembled here. Whereas most mothers might have some uncertainty that their child would survive birth, or the first few years of life, we do expect this. More than that, most of us expect a live, unimpaired child each time. All of these expectations have contributed enormously to the changed character of childbirth in this society today. While most cultures have drawn heavily and respectfully on their pasts and traditions, our culture has made a virtue out of active rejection of past traditions, both our own and those of other cultures. In rejecting our dependence on the past, we have created a new form of dependence on what is essentially the unknown future: the continual production of new knowledge and technology by experts. What is more, our stance is also contributing to a change in other societies, whose goals and interests may be quite different from our own.

The dependence on technology and expertise, and the demand for a perfect child each time have created a climate of inevitability about our childbirth technology. But when expertise and technology fail, as they sometimes do, a woman has few resources with which to meet the resulting feeling of disillusionment and betrayal. Because we are women in a society with few interpersonal or community solutions to life's challenges, and because we are not experts, we cannot provide meaningful help to one another. Cut off from the support of other women—whether from her mother, or other women in her parents' generation, or from her own peers—each woman's dependency on experts, on technology, on industrial products of all kinds grows. Her sense of isolation, of vulnerability and inadequacy in managing the experience increases, and so does her vulnerability to psychological experts who not only guide her development, but also serve as arbiter for her child's.

Until very recently, trust in professional expertise has been virtually complete.[2] Yet practices do change. In our system, change generally comes out of the needs of those who manage the system and deliver the services. It can be argued that all prevailing technology is an expression of the ideology of those in power in any society, if not an actual instrument of social control over others. Although classically religion has exercised such control, law, medicine, and education have increasingly tended to replace or incorporate religion/belief elements in our society. Medicine in particular has retained the characteristics of belief, ritual, and dogma that are ordinarily associated with religion.[3] Organized medicine, obstetrics and gynecology in particular, has correctly interpreted its mandate to define and control women's reproductive functions, a mandate endorsed not only by government, but by the people as well: given a choice, most American women prefer the care of a specialist physician and prefer to have their babies in large, prestigious hospitals. So do the fathers. This pertains largely to the upwardly mobile middle class. Only at the bottom, before people have fully entered the mainstream, or at the top after they have come through the system and found the best of it wanting, is there any consistent preference for alternatives.

Therefore critics of science, technology, and modern institutions are almost all drawn from the upper middle classes or university-trained groups, where demystifying education and demystified peer experiences are available for comparison with the dominant ethos. In the case of childbirth, only a minority of this group has raised criticisms and called for changes. And even their efforts to resist the unyielding monolith of medicalized, institutional childbirth rarely last beyond their own personal experiences. For the rest, faith in science and "progress" is still too strong, or the sense of isolation and vulnerability is too powerful. The fear of punishment for deviance is very great. So we may be in some danger if we believe that we are speaking for all women, or even most women, when we condemn certain practices or advocate others.

The tools we have chosen for our critical work are also drawn from several drastically different origins. Some of us are relying on the very tools of scientific analysis and coming to contradictory conclusions. And some of us, whether we recognize it or not, rely entirely on faith, whether in science itself, or our own particular set of beliefs about what the human being, or human nature, or woman, is.

Out of this diversity of critical analysis some key themes have emerged, ethical in implication if not always in origin. We show here that power includes the ability to suppress evidence contradictory to one's interests and to produce evidence supportive of the preferred policies and interests of the dominant group. We also believe that science is not value-free. From that premise we emphasize respect for differences: the only ethical posture seems to us not only to permit and allow, but specifically to provide for individual and cultural preferences and diversity, for minority views. Another closely related theme is the right of self-determination, honored more in the breach perhaps in international politics, but at least recognized there as an ethical issue if not for women. Expressed another way, we might think of this as "the consent of the governed" or "the right of dissent." Implicit in all of these themes is a tenet basic to all politics and human ethics: the right of control over one's own body and person—to be free of bondage and slavery—and, by extension, the right to control one's destiny. Closely related to this theme is the notion that the quality of life is more important than life itself at any price or cost. A further theme might be called the ethics of redress: that when patently, or simply in the eyes of the abused, abuses have occurred, however unintended, redress is called for. And, finally, there are the ethics of civil disobedience and of nonviolent resistance—political codes certainly, but moral principles also well known to most of us. Are any of these values unique to women or unique to the childbirth experience? In the last analysis, they probably are not, but in their application by women to this experience all of these principles are precedent-shattering.

To be fully relevant and ethical, a totally new organization of the childbirth experience must be created, and created by women. We believe that if women are not constrained, such organization will balance safety in birthing with the quality of life—indeed, they will mutually reinforce one another. Our work here shows that these efforts have already begun.

Man-Midwifery and the Rise of Technology

The Problem and Proposals for Resolution

Dorothy C. Wertz

Dependence upon technology in American births began in the eighteenth century. Births in America entered the hospital several decades earlier than in other industrialized countries. Doctors took over the deliveries of upper- and middle-class women during the nineteenth century. Midwives virtually disappeared except as deliverers of the poor.

Women and men practitioners started out with different experiences. Women were associated with nature; men were associated with "art," or improvement upon nature through mastery and manipulation. In America, art was always considered superior to nature; art must triumph over nature. The end result would be a view of birth as a disease in need of medical treatment, rather than birth as a natural process.

More drugs and technologies are now used in "normal" births in America than anywhere else in the world. This reflects in part the desire to master, conquer, and control nature that was present among the colonists from the beginning.

Although colonial midwives brought with them English birth practices, their practice necessarily differed in one important respect from that of their English sisters: the Protestant authorities in American communities absolutely forbade anything resembling witchcraft or magic. This meant that much of the traditional "women's lore" or women's wisdom, associated with "good" witchcraft in England, was forbidden in the colonies. The techniques midwives were permitted to use did not depend on any knowledge particular to women. Therefore, a man was potentially just as adequate a midwife since both ultimately relied on Providence. In the late eighteenth century, when men began to claim that their version of midwifery was a science, the men began to appear superior in the eyes of the middle classes. By that time Americans had shifted their faith from Providence to science. Medicine's claim to be scientific rested largely on several new discoveries in the field of midwifery that ultimately led to men's taking over American births.

In the early colonial period, birth was a women's ceremony, attended and controlled by women, economically supported by the community. The midwife was paid by the town; the neighbors not only attended the birth, but took over the entire care of household and children while the mother rested for the three-to-four week "lying-in" period of recovery. At the end of lying-in, the mother feasted those women who had helped her, at a "groaning party." There are no records of husbands attending or participating in births, except on the frontier where there was no local community of women. "Social childbirth," in the sense of community participation, came to an end in the late eighteenth century, when settlements grew larger and more diverse and families started hiring attendants and servants instead of relying on the community to play a supportive role.

Many of the colonial midwives apparently performed very well indeed, at least according to the records preserved in folklore. Some are reputed to have delivered three or four thousand babies, and to have lost only one or two. A Maine midwife's diary[1] from the end of the eighteenth century describes over one thousand deliveries, in the course of which she lost four mothers and very few babies—hardly the kind of death rate now popularly attributed to pre-scientific maternity. Demographic records of New England towns indicate that birth, although sometimes dangerous, was not a major killer of women. More men died during the childbearing ages of 15–44 than did women, and after 1700 women had a greater life expectancy than men.[2] This improvement owed nothing to any changes in maternity care, because there had been no changes. Infectious diseases were the major killers of both sexes. Midwives would attend hundreds of deliveries without a death or a need to call for assistance. The midwife's experience of birth was that it was overwhelmingly successful, though sometimes prolonged or painful.

There is no analogy, however, between colonial birth and modern "natural" childbirth, because when something went wrong in colonial times it went very, very wrong. There was no technological backup on which people could depend. In the absence of techniques to deal with the few cases where nature failed, it was difficult to have confidence in the outcome of natural processes. If the baby were in an "unnatural" position, such as breech or transverse, a skillful midwife might be able to turn it around (version) or extract it with a loop of whalebone. If this failed, she would have to call for assistance from a "barber-surgeon," a man who owned instruments with which he would remove a (presumably already dead) fetus piecemeal. In a time of high infant mortality from infectious diseases during the first five years of life, there was no question that the mother's life was considered more valuable than that of the child. It is small wonder that the few men who were called by midwives to assist in births regarded birth as deadly and disastrous. They lacked the midwife's experience of hundreds of routine normal births that required no assistance. Midwives, on the other hand, saw instruments as invariably deadly, always to the child and frequently to the mother, who was sometimes cut accidentally. Figure 1 shows some of these destructive instruments, including a cervical dilator that goes back to Pompeii and hooks for dismembering

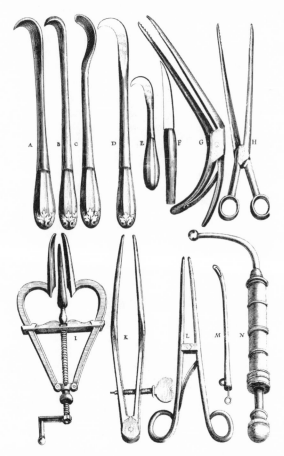

FIG. 1. Early instruments. The hooks and scissors at top were for destroying an impacted fetus. The *speculum matricis* at lower left was for cutting and dilating the cervix.

the fetus. When new instruments were eventually developed that enabled men to deliver a living child, most midwives continued to associate instruments with death and destruction.

The modern technology of birth had begun with seventeenth- and eighteenth-century French attempts to measure the birth canal in order to see if a woman's pelvis were sufficiently large. Precise methods of measurement were developed (Fig. 2) that not only enabled doctors to predict the outcome of birth, but contributed significantly to the development of the "clinical" view of the body as a machine. Unfortunately, the French measurements, though elegant, were useless for purposes of treatment once pregnancy was advanced.

The first practical technique that represented a genuine improvement came, not from university-educated French physicians, but from the trial-and-error experiments of the English barber-surgeons. They probably had observed that midwives sometimes used

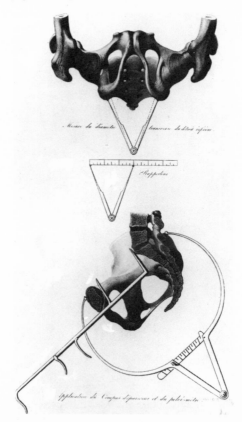

FIG. 2.   French techniques for measuring the pelvis.

spoons to try to deliver an impacted baby alive. In the seventeenth century a barber–surgeon named Chamberlen found that if two spoons were inserted separately, one on each side of the baby's head, and then locked together, this instrument, called a forceps, could deliver a living child. The Chamberlen family kept their instrument a proprietary secret for about one hundred years; it enabled them to become man-midwives or "accoucheurs" to the royal family.

By the early eighteenth century the secret of the forceps had become known. Physicians had their first demonstrable claim to a valid, life-saving procedure that could not be applied by family or neighbors. Most other medical procedures of the time were performed by the patients' families or even the patients themselves; especially, most people prescribed their own drugs and treated their own wounds and illnesses. Few doctors existed in the colonies before 1750. Those few had difficulty legitimizing their position when most procedures could be done by anyone and licensing laws were either nonexistent or not enforced.

Instruments were not only expensive, but also required at least a brief course of training before a man would try to use them. The gain for the medical profession was immense. Obstetrics (at first called midwifery) was the first specialty taught in American medical schools in the eighteenth century. Fees for obstetrics were higher by several hundred percent than for any other procedure performed by doctors before the Civil War. Doctors' ledger books indicate that it was the procedure itself, rather than the number of hours spent at the woman's bedside, that determined the fee. Doctors justified themselves by their claims to education, which was relatively rare and highly admired in the colonies, and by their new technology.

It may be asked why midwives did not adopt the new instruments. No laws prevented them from doing so, and one English midwife not only used them, but taught her students to do so.[3] Most midwives, however, regarded the forceps as an extension of the old, deadly instruments that midwives had never used and that were employed so seldom in the course of a midwife's practice that for her to buy them would have been an unnecessary expense. Perhaps the midwives were right, for early forceps were so crude that it is possible that they took more lives than they saved. Early forceps (Fig. 3) had no curve to fit the birth canal and frequently tore the mother. They were sometimes covered with strips of leather, which were ready carriers of infection in the days when no one knew how infections traveled. Sometimes, in the hands of undereducated or overly hasty men, they crushed the baby's head. The science itself, although potentially valid, did not tell men when to use it. The result was a great amount of overuse by men who were ill-acquainted with the resources of nature, or who wanted to

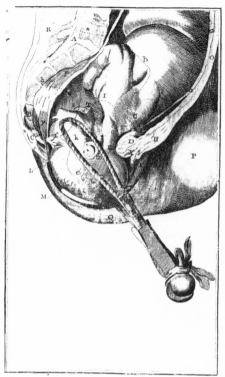
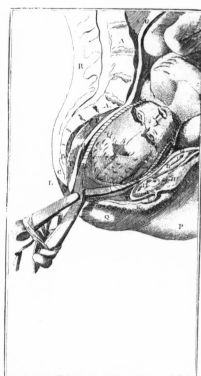

FIG. 3.   Early forceps. Note the lack of a pelvic curve.

demonstrate their superiority over midwives or to collect higher fees. Sometimes it was not the doctor, but the family who urged intervention, expecting the doctor to "*do* something."

In England, the midwives fought against the overuse of forceps by ill-trained doctors. Midwives wrote books lambasting "man-midwives" for incompetence and licentiousness, for using forceps because they were too "horse-fisted" to deliver with their hands as midwives did, and for turning "broken-down pork butchers and sausage stuffers" into "intrepid man-midwives" after six weeks' training on a wooden mannikin, without ever having seen a birth.[4] Doctors replied by accusing midwives of drunkenness, incompetence, and magical practices.[5]

In England the midwives continued to attend most deliveries throughout the nineteenth century. They were finally licensed and upgraded at the turn of this century. In America midwives themselves wrote nothing to protect their own occupation: there is no correlate of the English midwives' critiques of the man–midwife. Americans admired education and science to such an extent that they early shifted their allegiance to physicians. By 1830 it had become difficult to find a midwife of the middle classes in eastern cities. Families believed that it improved their social standing if they had a doctor, and most women preferred to have a physician of their own class rather than a midwife of a lower class. Changes in the roles of middle-class urban women had made midwifery no longer a respectable occupation for the daughters of the middle class.

Furthermore, in 1820 doctors mounted a campaign to claim to the public that women were inherently unsafe as practitioners of midwifery or medicine.[6] According to doctors, women were unable to remain cool in times of emergency, were too sympathetic with patients to make rational decisions, were too delicate to be educated in anatomy, and, most important, were mentally unstable or even temporarily insane when menstruating. In the first half of the nineteenth century, when the absence of regulations made medicine an entrepreneurial free-for-all open to absolutely anybody, women were the only group that "orthodox" educated physicians succeeded in excluding. Doctors feared, not without reason, that if women were admitted to the profession women patients would prefer physicians of their own sex, especially for childbirth.

Men gained control over birth during an historical period of great modesty and prudery about sex. They were able to do so by "practicing by the sense of touch alone," that is, by not seeing what they were doing. The Chamberlens had kept the forceps a secret by delivering under a sheet (Fig. 4); in the nineteenth century doctors continued to work by touch until after the Civil War. The gynecological examination (illustrated in Fig. 5) or "touch" was a source of embarassment to both parties; unless a woman had a large tumor, the procedure was of little medical value, but it helped the doctor to gain the woman's confidence. Having been placed in such a delicate situation, she was likely to turn to him for advice in many confidential matters. The doctor became women's confidential advisor, a position that he still holds. By gaining control over birth, doctors gained control over other aspects of women's sexual life. They became judges of women's moral conduct and proper fulfillment of their roles. A woman giving birth under the watchful eyes of men was judged morally and socially. If she felt too much pain, it was because she had not lived right: she had stayed up too late at night, played cards, eaten too many pastries, not exercised enough, not gotten enough fresh air, done something frivolous, or perhaps even worked. If she felt very little pain, it meant she was uncivilized, like the Indian woman frequently given as

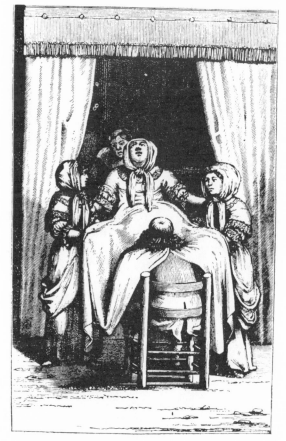

FIG. 4. Man-midwife delivering under a sheet to protect the woman's modesty.

an example of painless birth. The anxiety occasioned by having to perform correctly at birth, according to the expectations of one's social class and one's doctor, may have contributed further to the pain of birth in the nineteenth century.

The twentieth-century desire for pain-killing or memory-obliterating drugs is understandable only in view of what must have been a great deal of pain experienced by women just before American births began to take place in hospitals. Victorian women felt a great deal of pain. Some of this pain was the result of bad obstetrics, of men using forceps at the wrong time and causing tears between the vagina and bladder or rectum (vesico-vaginal fistula). This so "invalided" a woman that she was totally removed from society and often would rather have been dead. This is an example of "iatrogenic," or doctor-

FIG. 5.   The "touch" or gynecological examination. Early nineteenth century. Note the avoidance of eye contact.

caused, disease, which was not recognized as such at the time. Doctors like J. Marion Sims got credit from grateful women for developing repair surgery. A more frequent cause of pain was a prolapsed uterus, which necessitated the wearing of a pessary (Fig. 6). Women's life-styles contributed to painful births: middle-class women often had constricted rib-cages and pelves from wearing corsets day and night in order to achieve the fashionable sixteen-inch waist (Fig. 7). Vigorous exercise was discouraged for women of these classes.

Chloroform and ether, although used in some births since the 1850s, were only given at the last minute, as the baby passed through the birth canal (second stage of labor), after the woman had suffered for many hours. In most births, no anesthesia whatever was used. Doctors were fairly conservative in this regard. To women at the beginning of the twentieth century, control over birth meant the obliteration of pain, and the search for painless birth was an important factor drawing women into the hospital.

The doctors' takeover of American middle-class deliveries in the nineteenth century set the stage for the movement of births into the hospital in the early twentieth century. (In Europe most births

EVERY PHYSICIAN IS AWARE

of the trouble to himself and the discomfort to his patient in the treatment of uterine displacements by the old appliances, such as rings; pessaries, etc. Cases treated with pessaries and rings held in position by pressure against the vaginal walls receive no permanent relief from their use. The womb is held in place so long as the pessary or ring is in use, but on removal the case is worse than before, the walls of the vagina are dilated and weakened, the womb has lost its natural support from this course and falls lower in the pelvic cavity, and the only relief by the old method is to use a larger ring or pessary. By the new method, the McIntosh Supporter will raise the womb to its proper position in the pelvic cavity, allow the vagina and ligaments of support to contract and gain their normal tone, and although the instrument has been worn but a short time the uterus will keep its normal position if it be removed, though to insure a permanent result the supporter should be worn longer.

No instrument has ever been placed before the medical profession which has given such universal satisfaction as

 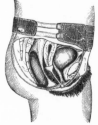

THE NATURAL UTERINE SUPPORTER   THE NATURAL UTERINE SUPPORTER APPLIED.

DR. McINTOSH'S Natural Uterine Supporter.

The combination is such, that the physician is able to meet every indication in the treatment of uterine displacements, Prolapsus, Anteversion, Retroversion and the Flexions.

FIG. 6.   A nineteenth-century pessary for prolapsed uterus.

remained in the home, attended by midwives.) The white, middle-class midwife had long since disappeared; only immigrant and black midwives remained. Between 1900 and 1930 these women came under attack from physicians who used racial and ethnic slurs of the lowest sort to discredit them as stupid, dirty, illiterate, or voodoo practitioners.[7] Ironically, as the New York Academy of Medicine pointed out in a study of maternal mortality in the early 1930s, the illiterate immigrant midwives of New York were safer birth attendants than the poorly-educated general practitioners who campaigned against them for control over birth.[8] These midwives ultimately disappeared as a result both of legal restrictions imposed by doctors and of acculturation to the American way, which meant having a doctor. This in turn meant giving birth in the hospital, "the doctor's castle."

As indicated in Fig. 8, urban births had already entered the hospital in the decade between 1920 and 1930, and the hospitalization of birth was completed in the 1940s. In the nineteenth century, most medical treatment of all kinds had taken place in the home, which physicians considered the best therapeutic environment. Hospitals

FIG. 7.   Corsets were the cause of much birth pain.

existed only for the poor or homeless, or those who needed quarantine. Nineteenth-century maternity or "lying-in" hospitals were founded largely for purposes of giving "moral treatment" to poor but deserving women who would otherwise have been forced to associate with incorrigibles in the almshouse. Hospitals accepted women having a first, but not a second, illegitimate child. But for physicians, hospitals offered the dual advantages of providing professional prestige (for only the elite attained a hospital affiliation), and unconstrained opportunities to do research on patients. Research could not be conducted in the home with the woman's family present.

Births remained in the home as long as infection (puerperal fever) remained prevalent. The home was considered safer from infection than the hospital. Pasteur's discovery in the 1870s of the

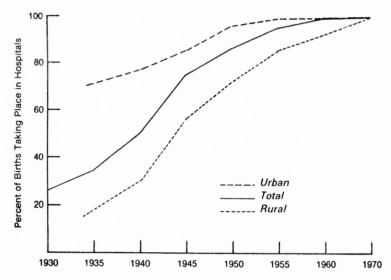

Estimated Percentages of Births Taking Place in Hospitals,
1930-1970

Sources: Donnell M. Pappenfort, *Journey to Labor,* Chicago, 1964,
Table 15, p. 49; AMA Council on Medical Education and
Hospitals, *Hospital Service in the U.S., IX-XV* (Chicago: 1936).

FIG. 8.   Graph showing percentages of births in the hospital.

bacteriological cause of puerperal fever and the development of
antiseptic and aseptic techniques made prevention (but not cure)
possible. The United States never suffered the major puerperal fever
epidemics that occurred in Europe because hospitals here were
relatively small. Nevertheless, many doctors' attempts to make birth
safer through the use of instruments and other interventions were
totally undone by infection before 1870. The causes of infection long
were regarded as mysterious. Although Oliver Wendell Holmes had
stated that puerperal fever was carried on doctors' hands, many
physicians attributed infection to the home slum conditions or
immorality of the patients. Infection remained the major killer at birth
until the mid-1930s.[9]

Nevertheless, hospitals began to be safer by 1900. In order to
support their charity wards, they began to advertize for paying
patients. They equipped rooms with the carpets and furniture found in
the upper-middle-class bedroom, representing themselves as gracious
hotels with room service. The mess, fuss, and bother of having the birth
in one's own home, and of having to hire servants for the occasion,
were eliminated by moving to the hospital. It offered twenty-four-hour

nursing service and an environment advertised as more germ-free than the home. Physicians in the early twentieth century were beginning to centralize their activities on the model of industry; it was more efficient and productive to have their patients come to them than to travel to patients' homes. Home-delivery services offered by hospitals became restricted to the poor, and were provided by medical students. After 1940, most such services were discontinued for lack of demand, and also because the supply of physicians during World War II dropped even more dramatically. Women had come to see all sorts of advantages in going to the hospital: they believed that it *was* safer than the home, especially after the development of equipment such as x-ray machines and incubators; that it was more comfortable; and also that it was the "modern" way to give birth.

A new method of pain relief, developed in Germany in 1914, gave impetus to hospitalization. This was "Twilight Sleep," a combination of morphine with scopolamine, an amnesiac that purportedly removed the memory of the birth altogether. To women at the beginning of this century, whose mothers had experienced so much pain, liberation meant relief both from pain and from the entire experience of birth. Feminists and women doctors joined women's campaigns to demand that physicians use Twilight Sleep. Society women such as Mrs. John Jacob Astor helped to found "Twilight Sleep Societies" to promote use of the new method; most of the members were upper-class women. Because this method required careful monitoring, it was best applied in the hospital; women eagerly entered the hospital in order to have its benefits. In Boston, one woman physician even founded her own Twilight Sleep Hospital (Fig. 9). By the 1930s, the method was extensively used by physicians, who found that patients who would remember little required less personal attention. As with the early forceps, the "new technology" of Twilight Sleep was at first considered an answer to a host of medical conditions, including slow labor and heart disease. Many also thought that it would be the answer to the declining birth rate among middle-class whites. Eventually, the morphine was replaced by other drugs because it was dangerous. By the early 1940s, the new spinal anesthesia was developed and killed pain rather than memory. Demerol, in some cases, replaced scopolamine.

Once in the hospital, women found themselves in a position of greater dependence than ever before. The timing and position of birth were arranged for the comfort of the staff; women had little or no control over procedures. Many hospital routines, such as the enema and shave, dated from the battle against infection fought early in this century. Others derived from doctors' incessant attempts to improve upon nature. Having lost the sense of nature a hundred years before,

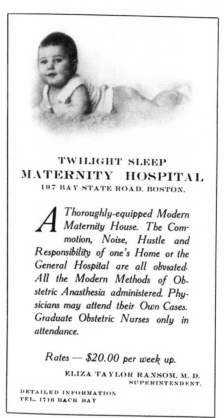

FIG. 9.   Dr. Eliza Taylor Ransom's Twilight Sleep Maternity Hospital.

doctors considered it inappropriate to let nature take its course. Experiments with induced labor go back to the 1890s. A balloon would be inserted into the uterus and inflated in order to bring on labor several weeks early. Presumably, the smaller baby thus produced would be born with less pain. The cesarean operation was another area for research after the introduction of antiseptics. By the 1890s this operation began to become a "safe" procedure. Prior to that time it had been invariably fatal for the mother and was therefore used only on mothers already dead. The new safety, and the possibility of saving the infant's life, led to overuse of cesareans in the decades between 1920 and 1940, when rates approached ten to fifteen percent in some hospitals. Many of these operations were performed by ill-educated or inexperienced general practitioners. Specialists agreed that overuse of this operation, along with overuse of other interventions, such as "high" forceps, was in large part responsible for a maternal death rate that remained unchanged between 1913 and 1935. As in the preceding century, the more experienced and educated doctors decried the overuse of new techniques by the ill-educated.

The specialists themselves urged such interventions as episiotomy and outlet forceps that became routine procedures in American hospital births. The rationale given by Dr. Joseph B. DeLee in 1920 was that nature was inherently flawed in birth. Nature, said DeLee, perhaps intended women to be used up like the salmon after spawning. Natural birth was equivalent to the woman's falling on a pitchfork and driving the handle through her perineum, and to the baby's having its head slammed in a barn door. It was far better to make a clean surgical cut (the episiotomy) that could be easily stitched together, rather than the otherwise inevitable jagged tear. It was far better to lift the baby out gently with forceps before its brain could be damaged by being rammed against the mother's tissues.[10] In 1920 mental retardation had become of national concern; parents had begun to plan smaller families, in which each child must be a work of art. The episiotomy and forceps procedures became standard, and remained standard even for women planning "natural" or "prepared" births in hospitals in the 1950s and 1960s. It has never been proved that these procedures affect mental retardation in any way; they have never become standard in other countries. In recent years there has been speculation that women tear because they are placed in an anatomically unnatural position for birth. The "lithotomy" or flat-on-the-back position used in American hospitals, while convenient for the physician, is conducive to tearing. The anxiety produced by some hospital surroundings may also contribute. If this is so, the episiotomy may be necessitated, not by nature, but by these other medical routines and the routine use of forceps themselves. This is the case with many birth procedures: there is a circularity of techniques that require other techniques either to correct their faults or to insure their safety.

In terms of maternal and neonatal mortality, the United States has always lagged behind other industrial nations. This has been true ever since the beginning of birth registration in this country in 1913. The reasons are largely socioeconomic, as is evident from the differences between white and nonwhite in Figs. 10 and 11. The United States has always had a two-class system of care. It has never developed a comprehensive plan of health insurance. Insurance and maternity leave plans developed far earlier in Europe; many other nations provide more government benefits for maternity. However, in the United States, doctors believed that all women had access to first-class care, whatever their ability to pay. To doctors the fact that they provided care made it first-class, whether clinic or private.

Reformers of the Progressive Era, however, were aware that many

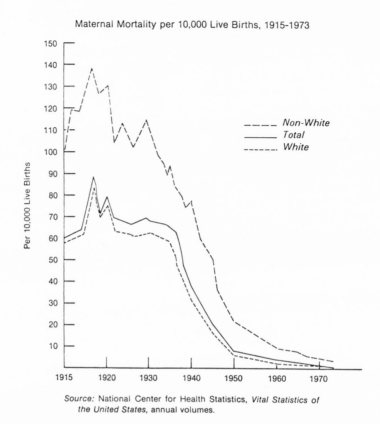

Maternal Mortality per 10,000 Live Births, 1915-1973

Source: National Center for Health Statistics, *Vital Statistics of the United States,* annual volumes.

FIG. 10.   Graph of maternal mortality, white and nonwhite.

women were not receiving first-class care, and advocated that the federal government protect maternity and infancy as it protected agricultural animals, by supplying matching grants to states.The enfranchisement of women and the advocacy of women reformers, such as Florence Kelley and Congresswoman Jeanette Rankin, led to passage in 1920 of the first federal law supporting medical care, the Sheppard-Towner Act "for the protection of maternity and infancy." In her introduction to the original bill, Rankin stated that maternity care was a right, not a charity. States used the Sheppard-Towner money largely for preventive medicine, by providing rural clinics for prenatal care, by educating expectant mothers, or by upgrading black or immigrant midwives or general practitioners. The Act was repealed in 1930 at the instigation of the American Medical Association, which considered it "creeping Bolshevism" and the beginnings of socialized medicine. When federal support for maternity care was reinstated in the Social Security Act of 1935, it took a very different form. Ever since

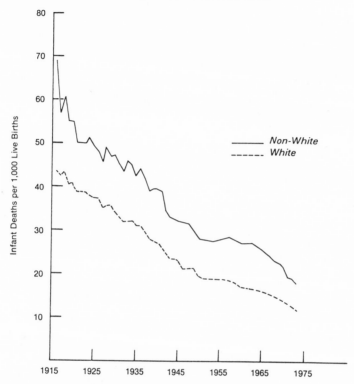

Neonatal Mortality (Infant Deaths under One Month),
1915-1973 (U.S. Birth Registration Area)

FIG. 11.   Graph of neonatal mortality, white and nonwhite.

1935, federal money has remained firmly under doctors' control. It is designated for research or demonstration projects of interest to doctors, and focuses on crisis care for "high-risk" births rather than the preventive care envisaged by the Sheppard-Towner Act.

The American doctors' reliance on crisis technology, coupled with the channeling of federal money into research rather than into patient care, often makes it appear that women of all social classes have equal access to crisis technology such as fetal monitors. It is too seldom realized that hospitals have always expected poor patients to "pay" for their care by allowing their bodies to be used for research. This has been true for 150 years; in the nineteenth century the provision of opportunities for research was a major reason for hospitals' existence. This means that poor women have frequently received the "latest" methods: induced labor or cesarean section in the 1890s, and fetal monitors and new drugs in the 1970s. The technologies used on poor women tend to be experimental; if successful, they are then rapidly disseminated to private patients. Too often it is forgotten that although the technology may be the same, it was used with different intent on poor and middle-class women.

The United States has consistently remained behind. In 1976, the most recent year for which statistics are available, the maternal death rate was 9.3 per 100,000 live births for white mothers, 15.2 for nonwhite mothers. The neonatal death rate was 9.7 per 1000 for white babies, 16.3 for nonwhite babies.[11] This reflects a gap that has existed ever since the beginnings of mortality statistics in 1915.

In 1977 the United Nations *Demographic Yearbook* listed fourteen nations with more favorable rates of neonatal mortality than the United States, and eight with more favorable rates of maternal mortality. These included the major nations of northern and Western Europe, and Australia. In neonatal mortality, East Germany, Spain, Canada, and Japan rank above the US. These rates are generally considered indicative of the scientific and social level of a nation's medicine and health. Saving some marginal infants shifts some mortality into the morbidity or birth-defect categories. Doctors in the United States do believe that improvement in neonatal death rates has been achieved within the last five years by saving the marginal babies through intensive technology.

Yet this technology is unable to prevent nonwhite women from having twice as many low birthweight babies, who are likely to need the new technology, as do white women. It is in the area of preventive medicine, particularly nutrition and prenatal care, that the greatest class differences exist.

The dramatic improvement in maternal safety between 1935 and 1945, as is evident from Fig. 10, too frequently has been credited entirely to technical advances and to the hospitalization of birth. It is true that two very important life-saving techniques were developed around 1935: blood transfusions and the first effective antibacterial drug, sulfanilamide. Perhaps more credit should go to the development of hospital regulations preventing the worst-educated physicians from doing cesareans, to the establishment of the first hospital investigating committees on maternal deaths, and to the provision of federal support. Nations that depended less on crisis technology also experienced a drop in death rates, even more rapid than ours. As a result, our international standing still lags behind many other industrial but less wealthy nations.

The ethical issues in birth technology today center on two basic questions: (1) who should have the ultimate authority to make decisions? and (2) should resources be used to provide high technology, such as fetal monitors, to everybody, or should there be a reallocation of resources toward providing basic care? The answer to these questions depends in part upon one's belief about nature. At present there is a complete polarity between most of the obstetrical profession, which seeks greater safety through more crisis technology, and a radical group of families who wish to avoid the conventional medical system altogether and to have their births at home. Doctors are redefining "high-risk" to include about half of all women, although obstetrical texts have always said that ninety percent of births are "normal." They are seeking further centralization by regionalizing intensive neonatal care and maternal care into fewer hospitals with more sophisticated equipment.

On the other hand, the home birth movement is attracting more adherents who argue that most births are natural and in need of no technology. If this polarity is ever to be resolved, women and doctors are going to have to agree about whether birth is a natural process or a potential disease, and about what percentage of births is normal. If the women's health movement has anything to say about this, the rate will be closer to 90% than to 50%. The problem is that medicine lost the sense of nature so long ago that it is going to be very difficult to regain it. There is very little research on normal birth outside the hospital environment. It is possible that we do not even know what normal birth is, aside from the elaborate structures that our technological culture has erected around it. If there is ever to be an agreement between the women's health movement and the medical profession, it will be necessary to take seriously the various procedures used by attendants in home births (family, lay mid wives, nurse-midwives, physicians), as being "basic technologies." Since technology is defined as the application of knowledge to human problems, these procedures need scientific comparison to hospital procedures. At present many home birth advocates are so alienated from the medical establishment that they regard all science as male-dominated, and reject any attempts at research on home births. These women believe that no reconciliation with the medical establishment is possible, and that they must undermine it in the most radical way, by removing themselves as completely as possible from its control.

The issue of control is the most basic issue in medical ethics today. Women want to make the final decisions for themselves and their babies, rather than being told that they are at risk and therefore must have certain procedures for the baby's sake. The evaluation of "risk" involves more than risks to physical safety. There are also psychological and social risks that may matter to the mother and to her relationship with the child. She may decide that she would rather take the physical "risk" of giving birth outside the hospital than take the psychological "risk" of giving birth in the hospital and of having a birth experience that she considers detrimental to the mental health of herself and her child. Even the physical risks so frequently cited by doctors to make women feel guilty for wanting a home birth or for not wanting a fetal monitor are open to question. The scientific literature is not at all clear about exactly who is at risk or under what conditions. Given this uncertainty, it is appropriate that the woman herself should have the power of decision over what risks she chooses for herself and her yet-to-be-born child. Although in some cases she will make a mistake, doctors also sometimes make mistakes. A woman who has done what she thinks best for herself and her unborn child should not be accused of "child abuse" if the outcome should be negative.

A shift toward emphasis on basic preventive care rather than crisis technology could help to overcome the current polarities. Although medicine does very well with the marginal or abnormal case, the greatest improvement in maternal and neonatal death rates is likely to come, not from expansion of crisis techniques to all, but from renewed emphasis on preventive care in the broadest sense. This means providing proper nutrition to poor women, eliminating the various kinds of pollution that exist in poor neighborhoods, and ultimately eliminating poverty altogether. Even so its effects upon maternal health may linger for several generations.

The personnel involved in preventive care need not be medical specialists. People from the community could become responsible for most aspects of maternity care, leaving the women in the few percentiles that are genuinely high-risk to the specialists. A shift of national priorities toward prevention could enable women and their communities to regain control over birth and to redefine it in terms of nature rather than disease.

The Electronic Fetal Monitor In Perinatology

Henry Klapholz

Electronic fetal monitoring is not a technology that is intended to raise the scalpel, but rather, one that permits the surgeon to withhold it. The objective of all technology is to effect timely and appropriate intervention while permitting nature to take its course in an otherwise uncomplicated event. Fetal monitoring is, therefore, a very difficult issue to address in today's times. Antitechnology feelings, while often appropriate, frequently interfere with objective evaluation of a potentially life-saving and life-enhancing technique.

Here I will try to present to you information and not opinions. I will deal neither with feelings nor with emotions, but simply with information that has been accumulated. I will attempt to show you the basis on which fetal monitoring has developed, what it can do, what it cannot do, and its limitations. It is not my intent to convert those of you who are strongly antitechnology, for it must be borne in mind that the chances for a successful labor and delivery are certainly 98 out of 100 or greater. For those who are willing to undertake such a risk, this entire discussion is simply unnecessary. For those, however, with the responsibility to advise, guide, and assist new mothers in deciding how to optimize the chances for their newborn child, this discussion may be of value.

It is well known that simply listening to the fetal heart in no way gives one an accurate picture of fetal status.[1] Much controversial literature has appeared purporting that simple auscultation of a baby intermittently with a fetoscope will produce a good outcome.[2] This is undeniable. It is also undeniable that simple intermittent auscultation does not permit even accurate counting.[3] When groups of experienced obstetricians were asked simply to count fetal heart rate, it was easily seen that there was a wide variation in individual observer counts and it was clearly demonstrated that individuals count best what they are familiar with, namely rates in the neighborhood of 120 to 130 beats per minute. Even if absolute heart rate is an indicator of fetal status, it would be very difficult to arrive at this number through mere auscultation.

Fortunately, or unfortunately, as the case may be, it turns out that the absolute fetal heart rate is, in fact, not a good indicator of fetal status. The development of modern technology and the ability to design small electrodes that attach to the baby's scalp and seldom cause damage, infection, or bleeding has given us the ability to calculate instantaneous fetal heart rate. By this I mean a computed rate based on only two heartbeats. This rate is recomputed every time the heart beats and the instantaneous rate is then plotted on a strip chart recorder.

Approximately fifteen years ago, commercial fetal monitors, as we now know them, were developed and their basic premise has not changed much. The information they supply us also has not changed much, but such a valuable indicator may quickly tell one the status of a baby at any given time in labor.

Heart rate is never constant in a healthy fetus as it is never constant in the adult. Instantaneous fetal heart rate has associated with it a characteristic referred to as fetal heart variability (Fig. 1). This pattern of variability, which is really an expression of the changes in instantaneous rate from beat to beat, is characteristic for any particular baby and is determined by fetal brain function. It is the fetal

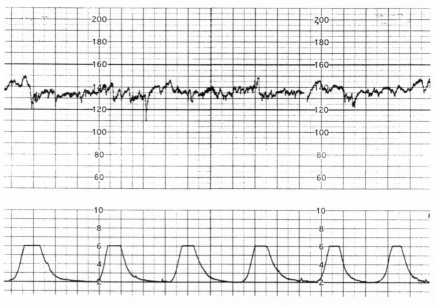

FIG. 1.   Fetal heart rate pattern showing normal amounts of variability. This pattern of variability is an expression of the instantaneous rate from beat-to-beat and is characteristic for any particular baby.

central nervous system that modulates neurologic activity that controls heart rate, and any damage to this controller will cause alterations in variability patterns.

What really controls heart rate? The entire nervous system, including the sympathetic and parasympathetic systems, affects fetal heart rate. Through the action of the vagus nerve (which slows the heart down) and the cardio-accelerator fibers (which are sympathetic in nature and speed the heart up), a fine interplay results that instantaneously controls heart rate to maintain fetal homeostasis. Surgical disconnection of any of these nerve pathways, or pharmacologic intervention by drugs—such as atropine, scopolamine or demerol (drugs that are unfortunately still used, in a few hospitals, routinely in childbirth)—act to modify neurologic control of heart rate. Once such agents are given, one sees heart rates that are completely flat, exhibiting no variability. This does not mean that the fetal brain is no longer functioning, but rather that it has been put to sleep. One can, however, infer that in a baby who has not been given such drugs, the brain may have been damaged by loss of oxygen, as is the case of the fetus whose heart rate pattern is shown in Fig. 2.

The above statement has, in fact, been verified, and it has clearly been shown that babies whose heart rates exhibit diminished amounts of variability have blood acidity levels (pH) that are lower than the norm. In addition, the Apgar scores of babies delivered after episodes of diminished heart rate variability are also considerably lower.[4]

Traditionally, a heart rate drop to 50 or 60 using auscultatory methods such as the fetoscope required immediate delivery. The obstetrician quickly rushed the mother to the cesarean section room,

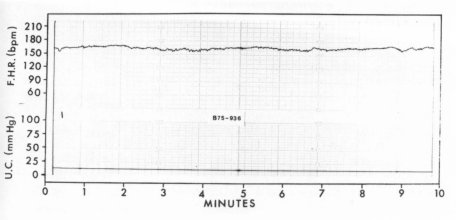

FIG. 2.   Fetal heart rate pattern without variability. This baby's brain may have been damaged by loss of oxygen or simply narcotized by a number of pharmacologic agents.

quickly performed an operation to deliver the baby, and then was justifiably proud of the results when a screaming, healthy young child was delivered. In fact, fetal monitoring has taught us that most of these operative interventions were probably unnecessary. However, in some hospitals, unskilled use of fetal monitoring may have contributed in its turn to unnecessary interventions.

Drops in heart rate to levels as low as 50 or even 40 do not necessarily predict a poor outcome. It is rather the pattern of *rate of change* with respect to time that is indicative of fetal well-being.

In order to understand more fully the value of fetal monitoring it is worth spending a few moments to discuss the several methods we have of obtaining fetal heart rates. External fetal monitoring detects fetal heart activity through the maternal abdomen. There are several techniques available including abdominal electrocardiography (which will pick up a fetal electrocardiogram directly from the mother's abdomen without connecting any wires to the fetus), phono-cardiography (by placing a microphone on the maternal abdomen), or ultrasonography (using a Doppler device that will determine movements of the fetal heart wall). These techniques are helpful when the mother lies still and does not move about. Unfortunately they are suboptimally effective in the ambulatory patient.

Maternal motion creates electrical interference to the external electrocardiographic technique, and simple movement of the fetus from beneath the acoustic transducers causes the fetal heart beat to be lost. Fetal position often affects the ability of a fetal monitor to pick up a fetal heart rate by external means as well. It happens to be true that most fetuses whose mothers are in the supine position can be well-monitored using external means; however, it has been well established that lying on one's back is the most unphysiologic position for labor and often the most uncomfortable as well.

There are two types of ominous heart rate patterns that must be understood. The first is referred to as a cord compression or variable deceleration pattern. This is a pattern of rate drop that can be seen when the umbilical cord is compressed. Such compression may be secondary, the cord being wrapped around the fetus' neck or arm, or even result from the trapping of the cord between the fetal head and the maternal pelvis. In rare situations when the umbilical cord is delivered before the baby (cord prolapse), fetal monitoring may detect the very first evidence of such an accident. Decelerations in heart rate produced by these events are rapid and deep. Figure 3 is representative of a fetal heart modified by cord compression. Decelerations, however, do not necessarily imply that the baby is jeopardized. They simply indicate that a neurologic reflex has taken place that has dropped the fetal heart

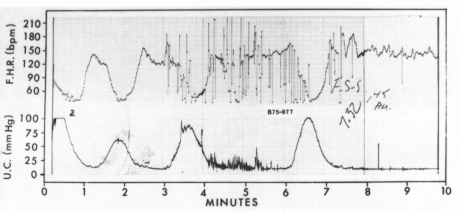

FIG. 3.   Variable heart rate deceleration patterns. This heart rate has been modified by umbilical cord compression but does not necessarily imply fetal jeopardy.

rate. The fetus whose heart rate pattern is shown in Fig. 2 was delivered with Apgar scores of 9 at one minute and 10 at five minutes and was a lively, vigorous baby that withstood 12 hours of such fetal heart rate patterns with no ill effect. Because the obstetrician who took care of this mother understood the meaning of this pattern, she was able to avoid an unnecessary cesarean section.

Another pattern (Fig. 4) that is seen is the late deceleration or uteroplacental insufficiency pattern. This circumstance can be likened to breath holding in the adult. Fetuses that are well oxygenated between uterine contractions do very well during the time that the uterus contracts, even though no blood is supplied the placenta at that time. This is perfectly normal.

However, fetuses whose placentas are insufficient, secondary to the effects of intercurrent diseases such as diabetes, hypertension, or advancing gestational age beyond the expected due date, do not sufficiently pre-oxygenate between contractions. The fetus does not withstand a 45-second lack of oxygen. When this occurs the fetal heart responds with a gradual but progressive delayed fall. It falls slowly, commencing its decline at least 20 seconds after the onset of a contraction. Heart rate then rises when oxygen flow has been reestablished. These late onset decelerations are clearly indicative of a reduction in uterine blood flow, a disturbance that is easily treated. It does not demand cesarean section in most cases, but rather invites repositioning the mother to maximize uterine blood flow, dictates administration of maternal oxygen by mask, and may even require intravenous fluids infusion in order to increase maternal circulating

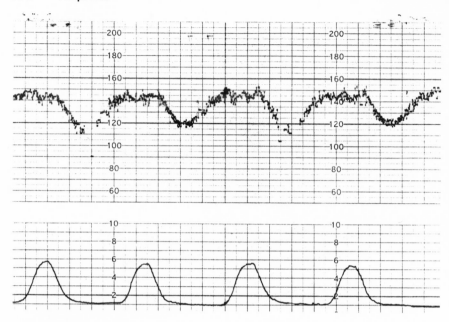

FIG. 4. Late deceleration patterns. The utero-placental unit is insufficient so that the fetus does not sufficiently pre-oxygenate between uterine contractions.

blood volume so that more red cells may reach the fetus in a given amount of time. Nine out of ten times, such late decelerations disappear with the aforementioned treatment.

It is clear that if one were merely to listen with the fetoscope, one would only hear a steady rate of 120 and 130 beats per minute with only minor changes. As a matter of fact, in the absence of variability the heart rate would sound very steady indeed. The ten or fifteen beat per minute deceleration that is clearly evident on the continuous tracing would hardly be appreciated through the fetoscope. It has been well demonstrated that the fetus exhibiting recurrent late decelerations accompanied by diminished variability is a fetus that is born acidotic and depressed.

Confirmation is essential in any scientific endeavor, and it is well that there is one additional tool that enables the suspicious tracing to be verified. Fetal blood may be easily sampled to check for acidity when there is a question of whether or not fetal distress exists. This biochemical augmentation of our diagnostic armamentarium permits the provider to single out those mothers who should appropriately be subjected to cesarean section. Simply performing such a major operation on a woman because her baby's heart rate alone has fallen is fraught with the potential for more excessive intervention. It has been claimed that the cesarean section rate throughout the country has been rising because of increasing intervention ascribed principally to fetal monitoring. Over the last ten years at the Beth Israel Hospital in Boston, it is true that the cesarean section rate has risen. It is interesting to note, however, that when one examines the indications for these cesarean sections, fetal distress is not responsible for the rise. The incidence of cesarean section for fetal distress has remained constant with the rise attributable to a reduction in use of forceps. What, then, is the role of fetal monitoring in this? It would appear that we are now performing cesarean sections on a *different* group of mothers. *True* fetal distress is now detectable. Many more mothers who could normally deliver healthy children vaginally are being permitted to do so. The injudicious use of forceps and oxytocin and the unindicated use of cesarean section have been markedly reduced. The sudden death during labor of an otherwise "healthy fetus with a steady heart rate of 140" has been virtually eliminated as well.

What then can one say about fetal monitoring? Statistical studies of its effectiveness in one class of pregnancy or another is not really the issue. Neither is cost the issue when it comes to saving the life of an individual fetus. No cost can be placed on the intellectual capacity or the quality of life of that individual child. If one is interested in gambling and taking that 2% chance, then fetal monitoring is unnecessary. If one is interested in optimizing the chances for *every* fetus, fetal monitoring is *essential.*

There are two questions that must be answered by every obstetrical care provider. They address the issues of: is the mother all right and is the fetus all right. The answer to the first is easy. It can be answered by examination of labor in progress, examination of maternal blood pressure, and examination of many other maternal parameters. The second question can be answered in only two ways. With fetal monitoring it can be answered with great certainty. Without fetal monitoring the answer must be, "I don't know, but I suppose it's all right." If this is a sufficiently satisfying response to the mother then one may proceed to traditional methods of fetal surveillance. If we are determined to provide a pregnant woman a chance for the *optimum* fetal outcome, modern technology can provide a valuable aid while maintaining human dignity and a sense of fulfillment for the mother.[5]

Drugs, Birth, and Ethics

Yvonne Brackbill

When fetal organs are developing, exposure to many drugs and other substances may produce behavioral, neurological, and structural changes. These agents are called *teratogens* when they produce physical changes and *behavioral teratogens* when they produce behavioral changes with or without accompanying physical changes. Figure 1 shows, for a rat fetus, the limited periods during embryogenesis when it is susceptible to physical deformity and the *longer* period, preceding and following birth, when the animal is vulnerable to central nervous system damage. In human beings, the period of vulnerability to central nervous system damage from exposure to drugs and chemicals lasts much longer. Even after birth, important areas of brain are growing and differentiating at a rapid rate and are still, therefore, especially vulnerable to damage. It has been estimated that the "growth spurt" in the cerebellum lasts for about 18 months, and that in the hippocampus, for about 4.5 years.

Unfortunately, in the last decade the number of drugs mothers consume during pregnancy and delivery has increased. (Note 1 for this

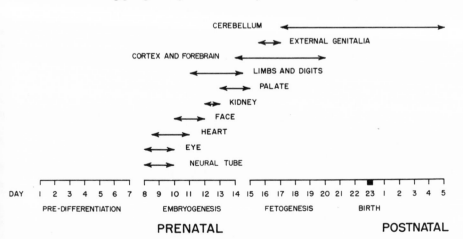

FIG. 1.   Sensitive periods in the development of the rat.

article contains a list of standard bibliographic reviews of studies of teratogenic, behaviorally teratogenic, and toxic effects on animals and humans of prescription and nonprescription drugs, as well as the effects of a variety of other substances.) Table 1 shows drugs and chemicals frequently indicted in these teratogenic studies.

In the present work, I will concentrate on perinatal drugs, i.e., drugs administered during labor and delivery. Table 2 contains a bibliography of studies on behavioral changes in infants and young children following their exposure to drugs at birth. As you can see, most of the studies in Table 2 show significant outcomes following drug administration, and several of them demonstrate drug effects well beyond the newborn period. It is difficult to believe that just a single dose of narcotic or 16 minutes worth of inhalation anesthesia could bring about such long lasting, if not permanent, changes. How could this happen?

The newborn's central nervous system is immature, still developing rapidly, and therefore still susceptible to damage. In addition, drugs cross the placenta rapidly and also cross the immature blood–brain barrier without difficulty. They lodge to a disproportionate extent in the highly perfused brain structures. They are not readily transformed into nontoxic compounds since the necessary liver functions are immature. They are not readily excreted because of still inefficient kidney function. Altogether then, drugs enter the

TABLE 1

Classes of Prescription and Nonprescription Drugs or Chemicals in Which More Than One Member Has Been Associated With Teratogenic, Behaviorally Teratogenic, and/or Toxic Effects in Studies of Animals and/or Human Offspring[a]

Antacids	Narcotics
Allergy, cough and cold medicines	Sedatives
	Tranquilizers
Analgesics	Vaccines
Anesthetics	Miscellaneous:
Anticoagulants	Alcohol
Antimicrobials	Caffeine
Appetite suppressants	Cigarette smoking
Cardiovascular medications	Environmental pollutants
Cytotoxic and cytostatic agents	Herbicides
Diuretics	Illicit drugs (LSD, marijuana,
Hormones and agents affecting hormones	mescaline, etc.)
	Vitamins A and D
Laxatives	in large doses

[a]For references see Note 1.

TABLE 2
Literature on Obstetric Medication and Infant/Child Behavior

Significant drug effects?	Test age ≥ 10 days?	Reference
Yes	Yes	Aleksandrowicz, M. K., and D. R. Aleksandrowicz, *Merrill-Palmer Quart.* **20,** 123 (1974).
Yes		Bakeman, R., et al., SRCD Paper (1975).
Yes		Borgstedt, A. D., and M. G. Rosen, *Am. J. Dis. Child* **115,** 21 (1968).
Yes		Brackbill, Y., et al., *Anesth.* **40,** 116 (1974).
Yes		Brackbill, Y., et al., *Am. J. Ob. Gyn.* **118,** 377 (1974).
Yes	Yes	Brackbill, Y., *Dev. Psychobio.* **9,** 353 (1976).
Yes	Yes	Brackbill, Y., and S. Broman, unpublished results.
Yes		Brazelton, T. B., *J. Ped.* **58,** 513 (1961).
Yes		Brazelton, T. B., et al., *Ped.* **63,** 279 (1979).
Yes	Yes	Broman, S. and Y. Brackbill, unpublished results.
Yes		Brower, K. R., et al., *Anesth. Anal.* **57,** 303 (1978).
		Brown, J. V., et al., *Child Dev.* **46,** 677 (1975).
Yes	Yes	Conway, E., and Y. Brackbill, *Monogr. SRCD* **35,** (137), 24 (1970).
Yes		Dubignon, J., et al., *Child Dev.* **40,** 1107 (1969).
Yes		Emde, R. N., et al., *Arch. Gen. Psychiatry* **32,** 780 (1975).
Yes	Yes	Friedman, S. L., et al. *Merrill-Palmer Quart.* **24,** 111 (1978).
Yes		Hodgkinson, R., et al., *Soc. Obstet. Anesthesia Perinatal* paper, Orlando, FL (1976).
Yes		Hodgkinson, R., et al., *Anaesth.* **31,** 143 (1976).
Yes		Hodgkinson, R., et al., *Intl. Anesthesia Res. Soc.* paper, Phoenix, AZ (1976).
Yes		Hodgkinson, R., et al., *Can. Anaesth. Soc. J.* **25,** 405 (1978).
Yes		Hodgkinson, R., et al., *Ped.* **62,** 294 (1978).
Yes		Hollmen, A. I., et al., *Anaesth.* **48,** 350 (1978).
	Yes	Horowitz, F. D., et al. (Israeli study), *Child Dev.* **48,** 1607 (1977).
Yes		Horowitz, F. D., et al. (Uruguayan study), *Child Dev.* **48,** 1607 (1977).

(continued)

TABLE 2 *(continued)*
Literature on Obstetric Medication and Infant/Child Behavior

Significant drug effects?	Test age ≥ 10 days?	Reference
Yes		Hughes, J. G., et al., *Am. J. Dis. Child* **76,** 626 (1948).
Yes		Hughes, J. G., et al., *Am. J. Dis. Child* **79,** 996 (1950).
Yes		Kraemer, H., et al., *Dev. Psych.* **6,** 128 (1972).
Yes		Kron, R. E., et al., *Ped.* **37,** 1012 (1966).
Yes	Yes	Lester, B. M., et al., unpublished results.
Yes		Moreau, T., and H. G. Birch, *Dev. Med. Child Neurol.* **16,** 612 (1974).
Yes		Palahniuk, R. J., et al., *Can. Anaesth. Soc. J.* **24,** 586 (1977).
		Parke, R. D., et al., *Proceedings of the 80th APA Convention,* 85 (1972).
Yes		Richards, M. P. M., and J. F. Bernal, *Ethological Studies of Child Behaviour,* N. B. Jones, ed., Cambridge University Press, p. 175.
Yes		Scanlon, J. W., et al., *Clin. Perinat.* **1,** 465 (1974).
Yes		Scanlon, J. W., et al., *Anesth.* **45,** 400 (1976).
Yes		Standley, K., et al., *Science* **106,** 534 (1974).
Yes		Stechler, G., *Science* **144,** 375 (1964).
Yes	Yes	Tronick, E., et al., *Ped.* **58,** 94 (1976).
Yes		Turner, S., and A. McFarlane, *Dev. Med. Child. Neurol.* **20,** 727 (1978).
Yes		VanderMaelen, A. L., et al., *Dev. Psych.* **11,** 711 (1975).
Yes		Yang, R. K., et al., *Dev. Psych.* **12,** 6 (1976).

developing central nervous system easily and, once there, are relatively more difficult to transform and excrete than is the case for the mature central nervous system.

All these considerations increase the probability that behavioral changes will result even from a single administration of drugs. Such changes are listed in Table 3.

What general conclusions can be drawn from these results? One of the most striking things about the results is their consistency. For those studies finding significant effects of obstetric medication, the direction of the effects is uniformly negative. Drugs affect all behavior adversely. *None* of the studies has shown that obstetric medication improves normal functioning. Not only are the effects consistent, but they are, in

TABLE 3
Behavioral Changes Following Perinatal Drug Administration[a]

Ability to inhibit responding
  Ability to shut down, be comforted, etc.
Habituation, response decrement (motor or heart rate response to auditory,
    visual or tactile stimuli)
Auditory responses
  Response decrement (see inhibitory ability, above)
  Sound localization
Behavioral items CPP rating scales, 4 and 7 years
  High assertiveness
  Low emotional reactivity
  Low frustration tolerance
  Withdrawal, uncooperativeness
EEG
  During stimulation
  Resting levels
Feeding, sucking, rooting
  Amount consumed
  Number of sucks; rate
  Pressure
  Responsiveness
Heart rate
Language
  Low reading scores, Wide Range Achievement Test
  Low spelling scores, Wide Range Achievement Test
  Verbal analogies, Illinois Test of Psycholinguistic Abilities
  Verbal items, Stanford-Binet
Motor functions
  coordination
  Gross motor activities
  Reflexes
Standardized tests
  Bayley Scales
  Brazelton Neonatal Behavioral Assessment Scale
  Collaborative Perinatal Project Pediatric-Neurological Exam
  Graham-Rosenblith Scale
  Prechtl-Beintema Neurological Exam
  Scanlon's Early Neonatal Neurological Scale
State and state lability
  Alertness
  Sleep
Visual responses
  Fixation time
  Response decrement (See inhibitory ability, above)
WISC Verbal IQ

[a]References can be found in: Brackbill, Y., Obstetrical Medication and Infant Behavior, in *Handbook of Infant Development,* Osofsky, J. D., Ed., Wiley, New York, 1979.

the main, substantial. I mean by "substantial" that most of the studies listed in Table 2 found significant drug effects for half or more of the dependent variables at one or more of the test ages studied. Drug effects are not transient; they persist in those studies that have followed babies beyond the neonatal period.

Another general conclusion that can be drawn from these studies is that the behavioral effects of obstetric medication are dose-related and potency-related. That is, stronger drugs and larger doses of a single drug produce stronger behavioral effects. For example, general anesthetics have stronger effects than local anesthetics, and local anesthetics have stronger effects than no anesthetic at all. This finding is apparent when drugs of different doses and potency are compared *within* studies and also *between* studies. In other words, studies showing the most substantially significant results are those using the most potent drugs given in highest doses.

The question can be raised whether these behavioral changes are related to other variables, or indeed whether they are artifacts of variables other than drugs, e.g., risk factors during pregnancy or complications during delivery. Almost all studies finding significant drug effects have studied healthy, full-term babies who came from risk-free pregnancies and whose deliveries were normal and uneventful. In other words, there is no evidence that the behavioral changes are produced by preexisting disease or pregnancy/birth complications. Likewise, there is no consistent effect of parity or of length of labor: differential drug effects still show up when infants are delivered by elective cesarean section. Likewise, they still appear when socioeconomic status is statistically eliminated or when comparisons are made within the same socioeconomic class. Finally, there are no consistent sex differences.

I want now to turn to some ethical issues that devolve largely on consumer information and on the consumer's right to decide whether or not she will consume drugs.[2]

The first ethical issue involves the Food and Drug Administration (FDA) and its regulation regarding the nonapproved use of approved drugs.[3] FDA requires proof of safety and efficacy from the manufacturer before a new drug is cleared for clinical use. Most drugs used for childbirth have never been approved for childbirth on *any* grounds. And certainly *no* drug has been approved on grounds that assess current neurobehavioral integrity or that predict future central nervous system dysfunction.

In 1972, FDA ruled that when a drug approved for certain specific purposes is used for a nonapproved purpose, the drug's status reverts to "investigational," i.e., experimental. When a drug approved for some other purpose is administered during childbirth (a nonapproved use), that birth literally becomes an experiment, and the mother and infant, experimental subjects. Under current Department of Health, Education, and Welfare guidelines for protection of human subjects' rights, the obstetrician–experimenter is required to disclose all information that bears upon the mother's giving informed consent for her own participation and proxy consent for her unborn child's participation. Thus, as an experimental subject, the mother is entitled to drug information both on moral grounds and legal grounds.

The components of informed consent that must be provided to her are these: (1) a fair explanation of the procedures and drugs to be used and their purposes, including identification of any procedures or drugs that are experimental; (2) a description of the risks to be expected; (3) a description of the benefits to be expected; (4) a disclosure of alternative procedures that are available (in this case, for example, natural childbirth, hypnosis, acupuncture, or no treatment); (5) an offer to answer any questions concerning the procedures or drugs; (6) an explanation that the mother may at any time withdraw her consent to further administration of experimental drugs or of any other drug or procedure; and (7) information regarding the availability of compensation and medical treatment for physical injury resulting from research participation. In addition, the investigator–obstetrician must avoid implying that he or she cannot be held responsible for negative consequences arising from the experiment. Finally, the consent should be documented. Do you know of any obstetrician who has obtained such consent before delivering a baby?

Another set of ethical questions apropos of unapproved-use drug research relates to the quality of research, since that research is not done within regulatory FDA guidelines nor is it typically supported by an agency requiring peer review of the research protocol. For example, nine American studies were published between 1975 and 1978 using beta-sympathomimetics to inhibit labor and corticosteroids to increase fetal lung maturity in preterms. These are two additional examples of approved drugs used for nonapproved purposes. None of these studies was funded by publicly or privately awarded research grants or contracts from agencies requiring peer review for that purpose. All were supported by the drug companies themselves.

A third ethical question raised by research using approved drugs for nonapproved purposes is whether the experiment taking place actually moves that use of the drug noticeably closer to FDA approval (or disapproval). For example, beta-sympathomimetics have been the subject of research on labor inhibition for 18 years, but are still unapproved for that purpose. If 18 years' worth of research has not produced a definitive answer on the safety and efficacy of beta-mimetics, then something must have been wrong with the design or conduct of a large number of experiments. On the other hand, if these experiments *were* designed and conducted properly, then there must be an answer definitive enough to approve or disapprove this use of beta-mimetics and thus to extend it to (or withhold it from) all women at risk for premature delivery whose offspring would benefit from its application (or nonapplication).

Cutting across the general ethical issues of information and decision-making is the important issue of conflict of interest when one person takes on the dual role of therapist and researcher. There is always a potential and often a real conflict of interest between the physician's fiduciary duty to a woman as a patient and his need to use her as a subject of research. This conflict of interest is exacerbated when the physician is connected in any way with a teaching hospital where there is enormous pressure to publish or perish—in fact, where doing research and publishing is the only route to professional advancement, the only route to salary increase, the only route to tenure and promotion. A further exacerbation of conflict of interest arises when drug companies fund this research, as is frequently the case.[4]

Finally, I would like to mention some ethical issues that also occur in teaching hospitals and in their affiliated institutions. A disproportionately large number of economically disadvantaged and minority women deliver as clinic patients at teaching hospitals because they cannot afford to be private patients anywhere else. Clinic patients are more likely to end up as research subjects than are private patients. In fact, one survey found that clinic patients are three times as likely as private patients to end up as subjects in research projects with "unfavorable" risk/benefit ratios, i.e., research in which the risks are high and the benefits are low.

One danger in using poor and minority subjects is that they may not have sufficient educational and experiential background to give fully informed consent. Thus, in a study of obstetric patients in a labor-induction experiment, one investigator found that twice as many clinic patients as private patients did not know that they had been used as subjects in a research project. Further, none of the black clinic patients with less than high school education understood that they had agreed to be research subjects upon being admitted to the hospital.

In summary, drugs are bad news for obstetrics. They have adverse consequences for behavior development, and they are an ethical threat to the treatment of mothers with the respect and dignity they deserve.

Benefits and Risks of Electronic Fetal Monitoring

David Banta

An analysis of electronic fetal monitoring (EFM) might best begin with a few comments designed to put it in historical perspective, especially since the dramatic successes of miracle drugs have led us into the situation of being insufficiently critical of what is done in medical care.

New treatments have been grafted onto medical practice—treatments that were largely developed by trial and error, were never carefully evaluated, and remain largely unproven. Some interventions were often so dramatic in their benefits, compared to what was already being done, that they tended not to be evaluated. Now we seem to be in a situation where we are adopting technologies with small marginal benefits in comparison with what is already being done, and these tend not to be evaluated either.

We do have the evaluative tools to use. Probably the most important is the randomized controlled clinical trial. It was first completely described in the 1930s, but it is still very little applied in the medical care system. The control group is very important because we lack complete knowledge of the evolution of illness; thus we cannot use an intervention and then say what would have happened without it. It's very important, too, in most cases, to randomize. There are many examples in the evaluative literature of self-selection or physician-selection with demonstration of benefit that later proved not to be real.

There are a lot of reasons that physicians—and other providers, too—claim efficacy: financial reward is among the reasons. But most important, I believe, is the psychological need the provider has for believing that what he or she is doing is worthwhile. This need for belief conflicts with the tradition of science, which calls for skepticism—for doubt, evaluation.

So, I think we have to doubt the claims of efficacy and safety until we see some standard of evidence. In the Office of Technology Assessment, we have now looked at well over twenty specific technologies, and we continue to look at other technologies. And we find that lack of benefit and the existence of risk are pervasive problems. Furthermore, with very few adequately studied medical technologies, even those that are efficacious may be used inappropriately. If the specific benefit is not known, the physician or any provider will tend to use a technology on everybody with that kind of condition. I believe that electronic fetal monitoring has some efficacy, but I'm also quite convinced that electronic fetal monitoring is grossly overused, and often inappropriately used.

Steve Thacker and I spent about eighteen months collecting the literature on electronic fetal monitoring, reading it, and analyzing it. We examined six hundred papers, books, and reports in detail, and summarized them. We had our paper reviewed by a number of people we consider to be our peers—that is, people who understand the use and interpretation of data, including obstetricians and pediatricians. The final publications were the HEW report[1] and a paper in *Obstetrics and Gynecological Survey*.[2] The full report includes discussions of cost, of diagnostic specificity and sensitivity, and of predictive value. Here I want to focus on the question of benefits and risk, and then come to some of the ethical implications.

Table 1 shows the array of commonly used techniques in electronic fetal monitoring (EFM). I emphasize electronic because I think it is very misleading and actually biased to say "monitoring" for electronic monitoring. Monitoring has been done for a long time by midwives and nurses, using the ear, and then later on, the stethoscope.

The impetus for the rapid diffusion of electronic monitoring clearly came from our position in infant—perinatal—mortality rates in relation to the rest of the developed world. You could show the same graph for perinatal mortality or infant mortality, but Fig. 1 shows

TABLE 1

Comparison of Standard Techniques Used for the Management of Labor

Method	Patient convenience	MD/nurse convenience	Patient cost[a]
Auscultation	+	−	−
External electronic monitoring	−	±	$25–35
Internal electronic monitoring	−	+	$25–35
FSB pH sampling	±	−	$15
EFM + FSB pH	−	±	$50

[a]In addition to basic nursing care. FSB refers to fetal scalp blood sampling.

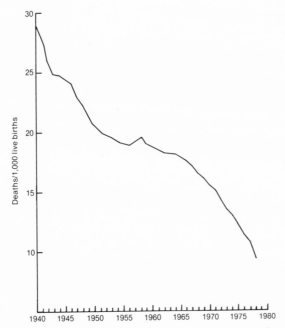

FIG. 1. Neonatal mortality rate change with time.

neonatal mortality over time. During the mid-1950s and early 1960s the rate of infant mortality stopped decreasing. That concerned a lot of people working in this field, particularly policymakers and a lot of obstetricians who felt that they could do better. The subsequent fall after the technologization of birth has been used as evidence of the success of electronic monitoring and the other techniques and technologies used in obstetrics.

EFM spread in use, and by 1976 was certainly available in just about every large obstetrics service in this country. There had been no reasonable evaluation of its benefits. There were certainly claims of its effecting reductions in infant and perinatal mortality and in cerebral palsy and mental retardation, but there was no good evaluative literature until the first controlled clinical trial, which was done in 1975 by Haverkamp in Denver.[3] And interestingly enough, Dr. Haverkamp saw the controversy developing. He believed that electronic monitoring was of value, and he did the randomized controlled clinical trial to prove it. Much to his surprise, he found no differences between the electronically-monitored and the nurse-monitored groups in terms of infant outcome. The studies shown in Table 2, by the way, are comparisons of electronic monitoring with monitoring by auscultation (monitoring by stethoscope). Auscultation itself has never been

TABLE 2

A Comparison of Selected Outcomes Among Women Monitored by Auscultation and Those Monitored Electronically in Four Randomized, Controlled Clinical Trials

Study	n	Apgar	Neonatal mortality	Convulsions	Neurologic followup	Cesarean section rate
Denver, 1973/75	483	—[a]	—	—	ND[b]	+
Melbourne, 1974/75	350	—	—	+	ND	+
Denver, 1975/77	695	—	—	—	—	+
Sheffield, 1974/77	504	—	—	—	ND	+

[a]— = no difference between the study and control groups.
[b]ND = not done.

evaluated, so there is certainly a possibility that it has limited benefit. But this is the dilemma with medicine now. With a lot of things that have never been evaluated, how do you evaluate new things? It is generally considered ethical to evaluate the new in comparison with the old. So that is really about all we can say. There have now been four randomized controlled clinical trials: two in Denver[3,4]; one in Melbourne, Australia[5]; and one in Sheffield, England.[6] There were no differences in neonatal mortality or Apgar scores. In the Melbourne trial, there were more convulsions in the group that was not electronically monitored. Only one study had neurological followup. That was the second Denver study, which found no difference after 9 months. In all four of the studies, the cesarean section rate was considerably increased with the use of the electronic monitor. The increase—except in the Australian trial—was more than double. In fact, it was almost triple in the Denver trials.

These trials have led to a re-evaluation of the possible benefits of monitoring. One way of re-evaluating that is to consider all the factors mentioned in the obstetrics literature that might have contributed to this fall of perinatal mortality, including changes in obstetric care or care of the newborn during that period (see Table 3). We do not know why infant perinatal mortality rates fell. But certainly there are too many factors to attribute the fall in any way to electronic monitoring. Another way of trying to sort this out is to look at the causes of stillbirths (see Table 4). The intrapartum causes for stillbirths are responsible for little more than a quarter of all the deaths. So intervention during labor and delivery could only be expected to influence at most about one quarter of the deaths.

TABLE 3
Factors That May Decrease Perinatal Mortality

General[a]	Obstetric[a]	Neonatal[a]
Abortion	Electronic fetal	Neonatal intensive
Contraception	monitoring	care units
Maternal nutrition	Increased attention	Regionalization
Patient education	to delivery	Therapeutic advances
	Prenatal care	(e.g., C-PAP)
	(e.g., amniocentesis)	
	Perinatal care (e.g.,	
	breech delivery by	
	cesarean section)	

[a]Public funding has facilitated access to these factors by the poor.

TABLE 4
Registered Causes of Perinatal Deaths in England (1971)—Percent
Distribution of Different Groups[a]

Causes of Death	Distribution, %		
	Stillbirths	First week deaths	Stillbirths + first week deaths
Congenital malformations	21.0	18.0	19.7
Immaturity	3.1	41.6	20.2
Intrapartum	29.9	28.2	29.1
Antepartum	24.2	0.7	13.8
Other	21.8	11.5	17.2
Total:	100.0	100.0	100.0
Total No.:	(9280)	(7303)	(16,583)

[a]Adapted from Alberman, E., *Clin. Obstet. Gynecol.* **1,** No. 1 (1974).

Putting this kind of data together has led a number of people to say that the maximum possible contribution of electronic monitoring to mortality is two to three per thousand.[7,8] That figure is based on using this kind of data on cause of death to ask what causes babies to die and where intervention possibly could make a difference. But actually to show a two per thousand benefit would require a very large study.

The other claimed benefit has been a reduction in cerebral palsy and mental retardation. There is no study of that subject, so you really have to deal with claims and logic. I have already mentioned the reduction in seizures in one randomized controlled clinical trial of electronic monitoring. That is potentially very important, because seizures are one of the most powerful predictors of mental retardation and cerebral palsy. But there are a number of reasons that one could cite against any EFM effect. The one that seems to be gaining credence is that a baby that is compromised and has asphyxia will die, and that intervention can make no difference. That is what is called the "all or nothing" effect. Another idea that has begun to surface is that, in fact, you *may* save some of those babies, but that they will be severely mentally retarded—which is another possible problem. Again, I want to stress that there are no data on this. These are speculations using epidemiological reasoning, statistics, and so forth. The National Institutes of Health group on EFM came to the conclusion that something of the order of two per thousand would be the maximum possible benefit from electronic fetal monitoring, because the other causes of mental retardation and cerebral palsy would not be affected.[8]

There is one other piece of evidence on benefits. In several clinical studies, low birth weight babies seemed to do dramatically better than one would expect when they are monitored electronically.[9,10] And that is something that we think deserves very careful study. It may be a real benefit, but it's only a suggested one at this time.

On the risk side, certainly the most important risk, we feel, is cesarean section. Figure 2 shows the cesarean section rate in the United States from 1965 to 1978. In 1965, 4.5 percent of births ended in cesarean sections; the most recent date is 1978, with a rate of 15.2 percent. I project that in 1980, about 18 percent of births will end in a cesarean. These figures are not from high-risk centers, but from the hospital discharge survey, a random survey of all hospitals in the country.

Why has this dramatic rise occurred? Many factors have been involved, including repeat cesareans, cesarean sections for all breech deliveries, and a reported rise in cesareans for cephalopelvic disproportion. In a situation of limited data, we feel strongly that the randomized controlled clinical trials have to be emphasized. Two in this country and one each in Australia and England consistently associate one outcome with electronic monitoring: the doubling of the cesarean section rate (see Table 5).

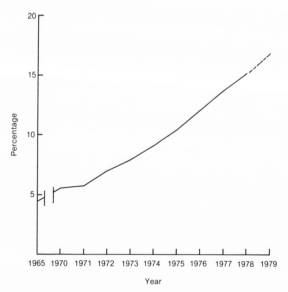

FIG. 2.   US cesarean section rate.

TABLE 5
A Comparison of the Cesarean Section Rates Among Women Monitored
by Auscultation and Monitored Electronically in Four Randomized,
Controlled Clinical Trials

Study	n	Cesarean section rates among		
		Auscultated, %	EFM, %	EFM + FSB,[a] %
Denver, 1973/75	483	7	17	—
Melbourne, 1974/75	350	14	—	22
Denver, 1975/77	695	6	18	12
Sheffield, 1974/77	504	4	9	—

[a]FSB refers to fetal scalp blood sampling.

TABLE 6
Risks to the Mother Associated with Electronic
Fetal Monitoring

Cesarean section	Infection
Laceration	Anxiety/discomfort
Uterine perforation	Death

TABLE 7
Risks to the Fetus Associated with Electronic Fetal Monitoring

Known	Potential
Amniotomy	Ultrasound
Laceration	RDS secondary to cesarean
Hemorrhage (0.3%)	section
Scalp abscess (0.1–4.5%)	Interference with maternal–infant
Sepsis	bonding
Death	

Table 6 lists the risks to the mother. Most are rare, but cesarean section and infection are not rare. Table 7 shows the risks to the fetus. The amniotic sac is often broken to insert the catheter, with infection, possible cord prolapse, and so forth. Laceration of the baby's scalp is rare, but happens. Hemorrhage and scalp abscess are fairly common. Sepsis isn't common, but certainly occurs, as does death, very rarely. Potential complications that are not proven must, I think, be of great concern. These include the effect on the fetus of ultrasound, the respiratory distress syndrome secondary to cesarean sections, and the possibility that all of this technology interferes with the bonding between the mother and the child.

Our general conclusions, then, are that there is no evidence of benefit attributable to electronic fetal monitoring in terms of measurable outcomes such as neonatal mortality and Apgar score. There is a suggestion of benefit, as I said, in selected high-risk groups— particularly low birth weight. There is an increased rate of cesarean section associated with electronic fetal monitoring. And there is a significant cost for routine EFM—we estimated a little more than 400 million dollars a year. We estimated that more than half of labors are now electronically monitored in this country. The National Institutes of Health group used our estimate and some other data to say 60-70 percent.[8]

These are our recommendations: that electronic fetal monitoring should be limited to specific high risk groups as part of carefully designed evaluative trials of efficacy. We also recommend that the impact of electronic fetal monitoring on the incidence of brain damage and cerebral palsy should be studied carefully, and that federal funding should be made available to study not only this technology, but other technologies as well. One recommendation that we have come to subsequently is that in this situation, where there is no good technical information on which to base a choice, the woman is the most appropriate person to make the choice.

A final note on the ethics of using experimental subjects: the randomized controlled clinical trial requires women as experimental subjects. This denies some of the controls access to EFM. This is often said, in the obstetrics literature, to be unethical when a technology is believed to be efficacious. It certainly raises general ethical questions. But in my value system, the ethics of using an unproven procedure on two million deliveries a year is very questionable. And I think that sort of ethical imperative has to outweigh the ethical problem of using women as experimental subjects.

Response

Hilary Salk

I want to offer some positive criticism of the conference, to say that I am very grateful to see that each of us does have a voice here—a place on the program to share what we do know. I think it's a sign that we do believe all women have something to say about their own bodies.

I find it mindblowing that Dr. Klapholz was originally in missile-building and comes to this very delicate subject from that kind of orientation. More and more, the people who are doing work that affects our lives come from an entirely different culture from those of us whose life the work directly affects. Also, it's very sad to me to see that he could not remain here to participate in any of the process that went on among us (in our Childbirth group), so that he doesn't have even these few days to understand something of women's culture. I do appreciate that there are some men here for that reason—despite the criticism that it would also be nice not to have them here.

I may seem somewhat messianic, but I cannot help it, because I feel that without the kind of contacts I was priviledged to have, I would not have had the kind of birth experiences that I did have. Talking last night with Helen Swallow, we agreed that much in our adult lives reflected the birth experiences we had had with our daughters, which were very positive. We knew we would not have had these positive experiences if we had depended entirely on the medical practitioners whom we thought we were supposed to depend on totally when we gave birth.

I am grateful to have heard about the research by Banta and Brackbill so that, if I need to come before the authorities who are still in control of birth, I will have some of the statistics necessary to show that a lot of that technology is absolutely unnecessary, if not harmful. However, I don't feel that I need the research for myself at this point, fortunately, in that I come from a completely different kind of orientation. I believe that our bodies, for the most part, are going to go through a natural process normally—that most of us will deliver without complications, and that we need to hear that constantly, because we hear from other sources that birth is a very dangerous process. But when we develop confidence in our bodies and in ourselves, and skepticism about interventions that lead to more interventions, I believe we contribute to a safer, more satisfying outcome. We constantly hear that our bodies cannot give birth without all these interventions invented for us. I think that more than ever in history physicians are trying to retain their monopoly over birth, so they come at us with a tremendous number of statistics about the dangers of childbirth. Yet, Klapholz' own statistics did indicate that 98% of women will have a normal birth even as he advocates the use of the monitor.

The question is why, then, should 100% of women be monitored when, in fact, we see from Banta's literature that it does cause certain risks to the mother? I was able to recognize that many of the routine drugs and devices that have been used up to the present day are unnecessary because I have—somewhere in me, in my own history—a belief in nature. Somehow, I have not lost that—although I needed much more than my own common sense to fight the isolation I had when I came to childbirth.

I was able to get support for my own belief in nature through contact with a childbirth education (cea) group twelve years ago. Without them, there would have been only my own common sense—and I'm not sure that would have been enough. Also, learning about other cultures has been extremely important to me, teaching me that birth in America is really just as ritualistic as the birth rituals you read about in other cultures; that there's nothing absolute about the way in which American birth is done. Such recognition is extremely helpful in stepping outside of the medicalization of birth in America.

The childbirth group provided me with tools for my birth: relaxation techniques, breathing techniques, and the confirmation that my body would work "right." It also provided ways of avoiding the technology that I would face in the hospital. We didn't think then about having birth outside of the hospital. After cross-cultural learning, three years later I had my second baby at home.

Another important tool I received from my cea group was a knowledge of how to negotiate my way through that medical hospital system. Now, when I'm speaking to other women about women's health concerns, I find myself talking about how to avoid this and how to avoid that, which I find incredible—because I am also working in my community with people who are concerned about limited access on the part of low income women to medical care. I am also concerned about the inability of certain low income families to pay for even basic health care needs. On the other hand, I feel it's so important to recognize the iatrogenic dangers of the very system to which so many community organizers are fighting for access on behalf of disadvantaged women.

The ethical issue that most concerned me when I began to think about birth, and which continues to concern me now, is: why am I privileged to this information that has transformed the birth of my children and transformed my life, when most of the women in my community are still submitted to a changing series of technologies that interfere with the birth process, that cause risks that would not be there without the technologies, and that rob them of the self-confidence that comes with knowing that they can be in control?

Despite working with other women for years to spread information about the alternatives to the medical model of birth, I know that the women who hear about these alternatives in a setting where they can *really hear* them are still too few and too often—as in this conference—white and middle-class. It also grieves me to say that we have lost some of the settings that we had even twelve years ago. Many childbirth education classes have been co-opted by the medical profession so that parents no longer control the nature of these classes as they did when I was giving birth; and women don't know that they're getting something second-rate when they go to a hospital childbirth education class or a completely professionally dominated childbirth education class instead of a community-controlled class.

I don't know how to get that message across, because there's no opportunity to communicate such a message using mass communication methods. So women are going to the hospital class thinking that they're getting a prepared childbirth experience, but they don't get the sense of power that came from knowing that they somehow contributed to the knowledge and can share in passing it on.

So the burning questions become not ethical questions, but political questions. How can we gain access to the communication tools to let women know of the dangers and travesties of our present system, and of alternatives to the system. How can we get control? Before we consider alternatives I wish to recall what Helen Rodriguez said: these alternatives are not going to be available for many, many, many years—if ever—to the large majority of people. And that's certainly an ethical issue that I hope we can deal with somewhere in this conference.

Ethical Issues in Childbirth Technology

Sheryl Burt Ruzek

A major task for this panel was to identify the ethical issues in setting priorities for research on childbirth technology and in the application of research. I am going to focus my attention on the uses, misuses, and political nature of research, and offer some structural explanations of why we are faced with many ethical dilemmas.

The fundamental issues are: Why are research funds allocated for developing high technology interventions such as electronic fetal heart monitors rather than low technology approaches to childbirth? Why is it that we routinely conduct enormous and expensive high technology experiments on childbearing women? Why don't we see experiments or serious controlled research on low technology interventions and low technology methods of childbirth? Why don't we research nutrition seriously? Why don't we investigate the social-psychological aspects of childbirth in various types of settings? Since as a society we seem comfortable with massive social experiments, I also wonder why we do not have experiments in community nutrition, or experiments in prenatal care. Ultimately the question becomes, why don't we have experiments in massive income redistribution? These are crucial questions because epidemiological data show that our high infant mortality rate (which we seem so concerned about because of our international standing) is directly related to income and education. Infant mortality is not going to be significantly improved simply by pouring money into things like electronic fetal monitors, even if the poor were the most likely to have access to the technology (which, of course, is not the case). We are also concerned that research on medical technology is done after the fact, after machines and procedures are widely adopted. Why is technology widely disseminated before we carefully research it?

We have tried, both individually and as a group, to come up with answers to some of these questions. The answers, I believe, ultimately lie in the structure of advanced industrial capitalism, in the social organization of the health industry, and in the organization of the academic research enterprise.

The self-interest of the drug and medical device industries is well known. In contrast, we have not focused adequate attention on the role of academic researchers and clinicians in society. In fact, we need to look very very closely at the ways in which medical professionals, both clinicians and academic researchers, create markets for their goods and their services. We need to recognize more fully that the more you intervene, the more you create a demand for your services and the greater the necessity of further intervention becomes. Yvonne Brackbill has already discussed the structure of academic research. I could not agree more that enormous ethical problems are generated by the reward structure of universities. A fundamental ethical dilemma is that the people researching and evaluating technology are in a position to gain not only financially or through connections to the drug or device industry, but also by aggrandizing prestige and power from their research results.

When professionals and scientists create the belief that we need elaborate technology for childbirth, they make themselves indispensible. When you use high technology equipment you do indeed need technical experts to manage that technology. Insofar as childbirth is defined by "the experts" as a high risk, high technology medical event, the relative power of the patient or the birthing family is predictably low. It is an inevitable problem. Only if childbirth is defined as normal and technological intervention is defined as unnecessary or undesirable except in extreme cases, can women in fact have any real power over what goes on during this crucial life event. I cannot overstate how profound a conflict this is, how serious an ethical issue it is to decide who has the right to define childbirth as high risk or low risk—parents, professionals, or academic researchers.

Given the research enterprise, one might hope that the results of research (at least when it is done properly) would influence or direct clinical practice. Historically, this has not happened. There is an enormous literature on the history of medicine that documents that technologies are adopted even when it is known that they are not particularly effective, and they continue to be used until they go out of vogue rather than until they are disproven scientifically.[1] The paucity of clinical benefit relative to risk clearly has not restricted use of electronic fetal monitors,[2] and we should recognize that this is not an isolated incident, but part of an historical pattern.

Overall, I believe that there are serious ethical questions in supporting huge research enterprises that do not have clear mechanisms for directing clinical practice. What is the point of research if it fails to shape what we do? On the other hand, if there were better mechanisms, we would still have to grapple with the problem of interpreting findings relative to diverse human values. Most research assesses safety and efficacy in terms that not everyone shares. Specifically, a growing number of parents and professionals alike reject the preoccupation with mortality statistics while ignoring morbidity in childbirth, especially for the mother, and while ignoring the social-psychological consequences of birth.

Henry Klapholz's suggestion that electronic fetal monitors are misused, that people simply are ignorant and do not know how to use them, is quite accurate. The minute you move *any* elaborate technology or any complex procedure out of sophisticated, research-oriented medical centers, there will, of course, be an immediate drop-off in the accuracy and efficacy with which the technology is used. If you look at open heart surgery done outside of major coronary care units, the mortality rate skyrockets. This phenomenon is repeated throughout medicine. It is not just a problem with childbirth technology. Indeed, as we consider all of the reproductive technologies we must keep in mind that the problems run through all of clinical medicine, not just obstetrics and gynecology.

The appeal of technology should not be underestimated. To be able—or better yet, to be mandated by society—to deploy complex technology in the interest of saving lives is appealing. Persons who engage in this kind of activity are rewarded in American society. Professionals who hold back are suspected of being backward by their colleagues and many of their patients as well. In this context David Banta made a very important point when he said that physicians have a psychological need to believe in what they are doing, whether that belief is founded or not. Hospital administrators and insurance companies have also jumped on the bandwagon to push high technology diagnostic techniques in the hope of finding ways to protect themselves against growing malpractice suits. Obviously this is not very effective. Many malpractice suits are filed because of the hazardous things done to people who have lost faith in physicians' trustworthiness. Significantly, small town family practitioners, general practitioners who maintain good personal relationships with their clients, are less likely to be sued for malpractice than technically more competent city specialists.

As a consequence of clinical medicine's reliance on "objective, scientific, computerized" diagnostic procedures, risk assessment and risk management for professionals centers on the potential hazards to *them* for failing to intervene. That is very important to remember. Professionals worry, "What is my responsibility if I do not intervene?" That obstetricians fail to succeed with their interventions is not the point I want to make. What I want to emphasize is that physicians want to *believe* that they can preserve life with complex technology and in the process become excessively reliant and dependent on technology to the extent that their clinical judgment becomes impaired. It is in part the physicians' value of preserving life that makes them subject women, often indiscriminately, to elaborate technology—just in case. "If you were one of that two percent, wouldn't you want to have your baby monitored?" they ask. The marginal utility of that "just in case" is very well documented in David Banta's presentation and elsewhere in the medical literature.

Many patients currently assess risk differently than do physicians. "What are the risks of intervention?" "What harm could come to me or my baby if I get caught up in the routine of hospitals where an intervention's complications lead to more intervention, which leads to further drastic action?" It is important to keep in mind that many of the benefits of home delivery or alternative birth settings are regarded as trivial by clinicians. It always strikes me as odd that "the constant support of a nurse or a childbirth attendant" is sometimes commented on as an explanation of good obstetrical outcomes in studies, yet providing this support is rarely proposed by physicians.

Clinicians simply have values and concerns different from those of many lay people. This value conflict is very apparent when physicians angrily ask home birth advocates, "Aren't you concerned that someone will die?" Physicians find it very difficult to understand or accept a lay midwife or a person birthing at home saying, "I understand that it's a risk; death is something that can happen." Physicians are very uncomfortable with the idea of death, often far more than patients. The crucial question, then, is who in society is allowed to define what constitutes an acceptable risk, including possible death?

In the past, it was largely assumed that medical men—and they were mostly men—knew best and were the only ones competent to interpret scientific data. Our experience as women, as feminist health consumers, and as participants in this conference certainly shakes that unwarranted belief. Now that laypeople are involved in assessing the evidence it is argued that the childbirth debate is politicized and polarized to the detriment of mothers and babies. This criticism has come largely from the medical establishment, which until very recently had almost a complete monopoly on the use of scientific evidence, or pseudoscientific evidence, for its own political interest. When outsiders want to do the same thing, the medics call "foul" and try to discredit critics by attacking their legitimacy and the validity of their scientific evidence.

The Brackbill-Broman study and the Banta-Thacker report provide interesting case studies. Brackbill-Broman's analysis has received a hefty dose of criticism for both methodological flaws and the authors' discussing their findings with the media rather than keeping it in "scholarly" publications.[3] Although the criticisms of methodology must be taken seriously, methodological flaws in scientific publications—even prestigious ones—are not unusual. The Banta-Thacker report, for example, details serious methodological problems in all of the studies on electronic fetal monitoring that are published in respectable professional journals. What is disturbing to me is that clinicians make sweeping promises and generalizations about the "scientifically" proven safety and efficacy of electronic fetal monitoring on the basis of these flimsy studies. Where is the scientific community's outcry over the methodological deficiencies of studies that purportedly establish the safety and effectiveness of medical devices?

To summarize, women's perspectives on the policy debate demand that we pay attention to the social organization of research and the delivery of services; that we question the ethics of having self-interested professionals set research priorities, define acceptable risks, and determine the appropriate use of technology. Consumers must have a larger say in these matters. Nonetheless, shifting the locus of control to consumers raises new ethical questions. What are the consequences of shifting the burden of choice, and perhaps guilt, to mothers, for making difficult decisions?

Solving many of the problems women see is difficult because we do not have a uniform health care system where valid scientific research data can be used to implement change, as can be done, for example, in systems such as the British National Health Service (although even there consumers have limited roles in these decisions). Consequently, we need to look for creative regulatory mechanisms while at the same time working for a national health system that would provide structural opportunities to mandate change both from the top down and from organized consumer pressure.

Women's health advocates need to organize and develop coalitions with both sympathetic professional groups and consumer advocacy organizations. Because organized medicine and its subsidiary organizations are well funded while consumer groups are not, public funds would be well spent financing consumer health groups whose representatives would be valuable consultants and advisors to legislators drafting national health coverage. Consumer involvement can no longer be conceived of as a strictly "voluntary" matter, but needs to provide opportunities for paid employment to facilitate the development of expertise and continuity of involvement.

Right now we have to discover practical ways to put pressure on existing regulatory agencies and on community institutions, and work to educate women to demand change in health services. Organizations that are represented here—including the Coalition for the Medical Rights of Women, NAPSAC, the National Women's Health Network, and others—have all had a fair amount of success in lobbying and getting regulations changed.[4] Currently, some women have decided that the hospital risks are too great and the only alternative is to give birth at home. There may in fact be risks associated with home birth, but because there is no definitive evidence that hospital birth is safer for normal birth, it seems only reasonable that the woman or birthing family should decide what type of childbirth setting is most appropriate.

Refusing to use conventional services is a powerful tool consumers hold to draw attention to the abuses of organized medicine. Withdrawal not only threatens medicine's economic position, but reveals what medical historians have long recognized. People who "go without" may actually be better off than had they exposed themselves to the hazards of medical treatment, an argument home-birth proponents regularly set forth.

Today, the social and economic consequences of supporting unjustifiable medical tinkering are so enormous that the pattern must be reversed. Organized medicine cannot be given license to continue to place its private wants over public needs. As the country moves towards either national health insurance or some form of national health service, health activists will look for opportunities to build in opportunities for pluralism and workable checks and balances to make providers accountable for their interventions. Although professionals, including physicians, will play major roles in the overall health system, priorities for health services need to be shaped within the framework of appropriate allocation of societal resources. Health activitsts, who have considerable insight into what many women actually need and want, clearly must be involved in setting priorities. Professionals object that involving outsiders "politicizes" health care, but then has it not been "political" all along?

Childbirth Technologies Discussion

Moderated by Margaret O'Brien Steinfels

Carol Korenbrot: How long after birth can the effects of these drugs last?

Yvonne Brackbill: They still appear in the NINCDS study at age 7 years, which is the last age at which the children were tested.

Unidentified Speaker: I'd like to know where you're getting your control groups of women that haven't had any drugs.

Yvonne Brackbill: Most of these studies are of correlational design. There are a few that are of experimental design, involving two or more experimental groups, or a control and an experimental.

Norma Swenson: There is a severe controversy going on in Boston about exactly what the cesarean section rates are. Some institutions have reported two different figures. Most institutions will not release their figures to the press or to anyone else. [The Massachusetts Department of Public Health has recently begun to collect these data.]

David Banta: These figures are not from high-risk centers. These data are from the Hospital Discharge Survey that is a random survey of all hospitals in the country. These are the only good national data and unfortunately they go only to 1976.

Anne Davis: What would have happened if the fetal monitoring and cesarean sections had not been done?

David Banta: No information.

Tabitha Powledge: But suppose the control groups, the auscultation groups, contained more low-risk women.

David Banta: They didn't. In all four of the trials a study group was selected: one was low risk; three were high risk. And then the women were randomized, hopefully with informed consent, to either auscultation or electronic fetal monitoring. The randomized, controlled clinical trial is the best technique, the most powerful technique for assuring comparability. Some of those studies have been criticized on various grounds for lack of comparability: the groups in the Australia trial clearly are not comparable; there are some criticisms of the first Denver trial; the other two trials appear to have very comparable groups.

Yvonne Brackbill: I want to say a few words about randomized clinical trials. There's no question that they're great, except for one little thing: it is not ethical to assign patients or subjects at random to groups unless the chances of risk and benefit are exactly equal for all groups. At current funding levels that is highly unlikely. The chances that any agency will fund a study that will probably not produce positive results is almost nil. The most famous case to be discussed lately on that was the development of "Ara A" for herpes simplex, as you probably know. And that points up another parallel for childbirth. In a situation in which a disease or a condition is relatively stable or progresses very slowly, there is perhaps no serious ethical problem in using an "A-B-B-A" design for the experimental and control groups or for the two experimental groups. But, when a condition proceeds very fast, as does herpes, or childbirth, it is not ethical to use a randomized clinical trial design unless the chances of benefit for the two groups are equal.

Gerene Major: On the table on outcomes of electronic fetal monitoring, "death" does not mean a direct cause–effect link, but deaths resulting from the cesarean or from infection, right?

David Banta: The deaths from electronic fetal monitoring would be primarily deaths from cesarean. Reported deaths from electronic monitoring and the complications from electronic monitoring itself are rare. But they certainly *do* occur. I was consulted in a malpractice suit in Arizona where the woman developed a uterine infection post-delivery and died. And her husband sued on the basis of negligence.

Tabitha Powledge: I was a member of the NIH task force to which Dr. Banta referred. As you know, David, we weren't as certain as you that it was monitoring alone that was driving up the C-section rate, although it seems to me quite obvious that in some hospitals that is the case. What we *were* certain about was that it probably was a risky procedure for low-risk women. Having decided that, a group of us in that task force then fought tooth and nail for some kind of definition, in the final report, of "high-risk" or "low-risk." I would have been happy to settle for either one, just so as to provide some sort of guidance for physicians. We were only partially (and in my estimation inadequately) successful in achieving that definition. The question of defining risk is a tremendously difficult problem and I don't know quite how we should go about it.

Is it possible to retain this technology for those few women and their babies who really might benefit from it, and not get into a situation, as is the case in some hospitals, where eighty percent of the births are monitored? I would like not to have to throw out this technology with the bath water. The real question is whether we can make proper use of it.

Norma Swenson: Can you give us a simple summary of the report?

Tabitha Powledge: Our high-risk conclusions were similar to David's. We decided there probably were some benefits for some high-risk women. The way we handled the definition problem is that we gave examples of some things that might constitute "high-risk"—high parity, diabetes, the conventional things that people know about. We also concluded on the basis of some of the epidemiological data that it would take a clinical trial involving 120,000 women to establish whether or not there was any benefit at all in "low-risk" women. There was some evidence of risk for these women for the reasons that Dr. Banta has alluded to.

There was a lot of internal discussion in the committee about how compatible these technologies are with family-centered childbirth (in the hospital, of course, needless to say, not homebirth). The internal monitor, which allows for some ambulation, and the experimental methods that are now being used, involving things that you can strap on yourself and walk around with, might mean that you wouldn't have to be in the prone position necessary with external monitors. But, on the other hand, it also seems to me quite clear that in most situations the monitor will in fact *not* be used that way. And that's really the problem I'd like to deal with here. How do we get people to use this stuff right? Or do we just have to dump the whole thing?

Norma Swenson: Having heard that, I think there are two things that we need to be thinking about when we think about the risk problem. There is, of course, the classic risking that medicine does, in terms of identifying certain kinds of conditions. And that can get very sophisticated, and it's getting more sophisticated as more experiments are done with out-of-hospital births. But we need to remember that our best predictors of outcome are still socioeconomic. If you want to start talking about mortality you've got to look at socioeconomic class.

Tabitha Powledge: It's very interesting that I pushed very hard for that as our definition of "high-risk," but that was the thing people wouldn't accept because of course that's racist.

Norma Swenson: Well, not only that. It can have controlling effects on any people so labeled. You talk about the problem of defining "high-risk," but we haven't talked about what would happen once we made that definition, what kind of power that would have over all women. First you have to look at to whom this is happening: Where in the population are these deaths? Then you have to look at where they happen. Intrapartum death is the thing that would not yield in all the long period of unchanging infant mortality. Now we know that primarily premature, primarily low-birth-weight babies, die intrapartum. Those will yield, to some extent, to appropriate prenatal care and nutrition, which is associated with socioeconomic class. So we know how to do it. And the idea of monitoring those high-risk women, those low-birth-weight babies, instead of feeding them—that is, I think, one of the ethical questions we have to raise.

Tabitha Powledge: So then your policy would be that the technology ought to be abandoned.

Norma Swenson: I'm not saying that. I'm pointing out to you that we have a means other than monitoring for assuring a better outcome for some of those babies. And there are three percent that will not yield and we know that. They'll never yield: that's what David's stillbirth figures were all about. They're in our biology and they're across all groups of people everywhere in the world. Whether we want to save every last one of them, and at what cost, is another question.

Diana Axelsen: When we reviewed the pain and traumas of white women in the eighteenth and nineteenth century, not a word was said about the situation confronted by the slave and other nonwhite populations. An example that comes to mind is the development of surgical techniques and of the speculum, through experiments with slave women. The only consent required was the slave owner's. I understand why there is frustration with the feminist movement when we hear that kind of historical analysis coming from white feminists. When we're doing medical history, let's remember that it's not just the history of white people, or white women, that we should consider.

Dorothy Wertz: I should add that some of the gynecological surgery Dr. James Marion Sims perfected was on black women who had forty operations before the discovery of anesthesia. He owned them; he bought some of these patients so that they would be readily available for surgery. Now *he* claims that they volunteered: they came in and said would you please try again. But we only have his side of the story.

Mary Ampola: I'm a pediatrician, a geneticist, caring for children in a birth defects center for the past 12 years. We care for children with mental retardation, cerebral palsy, learning disabilities, etc. I can't tell you how many times I've sat and taken histories on these children and their mothers and obtained a history of a perfectly normal pregnancy and a healthy mother, but something that went wrong during labor— the cord prolapsed, the doctor couldn't hear the heartbeat for a while and then it was okay, there was overdosage of medication and the baby came out limp and blue, there was trouble resuscitating the baby, the birth was long and difficult, etc. I think the answer to the association between difficulties during labor and damage to the baby later on is not known because people have not looked at the right population. You can examine a baby up, down, and sideways and think it's perfectly normal, but not until the later years of early childhood can one really assess what has really happened to those children. And that kind of study has not been done. Potentially, as far as I'm concerned, the few hours of labor are in fact the single most dangerous period in the human lifespan. So I have concerns about the *baby* and I think those concerns should be foremost.

Birth can be a beautiful and rewarding experience no matter where you have it, if you *make* it that, and that includes being in a hospital. I think that there is a way that one can compromise on this thing. What I envision is something on the order of delivery suites, where there are private rooms, where the husband can stay, where there is natural chldbirth, where there's a well-trained midwife, where one can use Lamaze, where one can have the siblings in after the birth, and from which one can send the baby and the mother home the next day if they're healthy. However, the absolute minimum that that baby deserves for those few hours of labor are four things immediately available: blood, an obstetrician if there is difficulty, a C-section room ready if there is truly a problem, and finally, resuscitation equipment if the baby doesn't start breathing on its own.

Susan Bell: One of the points that has been raised is whether we should throw out technology. I think that better questions are, "How do we make projections for future research?" "Do we try to improve what we have or do we question why the technology that we have was developed?" "Why do we have the choices we have now?" "And could it be otherwise?" By asking these kinds of questions we can make better suggestions for the future. In addition, we should be looking at ways to create better socioeconomic conditions and not ways to create more technology and more "miracle drugs."

Section 2
Social Control of Childbirth

Organized by Norma Swenson

Introduction

Barbara Hilkert Andolsen

In this section we consider alternatives to high technology childbirth—alternatives that are available to some women in a variety of cultural settings.

Some of the same issues raised in the chapter on high technology childbirth reappear here in a different light. Who defines the birth experience, its meaning, its value, its significance? Who defines the costs, the risks, the benefits of various alternative means of birthing? What counts as a cost? What counts as a benefit? How are those weighed and who should do the weighing? What's best for a woman and who determines that? Is what's best for the woman giving birth always best for the child being birthed? How are those tensions adjudicated? What about a woman, not just as a solitary individual undergoing a physiological process, but also as a member of a community of loved ones, of friends, of other people sharing her cultural background, of health care providers with whom she has, or has not, some kind of satisfactory relationship? How do we see the woman in the context of her growing circle of relationships?

Every woman on this panel, in addition to the other riches she brings to it, has borne a child herself and so has had personal experience with birth. We echo the plea that the system of health care in this country include access to good quality care for all women and their children, regardless of their income level, regardless of their ethnic background.

211

A Report on Birth in Three Cultures

Susan Cope Ekstrom

INTRODUCTION

When I told a friend, the mother of two children and a childbirth educator, that I was writing a report on birth in different cultures, she laughed and said, "What are you going to write about? After all, doesn't the baby come out the same way no matter where you live?" Her response, which was that of an experienced and informed participant in childbirth, illustrates perfectly Brigitte Jordan's contention in *Birth in Four Cultures*[1] that there is a need for studies of childbirth that are both cross-cultural and what she calls "biosocial." This paper is largely based on Jordan's work, though the selection and arrangement of material for presentation are mine.

By the *biosocial* nature of birth, Jordan means to draw attention to the fact that birth is a phenomenon that involves not only biological process, but also social organization. The friend I mentioned above was in one sense right. The physiological process of parturition *is* in a way universally the same for parturient members of the human species everywhere. But in another sense, my friend was also wrong, for, this species-universal biological function of birth is everywhere socially managed in strikingly different ways by different groups of people. Although we can't totally separate what is biological from what is social in birth, unless we try to distinguish between these two aspects of the process, there will be a tendency (as indeed there is) to assume that we can learn all we need to know about birth simply by looking at how "we" (whoever "we" are) do it.

Birthing systems, as systems, share a common characteristic, one which is illustrated by my friend's remarks. This is, in Jordan's words, "the extraordinary extent to which practitioners buy into their own system's moral and technical superiority."[2] That is, so long as any given system is functioning and stable, every set of practices in that system will be experienced *from within that system* as being morally and technically superior to any other conceivable way of doing things. Participants in that system will tend to see their own way of doing birth

213

as the correct way, the right way, indeed the *only* way of bringing a child into the world. Besides limiting exposure to birthing practices to those current in their own system, experimentation is discouraged (and in fact usually made impossible), since any tampering with the "right" way of doing birth will be seen as being unethical, exploitative, dangerous, bad medicine, and the like. Therefore, the participants in any given system are *systematically* kept uninformed about alternate birthing practices and ways of doing birth.

Given these two considerations—namely, that birth is not simply a biological function and that there exists in stable, functioning systems no opportunity for generating and evaluating alternatives— the value of, and need for, cross-cultural studies of birth that are also biosocial should be evident. They can provide us with a broader understanding of birth than that available from the point of view of any particular system. More urgently, however, the information provided by such studies can help us in constructing a useful and much-needed conceptual framework for evaluating and guiding the presently observable changes in childbirth practices that are taking place both in this country and abroad.

Traditional birthing systems in the so-called developing countries are under great pressure to change owing to the influence of Western medicine. At the same time, as Jordan points out, "some of the very obstetric practices that are currently exported to developing countries by the medically oriented, technologically sophisticated nations have ironically taken on a controversial status at home. In the United States, in fact, the appropriateness of the medical model for the entire conception of birth has become questionable."[3]

Unfortunately, the recently observable changes in birthing systems around the world have tended to take place in an all too often haphazard and unplanned way. The high-prestige, Western medicalized model of birth has recently been overwhelmingly, and usually uncritically, adopted as the standard to which to aspire, usually leading to a devaluation of traditional ways of doing birth. As a result, the possible contributions of traditional birthing practices in both modernizing and modernized societies are ignored. Some of the criticisms of Western birth practice, on the other hand, seem to be based on an unfavorable comparison of American birthing practices with so-called "primitive" childbirth. Whether or not the criticisms themselves are valid, the notion of "primitive" childbirth in such comparisons is not founded on actual research data, but rather on romanticized and idealized misconceptions of "primitive" childbirth.[4]

What is needed, then, is a way of assessing birth practices, both our own and those of other systems. The kind of biosocial, cross-cultural research on childbirth that Jordan is pursuing is in fact intended to help us formulate a "mechanism for generating change strategies which acknowledges and preserves what is useful in both [the Western medicalized system and the traditional] systems, under local conditions and for the people involved."[5]

It is toward this end that an initial list of biosocial features of birthing systems for a cross-cultural comparison of birth may be proposed (see Appendix). For this report, I shall briefly discuss two of these features: the definition of the event, and the nature and locus of the decision-making process; and I shall illustrate them with examples drawn from three different birthing systems. I shall conclude with a brief analysis of the current pressures for change on the American system.

THREE BIRTHING SYSTEMS: AMERICAN, DUTCH, AND YUCATECAN

The descriptions of each of the three systems discussed here are based on fieldwork done in the United States, Holland, and the Yucatan peninsula in Mexico. I omit the fourth of the systems in *Birth in Four Cultures,* because subsequent research has led Jordan to modify some of her conclusions concerning the Swedish way of birth. The American field work was done in several large teaching hospitals, and specifically did not include various alternate methods available to some segments of the population, such as natural childbirth, family-centered perinatal care programs, home births, and the like.[6] In this system, birth is located in the hospital and is attended by a physician. The Dutch system includes both home and hospital births, though the majority of births (55%) take place at home. Most births, however, regardless of location, are attended by midwives. The Yucatecan system is that practiced by the Maya Indians of Yucatan, Mexico. In this system, birth takes place at home and is attended by a midwife.

Since most of us are likely to be familiar with the American system, I will first describe the biosocial features as they appear in the American system and then as they appear in the Dutch and the Yucatecan systems. They are summarized in the Appendix, pages 220-221.

The Definition of the Event

A society's way of defining the event of birth powerfully shapes and is shaped by the other locally invariable features of birth in that society.[7] Thus, the local conceptualization of birth determines and serves as justification for that system's particular birthing practices; at the same time, this conceptualization is determined by those very practices.

The United States. As many people have pointed out, birth in the United States, like most physiological processes, is seen as a medical event.[8] By including pregnancy and childbirth in the medical realm, however, the pregnant woman becomes a "patient" and is subject to the kind of institutionalized expectations described by Talcott Parsons.[9] Among these expectations held in common by all participants with regard to the sick role are the following: (1) that the pregnant woman, as a patient, is relieved of responsibility for her status (and thus, to a considerable extent, of her normal responsibilities with regard to herself and to others); (2) that she is incompetent to handle the (medical) problem at hand (since, by definition, laypeople lack medical expertise); and (3) that she is obliged to seek out technically competent help (i.e., a physician) for her condition and to submit to that expert authority. The physician, too, is subject to a complementary set of expectations. Since his[10] competence is medical—which is to say, concerned with the management of pathology by surgical, pharmacological, and technological means—he is expected to put his medical expertise in the service of his patient's problem. This means that, as the authority with crucial and specialized knowledge, he is committed to taking total responsibility for the management of an essentially passive patient, monitoring the physiological process of birth for pathological deviation.

Holland. In Holland birth is viewed as a natural process that is best aided by letting nature take its course. The Dutch system distinguishes between normal and natural pregnancy and birth on the one hand, and abnormal and medical conditions of pregnancy and birth on the other. In the former case, the woman is treated (and views herself) as being competent to manage and actively participate in what is seen as a natural, normal physiological process. In the latter case, she is seen (and sees herself) as needing medical treatment for her medical problem, but only insofar, and only for so long, as the problem is medical, that is, pathological. The responsibility (and credit) for the course of normal pregnancy and birth is thus located primarily in the birthing woman.

Yucatan. In Yucatan, birth is seen as a stressful but normal part of family life, whose management and problems alike are properly handled within the family or woman's community. The doctor and hospital are used only in cases of dire emergency, when all else has failed. Understandably, this often results in a high medical failure rate, which then reinforces the Mayan Indians' reluctance to utilize the resources of the medical profession.

The Nature and Locus of Decision-Making

From the definition of birth in each of these three systems, the nature and locus of the decision-making process during birth follow directly.

The United States. In the United States, decisions concerning birth are subject to medical decision-making criteria. Owing to the systematic failure to distinguish between normal and pathological births, birth attendants' decisions exhibit a definite tendency to intervene medically in the birth process with procedures directed to correcting or alleviating pathological conditions. Since, moreover, participants in the system do not recognize the existence of lay competence in what are defined as medical matters, the birthing woman, as a patient, neither has, nor expects to have, nor is expected to have, any part in the (medical) decision-making process. This is true throughout her pregnancy, but it is perhaps most clearly illustrated when she actually goes into the hospital for labor and delivery. Upon entering the hospital she not only automatically cedes all decision-making power and authority to her physician and any on-staff physicians, including residents and interns, but also accepts the routine of "standard hospital procedure." Thus excluded from the decision-making process, the woman is seen (and sees herself) as being responsible for neither the conduct of her labor, nor the outcome of her birth.[11]

Holland. In Holland, where a mechanism does exist for separating pathological conditions from normal physiological processes, decision-making in routine birth is separated from strictly medical decision-making. Birth attendants tend to refrain from interfering with the birth process in the belief that, given enough time, nature works best.

At the same time, however, many decisions are also institutionally managed, including selection of birth attendants and birth location, and the use of medication for pain relief. The birthing woman is, for example, expected to be accompanied through her labor by a nonspecialist companion (usually her husband). Whether she gives birth at home or in a hospital will be decided upon the basis of a recognized set of medical and social indicators.[12] And she will not get, nor will she expect, any medication for pain relief. If current or foreseeable pathological conditions are diagnosed during her pregnancy, labor, or birth, the decision-making process is viewed (by the woman and by her specialist and nonspecialist attendants) as being properly medical, and is taken over by the specialists in attendance.

Yucatan.   Among the Yucatecan, decision-making throughout pregnancy, labor, and birth (including the diagnosis and management of abnormalities) remains primarily with the woman and her family. The participants in the Yucatecan system prefer to let nature take its course rather than intervene. Though the midwife's opinion carries considerable weight, decision-making is always the result of a consensus that recognizes the competence of all participants, both specialist and nonspecialist. And while the midwife has preferences of her own, she stresses again and again that in birth every woman has to *buscar la forma,* find her own style.

CONCLUSION

Jordan contends that the current pressures for change in the American system are in the direction of adjusting the system to changing views of the position and competencies of the women and couples involved in birth. So long as women hold in common with other participants of the American system of birth a medical view of the proper conduct of birth, one might expect that the parturient woman would be reassured by and satisfied with the medical conduct of her birth. But, Jordan says, "It was precisely the grossly visible incongruity between women's attitudes and expectations on the one hand and those of their attendants on the other that alerted [her], more than anything else, to the nature of the difficulties which beset the American system."[13] In the United States, the Women's Movement of the 1960s and the health care consumer movement have had a major impact on current notions about the position and competencies of women and patients.

"For many years, American women had regarded their individual unsatisfactory childbirth experiences as unrepresentative personal failures, due to their own ignorance, to a 'low pain threshold' or to idiosyncratic physiological problems."[14] However, with the emergence of the Women's Movement of the 1960s, this kind of discounting of women's personal experience began to change: "The Movement served as an arena for restructuring women's own self-image through consciousness-raising and political action. The proposition became prevalent that women's individual complaints about their birth experiences are not based on rare and special circumstances but are the systematic outcome of ordinary standard medical practice." She concludes that "this collectivization of previously idiosyncratic dissatisfaction has produced powerful and visible pressures on the American obstetric system as well as providing a political power base for activists' demands for change."[15]

A small but growing health care consumer movement has, in recent years, begun questioning the distribution of power and authority in the conventional doctor–patient relationship. As the feminist health movement demands for women the right to self-determination in matters regarding their bodies, the health care consumer movement argues for a greater degree of self-determination and a more active role in the decision-making process for the patient. Dissonance between the woman's conception of herself and the treatment she is accorded by her medical attendants during the childbearing years accounts for the pressures for change being brought to bear on the American way of birth.

The growing visibility of the various forms of natural childbirth, increasingly frequent efforts to restructure the physical design of obstetric wards, and the initiation of family-centered perinatal care programs may all be seen as moves in the direction of trying to reduce this dissonance and thereby to produce a significant increase in maternal satisfaction.[16] It remains to be seen whether this will indeed be the case. What is clear, however, is that the American system of birth will change; indeed, it is already changing. What is urgently needed is a way to assess rationally and to direct this change so that childbirth can be made both emotionally rich and medically safe.

APPENDIX I
SOME BIOSOCIAL FEATURES OF BIRTHING SYSTEMS[a]

	United States	Holland	Yucatan
Definition	Medical event	Natural process	Normal family event
Prenatal preparation	Physician supervision for all pregnancies	Midwife supervision for normal pregnancies, medical specialist for abnormal conditions; routine instruction for natural childbirth	Midwife visits woman in her home; instruction given only during actual labor, and by all attendants present
Attendants	Physician and medically trained physician support personnel	Woman's husband (or other relative or friend) for all births; midwife and her assistant for normal births; medical specialists for abnormal conditions	Midwife, woman's husband, and woman's mother for all births

	Hospital	Home (55%) or hospital	Home
Location			
Technology[b]	Forceps Delivery table	Vacuum extractor	Mostly from household (e.g., hammock for labor, chair for birth)
Decision Making	By physician for all births	By midwife in consultation with birthing woman for normal births; by medical specialist for abnormal conditions	Jointly by birthing woman, her helpers, and the midwife (both for the conduct of normal labor as well as the diagnosis and management of "trouble")

[a]From Jordan.[1]
[b]Since a comprehensive assessment of technology of American birth was beyond the scope of the discussion in *Birth in Four Cultures*, Jordan selected two objects that are an integral part of the American birthing system and contrasted them with their counterparts in other systems.

Community Alternatives to High Technology Birth

Ina May Gaskin

Every birth is a holy occasion. The management of the spiritual energy that is present whenever a baby is being born is as real a factor in the outcome of the birth as is the size of the baby, the size of the mother's pelvis, and other purely physical factors.

Modern medical science does not recognize the existence of spiritual energy because of the impossibility of measuring or describing something nonmaterial yet causative. But spiritual energy exists whether or not scientists can measure or describe it. The level of spiritual energy at a birthing depends, among other things, on the presence or lack of love between the mother and the other people attending the birth.

My researches in the management of spiritual energy began in 1970 when I began my community's midwifery service by delivering babies for my friends who were traveling around the country in the same group as I. We began with nothing more than a hemostat and a pair of scissors—in other words, almost zero technology. There was, however, a lot of love between the mothers I was delivering and me.

Since that time, we settled on the Farm, a 1750-acre piece of land in Tennessee and have grown to a spiritual community of 1300. Our midwifery service has expanded and developed to what we feel is a comfortable and safe level of technology for normal births and for detection and transportation of complicated births. We now have eight midwives, two physicians, twenty midwife trainee-labor coaches, a crew of nurses, twenty-four-hour emergency medical service with two back-up ambulances, a neonatal intensive care unit, an infirmary, a laboratory, a pharmacy, a maternity clinic for high-risk births, and an outpatient clinic for prenatal and pediatric care. All these services are offered for free. We plan to have an operating room on the Farm eventually so that any cesarean sections needed can be done by our own doctors. At present these are done free of charge by a doctor friend at one of our neighboring hospitals.

223

Table 1
Statistics for 1000 Births Managed by Farm Midwives
(10-8-70 to 3-13-79)

Total Births	1000	Reasons for transfer to hospital	43
Single mothers	131 (13%)	Transverse lie—2 mos. premature	
Non-Farm residents	468 (47%)	(c-section)	1
First-time mothers	434 (43%)	Marginal placenta previa	
Doctor present at home birth,		(c-section)	1
With midwife delivering	22 (2%)	Abruptio placenta (c-sec.)	2
Doctor deliveries at home, hospital,		Prolapsed cord (c-sec.)	1
or Farm Maternity Clinic ("FMC")	51 (5.1%)	Kidney infection (c-sec.)	1
Delivered at home	925 (93%)	Previous uterine surgery (c-sec.)	2
Delivered at FMC	32 (3%)	Cephalopelvic disproportion	
Delivered in the hospital, by doctor		(c-sec.)	1
or midwife	43 (4%)	Lack of progress—influenza	
Vertex presentation	948 (95%)	(c-sec.)	1
Face-up position	16 (1.6%)	Repeat c-section	3
Breech presentation	32 (3%)	Previous c-section, delivered	
Face presentation	2	naturally by midwife	1
Transverse lie	1	Fetal distress (c-sec.)[2]	2
Footling	1	Breech (term delivery)	10
C-sections	15 (1.5%)	Premature and breech	3
Forceps deliveries	3 (.3%)	Premature (2 mos.)	2
Induced deliveries	7 (.7%)	Suspected premature	1
Death in utero (Pitocin IV)	4	Suspected multiple gestation	1
Mild pre-eclampsia (snorted		Prolonged 2nd stage	2
Pitocin at FMC)	1	Anencephalic baby	1
Early rupture of membranes		Parents' request	2
(snorted Pitocin at FMC)	2	Other[3]	1
		Fetal death in utero (induced labor)	4
Breeches	32 (3.2%)	**Other complications of labor at home**	5
Home	7	Marginal placenta previa	1
FMC	11	Premature separation of placenta	3
Hospital	14	Hematoma in birth canal	1
by c-section	1	**Maternal Mortality**	0
with anesthesia	2		
without anesthesia	30	**Maternal complications**	63 (6%)
with episiotomy	16	(7 ladies had 2 complications)	
without episiotomy	16	Postpartum infection	31 (3.1%)
First-time mothers	17	Hemorrhage	27
Mothers over 30	6	stopped with oxytocin	
External versions,		(less than 500 cc)	21
breech to vertex	5	needed transfusion (more	
Premature (at least 4 weeks early)	27 (2.7%)	than 500 cc)	6
Home	16	Retained placenta	6
Hospital	8	Subcutaneous pneumothorax	1
FMC	3	Inverted uterus	1
Reasons for doctor del. at home	9	Severe tear	5
Breech	4	Prolapsed cervix	1
Prolonged 2nd stage	2	Treated at home	45
Other[1]	3	Treated at FMC	4
Reasons for transfer to FMC	28	Treated at hospital	14
Breech	10		
Suspected multiple gestation	5	**Complications of pregnancy**	10
Mild pre-eclampsia		Pre-eclampsia	2 (.2%)
(induced labor)	1	Polyhydramnios	3
Suspected premature	7	Incompetent cervix (cerclage)	2
Premature rupture of membranes		Prolapsed cervix	1
(induced labor)	1	Down's Syndrome	1
Premature separation of placenta	1	Retro-bulbar optic neuritis	1
Influenza	1		
Mothers choice	1	**Meconium staining**	45 (4.5%)
For Video	1	with complications	15
		without complications	30

(continued)

Table 1 (*continued*)

Total Perinatal Deaths[4]	15 (15 per 1000)	Shortest labor	1½ min.
Stillbirths	7 (7 per 1000)	No tear, no episiotomy	538 (54%)
Deaths in utero	4 (4 per 1000)	Tear	264 (26%)
toxemia	1	1° 166	
placental infarction	1	2° 94	
cord accidents	2	3° 4	
Deaths during labor	3 (3.0 per 1000)	Episiotomy	199 (20%)
anencephalic	1	1° 120	
prolapsed cord	1	2° 70	
premature separation		3° 9	
of placenta	1	Apgar (recorded for 497 births)	
Neonatal deaths	8 (8 per 1000)	Apgar of 10/10	244 (49%)
premature (10 weeks early)	1	Apgar of 10 after 5 min.	393 (79%)
RDS (premature)	2	Apgar of more than 6 at 1 min.	432 (87%)
Lethal congenital defects	3	Nursing mothers	99%
(1 anencephalic, 2 unknown		Ladies who had babies on Farm	
but probable)		and left them	6
Cause unknown	1	Postpartum depression	3
(1 month premature)			
Crib death	1		
Neonatal complications in			
living babies	17		
RDS	7		
Congenital abnormalities	6		
supernumerary digits	1		
Spina bifida	1		
Polycystic kidney	2		
Harelip	1		
Phocomelia	1		
1 ear	1		
Birth injury (broken arm)	2		
Hemolytic anemia (ABO			
incompatibility requiring			
transfusion)	1		
Biggest baby	11 lb. 4 oz.		
Smallest living baby	2.lb. 10½ oz.		
Oldest mother	42 years		
Youngest mother	16 years		
Average weight			
boys	7 lb. 8 oz.		
girls	7 lb. 4 oz.		
Mothers' average weight gain	25 lb.		
Average age of mothers	24.6 years		
Average length of labor			
First-time mothers (for 316 births)	11 hr.		
1st stage ⎫ for	10 hr. 12 min.		
2nd stage ⎬ 111	1 hr. 8 min.		
3rd stage ⎭ births	18 min.		
Second or later baby			
(for 380 births)	7 hr. 27 min.		
1st stage ⎫ for	6 hr. 36 min.		
2nd stage ⎬ 172	21 min.		
3rd stage ⎭ births	14 min.		
Longest labor	72 hrs.		

1. One was our midwife at our Wisconsin Farm. There was no other midwife available. Two Mennonite ladies from the area were delivered at home by our doctor. Now they are delivered by our midwives.
2. This was a repeat c-section. The doctor was going to try vaginal delivery but the FHT dropped.
3. Normal term delivery by midwife. The doctor wanted it done in the hospital because of drugs he'd given earlier to stop premature labor.
4. These include the 37 deliveries which the midwives considered high risk and which were delivered in the hospital. Many hospitals and clinics would not include in their statistics those cases which were transferred to another institution. Of the 926 babies delivered at home or in the Farm Maternity Clinic, there were 8 perinatal deaths, a rate of 8.6 per 1000 (1 stillbirth and 7 neonatal deaths, 3 of which were lethal congenital defects).

Here are some sample statistics for perinatal mortality from *Obstetrical and Gynecological Survey*, March 1977. Bronx Municipal Hospital Center, 1966: 36.3/1000; 1973: 21.7/1000. The Medical Center Hospital, Columbus, Georgia, 1970: 32/1000; 1972: 28/1000. Infant mortality in the State of Tennessee, 1977: 26/1000.

Our entire technical kit for home and Farm maternity clinic births in 1979 includes:

Portable oxygen units for home births	Suturing equipment
Two incubators, and 1 transport incubator	Doppler fetoscopes
Bilirubin lights	Blood pressure cuffs
Forceps	Umbilical catheter supplies
	DeLee suction catheters
	iv Equipment is available if needed

For communication we have citizens' band radios, an inner-Farm phone system, and video equipment that we use for educational purposes.

Our statistics for the first 1000 babies delivered have been excellent. About half of these births were for women who did not live on the Farm, who asked to have their babies under the supervision of Farm midwives. There were 15 perinatal deaths, for a perinatal mortality of 15/1000. Perinatal mortality in the State of Tennessee for 1977 was 22.4/1000. Ninety-nine percent of babies born in Tennessee are born in hospitals. All of the figures given include high-risk women who were transferred to the hospital for delivery. When only the 957 infants born at the Farm clinic or at home under the midwife's supervision are counted, the mortality drops to 8/1000. Screening for mothers too high-risk for birth out of the hospital is done by the midwives with the backup of the Farm doctors. Maternal mortality has been zero.

Instead of the American obstetrical practice of delivering most breech babies by cesarean, we deliver them naturally. There have been no forceps or induced deliveries for breech babies and only one cesarean. Seventeen of the thirty-two breech deliveries were first-time mothers; six were mothers over thirty. Only fifteen cesareans were necessary out of 1000 births, 1.5 percent of the births. The reasons are listed in Table 2.

No anesthesia was used, except for the cesarean deliveries and for one breech delivery. Deep massage and loving support have been sufficient for all of the rest.

Amniocentesis has been used only once, by order of our local surgeon friend, who wanted to determine the maturity of a cesarean baby about to be delivered. We think there is considerable danger to mother and baby if the use of this diagnostic test becomes routine.

Nine hundred ninety-nine of the births happened with no electronic fetal heart monitoring, internal or external. A traditional horn-type fetoscope was used for prenatal checkups and for some

Table 2

HIGH RISK PREGNANCIES

Home	79
Hospital	43
Farm Maternity Clinic (FMC)	24

Breech	32
Home	7
FMC	11
Hospital	14
Births with anesthesia	2
C-sections	1
Premature (4 or more weeks early)	27
Home	16
FMC	3
Hospital	8
Induced deliveries	7
Death in utero - hospital	4
Pre-eclampsia - FMC	1
(snorted Pitocin)	
Early rupture of membranes	2
(gave castor oil)	
1 home; 1 hospital	
Prolonged 2nd stage -	2
(doctor deliveries at home)	
Low forcep deliveries	2
1 home; 1 hospital	
Vacuum forcep delivery (prolonged	
2nd stage, small pubic arch)	1
Multiple gestation	6
2 home; 4 FMC	
(one lady also had severe vulvar	
varicosities)	
C-sections - hospital	15
(1 transverse lie and premature	
2 months; 1 marginal placenta	
previa; 2 abruptio placenta; 1 pro-	
lapsed cord; 1 kidney infection;	
2 previous uterine surgery;	
1 cephalopelvic disproportion;	
1 lack of progress; 3 repeat c-sec.;	
2 fetal distress; 1 prolonged	
2nd stage)	
Prolonged 2nd stage - hospital	1
Anencephalic baby - hospital	1
Parents' request - hospital	1
Normal birth (doctor wanted it done	
in hospital because of drugs he'd	
given to stop premature labor)	1
Marginal placenta previa - home	1

Probable premature separation of	
placenta (death during labor)	1
16 year-old mothers - home	3
40-year-old mothers - home	3
Lady with epidermolysis	
bullosa - home	2
Lady with double uterus and	
double birth canal	2
Influenza and high	
blood pressure - FMC	1
High blood pressure	1
Pre-eclampsia - FMC	2
Polyhydramnios - 3 home; 1 FMC	4
Incompetent cervix - home	5
(2 births after cerclage and 1 neo-	
natal death at 6½ mos. gestation)	
Prolapsed cervix - home	1
Premature rupture of membranes	18
13 home; 1 hospital; 4 FMC	
Herpes Virus II during pregnancy -	
home (no open lesions at	
time of birth)	6
Small pelvis - home	1
(baby went to hospital - fine)	
Told pelvis too small by doctors	3
home	
Previous prolapsed cervix - hospital	1
Bleeding during pregnancy (cause	
unknown) - home	2
Prediabetic - home	2
Edema - home	1
Kidney infection in 9th mo. - home	1
Lady with history of pre-eclampsia	
causing placental insufficiency -	
home (1 stillbirth)	3
Uterine infection - home	1
18-year-old welfare patient - home	1
Ladies with severe varicose veins -	
home	2
Premature separation of placenta	2
1 home; 1 FMC	
Hematoma in birth canal - home	1
Lady whose 1st baby had ABO	
exchange transfusion - home	1
	168
	-23*
TOTAL HIGH RISK PREGNANCIES	145
	or 14.5%
*19 ladies had 2 complications;	
2 ladies had 3 complications	

births. A small doppler fetoscope was used during approximately one-third of the prenatal checkups and labors.

We think it is significant that these results were accomplished by amateurs, who took the trouble to teach themselves a discipline with almost no use of the technology that American obstetrics is trying to prove to the world is minimal. We do not use X-ray equipment in obstetrics. We think that the risk of low-level radiation to the baby (such as that produced by the X-ray equipment) is sufficient to limit its use during pregnancy only to immediately life-threatening situations. Determination of fetal and pelvic size and of fetal presentation is done manually. That the midwives have been able to internalize the many factors of measurement that must be considered in determining whether passage of the baby is possible is demonstrated by our statistics. There has been only one case of the baby's head being too big to fit through the mother's pelvis.

Because we are doing and paying for our own health care as a community, there is no tendency for us to accumulate expensive equipment. One of our transport incubators was built by a Farm member for a total cost of $60. It does not look as fancy as the $2,000 commercial model available, but it functions just as well. Instead of having a several thousand dollar fetal heart monitor and leaving a laboring mother alone, with a nurse or resident to come by and check her labor graphs every fifteen minutes, we have attendants with the mother continuously, who can check the baby's heart tones with the doppler fetoscope anytime they need to, continuously, if need be.

OTHER ASPECTS OF SUPPORT GIVEN TO MOTHERS

The Farm has no psychiatrist. There are a few people in the community who have grown to be good psychological counselors who, with the midwives, take this kind of responsibility in the community.

There is no need for a group to promote breast-feeding. The midwives have kindled a close sisterhood among the Farm women. The knowledge of how to breast feed is mainly transmitted from woman to woman, with help to new mothers initially given by the midwives.

There is no center for battered women on the Farm, as there is no need for one. The midwives provide protection and counsel, with the support of Farm men, for all of the other ladies and girls. Any man who strikes his lady is asked to leave the Farm for thirty days.

There are other ways that Farm life makes a low-technology system of birth work safely. Birth control counseling and education using the sympto-thermal method means that the midwives are not faced with risky deliveries for women who have had too many pregnancies. Tubal ligations are allowed, but not at this time performed on the Farm.

Sexual and marital counseling is provided by the midwives. We think that this counseling is largely responsible for the lack of incidence of post-mature babies. Onset of labor can be delayed by emotional factors. This type of counseling also is responsible for the total absence of arrested labor and partly explains why such a large group of mothers were able to give birth without anesthesia, forceps, or surgery.

Sex education for teen-agers is provided both in the homes and at school. This education includes the area of sexual responsibility on the part of both boys and girls. Although we have a lot of teen-agers living on the Farm, we have had few pregnancies in young teen-agers.

We think that the era of medical care for profit is coming to an end. Our collective system has proven to be far superior statistically and economically. Health care for the average American cost $875 per person per year in 1978. On the Farm, the cost was $75 per person per year for total health care, maternity care included.

It is obvious that American hospital obstetrics is a man's profession. It has been designed by men; it is controlled by men. It is practiced on women. It is a highly profitable business, both for the men who handle the birthings and the men who own and run the hospitals. Obstetricians are among the highest paid of all American doctors. To any families who wish for an alternative way to give birth, the medical and hospital system looks like any other monopoly, the doctors' associations such as the American Medical Association, the American College of Obstetricians and Gynecologists, and the American Hospital Association functioning as some of our most powerful trade unions, with the people's health and welfare at stake.

We believe that it is time for true freedom of choice for women in all aspects of health and maternity care. We feel that returning the major responsibility for normal childbirth to well-trained midwives rather than have it rest with a predominately male and profit-oriented medical establishment is a major advance in self-determination for women.

Contrasts in the Birthing Place

Hospital and Birth Center

Byllye Y. Avery and Judith M. Levy

I (BYA) was born in my grandparents' house on October 20, 1937, in Waynesville, Georgia. My mother was attended by a white country doctor who, along with several grannies, served this rural community. My grandparents' house was the birthplace of my mother, her six sisters and brothers, and eighteen of my cousins. Childbirth was perceived as a natural process; midwives were respected members of the community—they were the wise women, the healers. Home was the expected place of birth; doctors and midwives assisted women at home and were involved with birth as a family event and a social celebration.

Forty-one years ago, in the South, life was simpler and birth more humanistically oriented.

It was a time when midwives were being licensed to practice and there was physician support for midwifery. For in this country, midwives have always been allowed to practice with poor people and in areas where doctors did not want to go. While obstetricians in cities were persuading women to have their babies in hospitals, in the deep South, particularly in rural areas, the home was considered a legitimate place for childbirth.

I remember when my brother was born at home in Florida. The night before his birth, Ms. Henrietta Griffin, the midwife, came to our house when my mother was in early labor. Around noon the next day she found me at a neighbor's house and excitedly told me that I had a baby brother! When I reached home my mother was lying in the glow of childbirth showing both fatigue and elation. That night Ms. Henrietta Griffin fed me, tucked me in bed, and spent the night so my mother could rest.

It was a simpler time in the forties and birth was more humanistic.

In 1960 I became pregnant and my birth experience parallels the "mobility" of blacks in the South. I had two options: I could attend a segregated hospital in Jacksonville where I lived, or a segregated hospital in Macclenny, Florida, where I worked. Brewster Methodist Hospital in Jacksonville served the black community the way other Jim Crow institutions served the blacks: inadequate staff, insufficient facilities, and poor patient care. Fraser in Macclenny, Florida, on the other hand, was a small newly constructed rural hospital serving both racial groups, albeit on segregated wards. It was easier to get a doctor's appointment in Macclenny and prenatal visits were more convenient near work. Fraser also offered rooming-in, rather unique in the sixties, but this was really not a determining factor in my choice.

During my first pregnancy I was apprehensive, anticipating a painful birth. I was *very* afraid of being awake during birth. For although I come from a tradition that recognized that birth is a natural process, I also carry with me in my history and in my psyche the deaths of my Aunt Laura and my cousin Jewel Mae during childbirth. Maternal mortality rates are not abstract statistics for black people.

When I came into the hospital in early labor, I was prepped and enemaed. My husband was allowed to remain with me during labor, and he offered emotional support while nurses came in and out of the room checking my progress. When the doctor came to examine me, he informed me that I "got him off the fish creek." My husband, Wes, notified the nurses when the baby was crowning; they came promptly, held the baby's head back, told me to stop pushing, put Wes out of the room, and rolled me to the delivery room—my last memory before I woke up in my room back on the ward. Wes saw our son before he was cleaned up and this is something that he often spoke proudly about.

I was less anxious during my second pregnancy. My labor and delivery were shorter and my need for anesthesia was less. Just before delivery I removed the ether mask from my face and was awake for Sonja's birth. I did not breastfeed either of my children. For blacks in the sixties, breast-feeding was as old timey as granny midwives.

In the sixties life was becoming more complex and birth less humanistic.

As hospital births became more prevalent, the practice of midwifery declined. Doctors withdrew their support, but midwives continued to attend the poor or those in outlying areas where the doctors did not want to go. And the black community fit both criteria.

Rebecca Wallace, a 76-year-old black woman in Alachua, Florida, learned midwifery from her mother, who had practiced for 56 of her 104 years. "I started early! . . . I kept the birth certificate. The first baby I caught was when I was 18 years old. My mother had to check on another woman so she left me in charge. When she got back, the baby was delivered and everything was done." Mrs. Wallace has caught some 1500 babies in her 50 years of practice.

Sometimes midwives and their patients were incorporated into the system. In 1958, the University of Florida School of Medicine and the Shands Teaching Hospital and Clinics were established in Gainesville and "teaching material" was needed. Mrs. Wallace remembers: "The doctors told me to bring in my list of patients and they would give me a job there. I worked at Shands on the OB ward as an aide." Her patients became the population upon which young doctors-in-training worked.

Mrs. Wallace left Shands three months later and began to deliver babies again. She used three rooms in the seven-room house as birthrooms. "The women who lived far away would come here and I could take care of them all together. One night I delivered three babies right here in this house. That's the most I've delivered in one day. That was an exciting night. If a baby was born before they got to the house or the hospital, we called that an outside baby," says Mrs. Wallace. Babies delivered by a midwife in the family's home were from poor families who were unable to pay. These babies and their families carried a stigma in the nineteen-sixties.

"The top price I ever got was $60," Mrs. Wallace noted. "If I found a destituted family I wouldn't take nothing. I figured the young child coming into the world needed it more than I did. No, I wasn't in it for the money."

Today the cost of prenatal care and a normal hospital delivery ranges nationally from $900 to 3200. Health care is distributed in this country on the basis of socioeconomic class. Thus prenatal care is available in a variety of clinic and private practice settings. Some women receive no care at all. The typical ob/gyn is a youngish white male who is building up a clientele so he can retire from obstetrics and practice gynecology, a more lucrative specialty with more regular hours.

When a woman's pregnancy is confirmed or when she thinks she might be pregnant and she chooses to have the child, she generally begins a course of prenatal care. Typically, on her first visit to the doctor she completes a medical history form, is weighed, and has her vital signs taken by a nurse. A urine specimen is obtained and lab work ordered. The woman changes into an unattractive hospital gown, sometimes disposable, and often is on her back and draped ready for a pelvic examination when she meets the obstetrician. The doctor reviews the chart and performs the physical exam. Then the woman gets dressed and sits across from the doctor who is at his desk. He discusses his findings, prescribes vitamins, and gives her a booklet about childbirth. Total time of visit, excluding waiting time, is ten to fifteen minutes. Subsequent prenatal visits last five to seven minutes, again excluding waiting time.

The doctor may or may not discuss with the woman the interventions he intends to use during labor and delivery. He may be open to requests or he may give lip service to requests, or he may be blatantly authoritarian as was one obstetrician who told a woman that her pregnancy was none of her business. Most physicians have routine practices that are established at the hospital and go into effect when a woman goes into labor. Usually prior to her due date the woman makes financial arrangements with the hospital. She may or may not be encouraged to take a childbirth preparation class or a tour of the hospital.

A hospital is an acute care facility, which is a profound message to the woman in labor. She enters through the emergency room and is admitted as a patient. She is given a number and wears a plastic identification bracelet throughout her stay, as does her baby. She is prepped, a presurgical procedure; an enema is usually routine as are the other procedures in what Suzanne Arms calls "just-in-case" obstetrics. "Just-in-case you need anesthesia, we won't feed you." The woman generally labors on her back to accommodate the fetal monitor which is now routine procedure in most institutions. Husbands or partners are now in many hospitals permitted to remain with the woman during labor, and more progressive settings allow him to accompany her into the delivery room. Vaginal examinations are intrusively and frequently performed.

When birth is imminent, the woman is wheeled to the delivery room, which often signals the first appearance of the obstetrician. The woman is placed flat on her back in the lithotomy position where she pushes against gravity. She's draped and stirupped; her arms are strapped down to prevent her contaminating the sterile field. She is often anesthesized, and forceps need to be used. Episiotomy is usually routine. The cord is often cut immediately. The baby is whisked away by the pediatric staff to be examined and footprinted; to get eye-drops, vitamin K, and her/his plastic identification. The placenta is often aggressively extracted. The mother is transferred to the recovery room and the baby to the nursery for observation. Hours pass before the mother and baby are reunited. Family members may view the baby through the nursery window at designated hours. Floor nurses may teach breastfeeding to the new mother although in many settings there is no encouragement or support.

Variations on this theme range from a few progressive and responsive physicians who respect the woman's wishes for a non-interventionist birth in a setting of optimal emotional support, to the situation at Charity Hospital in New Orleans less than ten years ago where no visitors were permitted on maternity and where mother and baby were separated for the entire hospital stay. Most hospital births fall somewhere between these extremes.

Inevitably, a reaction against this mechanized, assembly-line, impersonal birth environment had to occur. Beginning in the 1940's, the childbirth education movement sought to soften and reform hospital birth practices, but never challenged the idea of the hospital as the legitimate place to have a baby. The present alternative birth movement challenges the obstetrical dictum that the hospital is the best and safest environment for a woman and her baby. Starting about a dozen years ago on the West Coast, as an outgrowth of the counterculture critical of mainstream America, the alternative birth movement is sweeping the country, affecting mainstream obstetrics itself.

Birthplace, a free-standing alternative birth center, opened on October 15, 1978 in Gainesville, Florida. It is one of nine centers in the country, with many in the planning stage, that provide nurse-midwifery services in a homelike setting. These centers typically have strict criteria and screen women carefully. They are designed for healthy women sustaining normal pregnancies who are motivated for a natural childbirth experience. Because nurse-midwives are more uniformly trained than licensed or unlicensed lay midwives and because they can openly function in most states, nurse-midwifery centers are less vulnerable to attack by the medical establishment.

Birthplace has its roots in the women's health movement. The center is an expression of our belief that we have the right to make decisions about our bodies and ourselves. Without the fundamental choice to decide whether or not to conceive or whether or not to terminate a pregnancy, all other rights are illusory. The corollary of this is that it is our right to decide where to give birth, how the birth should be managed, who should be present, etc. It is our belief that traditional obstetrics, which places us on our backs, knocks us out for the delivery, and *robs us* of our childbearing experience, both symbolizes and actualizes the role of women in this society as passive victims. We reject this image as we reject the stereotyped pacing father and the newborn baby slapped on the ass. These are all social roles that are humiliating and demeaning.

At Birthplace we believe that childbirth is a natural process of the body, the mind, and the spirit. We attempt to create an atmosphere that enhances self confidence, control through knowledge, and trust in one's own body. We encourage the woman to be an active participant in her care—all information is shared, procedures and risks are explained, the charts are open, women do their own weighing and dipstick urinalysis; and they look under the microscope if there is a suspected vaginal infection. Childbirth preparation classes and prenatal yoga are offered; partners and support persons are encouraged to come to prenatal visits. A self-help mother's group has evolved. We have a well-shelved library open to participants as well as to the community.

The physical surroundings are esthetically pleasing. There is a play room for children as well as an outdoor playground. The birthing rooms have large double beds that accommodate the mother and her supportive person. Couches and pillows as well as kitchen facilities are available for families in waiting.

The initial prenatal visit lasts about two and a half hours, during which a detailed history is obtained and a complete head-to-toe physical performed. This sharing of information initiates a relationship of trust and friendship between the woman and the nurse-midwife. The second visit lasts for one hour with a review of the lab results and nutritional counseling if needed. Subsequent prenatal visits are from thirty to forty-five minutes. The non-authoritarian, non-elitist relaxed atmosphere, and the personalized interest by the entire staff make for a more humanistic, comfortable setting.

There are very few "routine" procedures since each woman's needs are different. Women labor and deliver in positions that are comfortable for them. Some women deliver lying on their side; some are propped up with pillows; some are in squatting position or on all fours; some are more comfortable standing up. Episiotomies are performed only when indicated and perineal massage and gentle directed pushing often prevent laceration or the need for the episiotomy. We usually delay cutting the cord with the baby placed on the mother's abdomen. The baby may be placed on the breast immediately to aid in the expulsion of the placenta. The father or partner's role is determined by the couple's relationship. The father may cut the cord or give the baby a Leboyer bath, or "catch the baby" with midwife's supervision, if he so chooses. The baby may be bathed with the mother if that is the choice. Vaginal checks during labor are minimal. Some births are photographed, some tape recorded. Some births have cheering sections; others are meditative and quiet. Children may be present if the mother chooses. Some women need very little external support; some need the energy of others to breathe through each contraction. The woman's stay at Birthplace varies with the time of birth, the length of labor, and the distance from home. One woman having her second baby went home an hour and a half after the birth; one couple stayed the weekend before traveling home to Alaska.

One of the gratifying aspects for us at Birthplace, as older women who are past the childbearing stage and whose children are almost grown, is the impact of the Birthplace experience on the grandmothers who were often anesthesized during their own childbirth experiences. As one grandmother wrote on her return to Santo Domingo:

> This "thank you" note expresses in only a token manner the gratefulness I feel towards Birthplace. On May 14, my younger daughter, Terry Wiggins, gave birth to *her* second daughter in such marvelous surroundings! Until then, I had not known that there was an alternative to a hospital birth, not that such an alternative was even desirable—the whole experience was astonishing for me and my enthusiasm is unbounded. Beth was so kind, so reassuring, competent and just plain nice—Judy's smile helped a great deal—and everyone was kind and helpful. It was a morning that will live in all our memories—

Women are rejecting the obstetrical model of birth in the hospital setting. Birth centers and home births represent an alternative to the hospital. In typical irrational frenzy, the medical establishment has denounced out-of-hospital birth as child abuse rather than understanding and responding to the changing consciousness of the birth experience. Ostrich-like, the obstetrical profession counter-proposes in-hospital "Family Centered Maternity Care"—the reforms that obstetricians bitterly opposed for the past twenty to thirty years are too little and too late. Fathers in delivery rooms or relaxation of stringent visitation rules or birth-rooms that try to de-emphasize the institutional hospital setting cannot stem the powerful trend of out-of-hospital birth.

And a new phase of midwife persecution has begun. Across the country, lay midwives are being legally harrassed. Currently in St. Augustine, Florida, Carolle Baya has been charged with practicing midwifery without a license, although with her experience she has attempted to get one for the past two years. She is also charged with practicing medicine without a license, ironically because she puts neosporin in the baby's eyes, a prophylactic measure that is a state law.

Whatever rationalizations the doctors offer indicating their professional concerns about the safety of home birth and the skill of the lay midwife, the real motivation is summed up by Dr. Anthony

Mussalem who pressed the charges against Ms. Baya: "I don't believe there's a place for a midwife in this community. We've got about eight or nine physicians in this town doing obstetrics and lots of them aren't even busy."

The roots of patriarchy go deep. Changing styles must not be mistaken for radical change. As Barbara Rothman has noted, "moving birth out of the institutions of medicine is not the same as moving birth out of the institutions of patriarchy." We must be on guard against a modern version of the traditional role of motherhood where mother is expected to provide all the emotional needs of the family. Alternative birth settings and the new birth consciousness may bring new prescriptions for the woman to bond immediately with her baby to ensure its intellectual and emotional development; new prescriptions that her childbirth becomes a sex educational setting for her older children; new prescriptions that the presence of the father will cement the marital relationship. We must avoid these rigidities. Childbirth—the bringing forth of new life energy—is quintessentially a woman's event.

Ethical Issues Relating to Childbirth as Experienced by the Birthing Woman and Midwife

Judith Dickson Luce

I am a woman; I am a mother. I have given birth three times. I am a midwife—a lay midwife. The purpose of this paper is to root a concept, "ethical issues," in the flesh and blood of women's lives, of families' lives, in the lives of midwives whose basic function is to help women in their birthing. Because I am both mother and midwife I find it difficult to separate these perspectives, so in this paper "they" may slip into being "we."

I want to deal not so much with ethical issues as with the people who make ethical choices. Only individuals can make decisions about what is ethical for them. In fact when these decisions are made *for* whole groups of people rather than *by* them we are faced with an ethical dilemma in itself. Rather than talk about what is "ethical," I want to talk about the efforts that women make to do what is right in their lives. Wholeness and harmony in one's life, living with integrity, being responsible, simply having one's life make sense: these are what concern women when they make choices about their childbearing, when they ask whether the "American way of childbirth" makes any sense.

So it is not just the armchair philosophers, the academicians, who are struggling with "ethical questions," for every woman whose birth I have attended has shared with me her struggle to be allowed to make choices and to make the right ones. Although an awareness of the larger issues—social control, medicalization of life, use and abuse of technology—has varied greatly, each has seen her decisions, her acts as connecting her to others and to a larger struggle of some sort.

As the mother of a three-day-old just commented to me on the phone: "I'm not sure how it's political, but I know when they can take birth from you they've got you." Her history is pertinent. Seven years ago, she gave birth to her first child in a small hospital in Pennsylvania.

She was 26. No one was allowed in the hospital with her. She was put into a bed and left alone for long periods of time and then told she "needed something." She was given demerol. At one point a doctor came in, checked and inquired, "How long has she been like this?" She was then wheeled to the delivery room, given general anesthesia and a large episiotomy. Forceps were used to pull her 6½-pound baby out. Her cervix was lacerated as was her vagina. She was unable to sit for three months without considerable pain. This time she stayed at home to give birth. She experienced a long and intense labor, but gave birth to an 8½-pound boy. She had no drugs and no episiotomy, but she did have a lot of support from her mate, friends, midwife, and 7-year-old son. One of her first comments after the birth was: "I feel so good. After Jamie's birth (first son) I never felt good about myself, never had a good sense of myself as a woman. My image of myself was sure bad."

I feel that the basic ethical issue is the right of women to make choices about how, where, and with whom they give birth. Who will decide what is ethical for women in childbirth? Who will control birth? I believe that the childbearing woman is best equipped to choose what is right for herself and for her unborn child—that she is most fully aware of the myriad values that can be brought to bear on the decisions she makes. (I also want to suggest that doctors and men are least equipped to do this.) How women make choices, what factors they consider, are things we must listen to. To birthing, as to dying, we bring our histories, our relationships, our rituals, and the deepest values and hopes that give meaning to our lives. We bring needs and values that relate to intimacy, sexuality, the quality and style of family life and community, and our deepest beliefs about birth, life, and death. The relative weight of these considerations cannot be medically assessed on a risk factor scale (although I am certain someone will try it). Quality of life is as important a consideration as the fact of life.

Historically it has been impossible to talk about birth without talking about midwives—wise women, healers, enablers of women, protectors of the process of birth. Today the midwife, particularly the lay midwife, exists to protect the right of women and families to maintain control of their birth experiences, to make choices. This is why I am a midwife.

From experience I want to suggest that becoming conscious of the values in one's life that one wants to protect and express, and being allowed to do so, has a direct bearing on the physiological process of labor and birth and the "outcome" (to use medical jargon). They are not just psychological and emotional factors extraneous to the birth process; to a great degree they make the process what it is. There used to be a saying—tell a first grade kid he is stupid and he will prove you right every time. Similarly, tell a woman she is a high risk and she will become a high risk. By definition, to be a woman has almost come to mean high risk or at least potentially so. By describing women this way we evoke fear of a process that most women are already alienated from, and fear creates problems in childbirth. Being afraid of natural bodily functions and processes, and dependent on men and machines, damages women in birth, just as forceps, drugs, and meddling hands damage newborns. And fear and the experience of failure keep woman distant from each other. Being bonded with other women, drawing strength from them has in many cultures been intrinsic to giving birth well. In Ethiopia there was an expression that a woman would always have as many women as she needed to "hold her up" in labor—not just physically, but emotionally and spiritually as well.

In this society birth has become defined for us by medicine in ways that narrow the experience. It becomes increasingly difficult to approach birth on our own terms in our own language. And in turn we see the professionalization and medicalization of roles and relationships that rightfully belong to mothers, fathers, siblings, and friends.

The ways in which responsibility and rights are weaned from women can be very subtle. And the struggle to reverse it can be difficult, leaving a woman feeling deviant or guilty. (All forms of social control do this in some degree.) I once heard a physician speaking eloquently and passionately of his concern and caring for the lives of unborn children as a defense of his use of fetal monitors. But we have to remember that no one cares about the life of an unborn child as much as the woman who is carrying that child. As obvious as this might sound, it has to be said because of the polarization that has taken place: women and parents who supposedly do not care (or are too ignorant to care effectively) versus the doctor in the hospital who allegedly does. We must re-establish who babies belong to: not doctors, not nurses, and not the state.

To further bring home this point I want to relate an incident involving a noted Boston physician who made a "Leboyer" type nonviolent birth film called "Gentle Birth." The film ends with him saying that we have not changed everything, but perhaps *we are creating more caring parents.* The statement was not made with any deliberate arrogance. After a lengthy discussion he still was baffled by my rage, unable to comprehend why I was disturbed by the remark. I think this exchange is a fair indication of how warped things have become. In fact, parents are not becoming more caring, but are again being allowed in certain ways and in certain controlled instances to express their caring. So in this film the baby is immediately placed on the mother's disinfected stomach, whereas when my first child was born and I instinctively reached out to touch him I was yelled at, and told I had broken the sterile field, and to put my hand back under the drapes. The worst part was I did. The woman in the film had become "more caring" than I was because the medical authorities allowed her to be.

A question of priorities must be defined and kept straight even in the few births that become medically complicated. For the woman giving birth, the medical dimension of what is happening is not the most important one any more than it is for the dying person. Life-supporting procedures cannot be allowed to impinge upon or replace values and experiences that are equally life-sustaining.

I worked with a young woman whose first child died in utero at the beginning of her ninth month. She knew the baby had died. Movement ceased and she sensed life going out of her. By the time the doctor confirmed what she already knew she had begun mild labor. She told him she still wanted to stay at home and give birth, and she would whether he came or not. Initially he refused, but reconsidered that night. She labored knowing her child was dead, she gave birth, held her girl child, touched her, examined every inch of her body, and wept. Together she and her husband buried their child. She wanted to stay home because in her words she had to carry things to completion. She did not want someone, out of a misguided concern, taking her baby from her to spare her; and she wanted to be with friends not strangers. I know this woman grew immeasurably from this experience. (And recently she gave birth to a healthy seven and a half pound girl at home).

Of course every woman should not go through this experience in order to grow. But when the doctors try so singlemindedly to eliminate all risk and possibility of death, or we become convinced that they've done this, we've lost a capacity for living. By "reducing risk" and guaranteeing a "life outcome," technology has created its own set of risks, and it damages women, babies, and families both physically and emotionally.

This woman's facing death in birth is not an isolated phenomenon. Most women I work with talk about the possibility of death or of a baby's being severely deformed. They say they want to stay at home so they will have some voice in what happens in either of these eventualities. They are very much in touch with birth and death as process; they resist the "product" mentality. The risks people take are linked to efforts to act responsibly, not foolishly. I am convinced that much of the intervention that takes place and much of the use of technology and drugs in childbirth grow out of the doctor's need to control birth and women's bodies. And much of the hospital ritual is rooted in the inability of doctors to face death, to see death as anything but a failure. Rescuing women from birth then becomes one of their successes.

Women have a right to choose their own level of risk—to choose what risks they are willing to take in order to live fully. Life is not risk free; birth is not risk free anywhere. Home birth carries a set of risks and rewards; hospitals carry their own set of risks. It is not a question of eliminating, but of weighing them. Taking risks has always been a sign of a full life. Now risk is something you are at before you are even born, a category you fit into. As a midwife I am frequently asked what "criteria" I have for "risking" people out. The language is just not appropriate for me. In my role as a midwife I give out a lot of information. I do a lot of teaching and explaining and a lot of listening and learning. I share my personal feelings and concerns about things, but in the end I believe a woman has a right to weigh all this and to make her own choice about where and how she gives birth. I also have a right to choose. Theoretically there are situations I would not be comfortable with, women I would not want to attend. I have rarely been faced with that.

Prenatal care is essentially the care a woman gives herself and the child growing in her. I offer feedback in my screening in specific areas, but the real preparation for labor and birth involves a woman's total life—the physical, the intellectual, the emotional, and the spiritual. These are totally ignored in traditional prenatal care. And they do affect "outcome" every bit as much as anemia, protein in the urine, weight gain, and all the other measurables and chartables.

So much that happens in institutions comes about without any consideration as to its "rightness." Practices become routine that are based on assumptions and values that someone else had (or did not have). They no longer, it is assumed, have to be thought about; or perhaps they never really were. The question of a woman's bodily integrity is a case in point. I want to recount a recent birth story because it was the experience of this woman that gave me a language to begin to talk about this issue.

A woman, pregnant for the third time, was in her ninth month. Her baby was in a breech position. She had entered the hospital for an evaluation to determine whether she should be allowed to deliver her baby vaginally. While there she went into labor. X-rays were done, but they were slow coming back. (As an aside, how many women are told that X-rays present a risk to their child and should be done only when absolutely necessary?) Meanwhile labor precipitated. While everyone, including the father, was out looking at X-rays the woman felt the urge to push. The obstetrician spoke of an extended head and something about pelvic bones (remember she had already has given birth twice to good size babies). He decided a section should be done. But at this point, time was of the essence. So instead of a spinal, general anesthesia was given. She had a C-section; the baby was delivered, but never breathed on its own and died within an hour because it had no kidneys. The woman's reaction to the whole experience was one of rage. She felt she had been raped. The loss of the child did not weigh as heavy as the loss of her bodily integrity, her sense of utter powerlessness. Men basically made the decisions about what would happen to her body. The issue is not whether a woman may choose to have a C-section in order to reduce the supposed risk to her child; it is that she is never asked to choose. An unknown life is given a value and priority over her life. It is documented that C-sections carry an increased risk to the woman in terms of mortality and morbidity. A woman is rarely told this while the risks to her baby are being enumerated.

Sustaining life at all costs is another rarely questioned assumption. While trying to sort out the ethical questions that arise when dealing with a small percentage of complicated births, I came upon an account that brought at least one issue into focus. I read of a woman, mother of two other children, who gave birth to a 2-pound baby, anoxic, retarded severely, who will probably never walk, who (at two years of age) still requires tube feeding, chest suctioning, and constant care. I did not know whether to cry or cheer at the marvels of modern medicine that kept this child alive. I know that in any other age, and born outside a hospital this child would not have lived. Technology keeps improving. Two pound babies/fetuses can be kept alive. But at what cost? Is it ethical to do this or is it playing God? Who should decide when it is women, primarily, who are called upon and expected to give the "constant care" to such children?

The modern industrial age has given us a whole new set of rules to play by. Many of the questions are difficult even to formulate. Hopefully this conference will be an aid in their formulation. I do not really know whether keeping the previously mentioned baby alive was ethical, even though it was possible. What I do know is that women must be directly involved in the clarification process, women who are doing the child-bearing and the care-taking.

Midwives in Many Settings

Helen Swallow

Many factors currently are forcing a reassessment of health-care policy toward home birth: the increase in family-centered care in childbirth, the developing awareness of woman's rights, the professional discomfort with the recent increase in numbers and the visibility of home births, the increased cost of medical care, technological medical developments, and the continued high perinatal mortality and morbidity rates.

In May, 1975, the American College of Obstetrics and Gynecology (ACOG) *did* officially acknowledge that childbirth was a normal physiological event, *but* claimed that it is so full of potential danger that all births should occur in the hospital. Last year, an interdisciplinary task force consisting of the American College of Obstetrics and Gynecology, the American College of Nurse-Midwives, the American Nurses Association, the American Academy of Pediatrics, and no consumers, issued a pamphlet encouraging the development of in-hospital family-centered maternity centers.[1] But in any particular hospital people involved in making changes in obstetric "policy" do not seem to have studied carefully the beliefs, the desires, the needs, and the characteristics of the population of people who would need and use those services.

The issue of home births and alternative births revolves around two questions I am going to treat: (1) to what extent is a given alternative safe or not safe, and (2) to what extent does an individual or family have the right to choose their own health-care? Both of these questions require answers framed in terms of ethics. They are social questions, and studies attempting to answer them are soft and never definitive.

SAFETY

The conflict between art and nature, between women's bodies and men's tools in childbearing today, is oversimplified by contrasting home birth to electronic fetal monitoring. In my experience in home, maternity center, and hospital birth as a mother, lay midwife, and certified nurse midwife I have found that delivery is neither as safe as the lay literature would say, nor as hazardous and full of peril as the medical world has claimed.

Let me tell you about my home birth service. In March, 1977, with the support and encouragement of an obstetrician from New London, Dr. W. J. Morse, Jr., I began seeing my own clients choosing home delivery in an office at his practice. He was available for consultation and always for referral into the hospital when I felt that was necessary. My population had the normal spread of the age of the childbearing population. Almost all were married and white. Of the last hundred registrants, 35 ended up in the hospital—which I found appalling and most discouraging. There is nothing worse than taking care of someone through her pregnancy, wanting her to have the baby at home nearly as badly as she does, and then having to go to the hospital and be an advocate—yet be polite enough not to get yourself thrown out the next time you might have to take a woman in. It is very painful to watch your patients be abused and even punished for trying to maintain control over their own bodies.

Besides the 35 that ended up in the hospital, eight had spontaneous abortions. I had four sets of twins: one set should occur only once in 88 births. I wonder how *they* found *me*.

The indications for transfer to a hospital were prematurity, heavy meconium staining of the fluid, failure to progress in labor, premature rupture of the membranes; elevated blood pressure, and one IUGR (intrauterine growth retardation) with an elevated blood pressure at 37 weeks.

Two of my mothers whom I took to the hospital had severe variable decelerations—sudden drops when the umbilical cord is blocked. I listened, and they both got worse with pushing, so we went to the hospital nearby. When we got there, the pediatrician who had to leave his busy practice a half-hour from the hospital, much to his displeasure—said, "What do you mean? You don't have a monitor at home, do you?" And I said, "No. I don't have a monitor at home." And he said, "What are you talking about?" When I plugged in the monitor, there were cord patterns. In one case the cord was around the neck three times, tightly, and the baby required considerable effort at resuscitation. The other had a frank knot in the cord and was fine at birth. So it's perfectly possible—with some wits and a lot of paranoia— to make that sort of a diagnosis at home with your own ears. In the large geographic area that I was trying to cover, my mothers really needed a network of support. The backup hospital was often an hour away.

At home if we ran into the kind of trouble where fast emergency attention was needed we might have had to go to the nearest hospital rather than to my backup hospital. Although that did not happen, I always dreaded the possibility of having to take one of my mothers to a probably hostile hospital and trust an unknown obstetrician to help out. So I was on call for my ladies 24 hours a day, seven days a week, driving 30,000 miles a year and barely paying the the gas, supplies, and phone. I did not close my service because home birth is not safe; I closed it because it was too hard to do.

Yes, I miss it. When everything was ok at home, the experience for mother, baby, father, and midwives was a peak human event. It is the best. But of the millions of births in the US annually last year there were only 43,000 out-of-hospital births.

Perinatal outcome figures are affected by many factors. The familiar ones well studied are: number of pregnancies, number of deliveries, weight before pregnancy, preexisting medical condition, age, how much prenatal care at what time in pregnancy, economic and social status, ethnicity, geographical location, marital status, heterogeneity of population, birth weight, Apgar score, nutritional history and status, contraceptive history, intrapartal care, post-partum care, and infant care. And then there are some other factors that are just beginning to be studied: who gives the care, what is the place of birth. One that really intrigues me is the congruence in attitude of the receiver of care and the giver of care. Rosengren found that when women thought they were sick and acted sick, and the doctor agreed that they were sick and treated them like they were sick, everything was okay. And when the women thought that they were well, and the doctor agreed that they were well, they were also okay. But when they disagreed in either direction, labor took up to twice as long.[2]

In the mid 60s, in Madeira County, California, a study of midwifery was done on a farmworker population.[3] Prior to the study the prematurity rate was 9.6%, and the infant mortality rate was 32 per thousand live births. A crew of nurse-midwives was introduced and given privileges for the duration of the study. They provided prenatal care, nutritional counseling, and health teaching. And in one year, the prematurity rate dropped to 6.6%, and the neonatal mortality rate to 10 per thousand. The project was discontinued because the California Medical Society would not continue to license midwives. Prematurity and neonatal mortality rose to the prestudy levels within one year.

Iain Chalmers[4] compared outcomes and interventions practiced in Cardiff, Wales, in 1965—before near-universal hospital delivery—and in 1973—after hospital birth became the norm. He found more toxemia in 1973 than there had been in 1965; Apgar scores were lower;

and there was no change in perinatal mortality rates or in causes of death. Before hospital care, the district midwifery service had a community midwife on call. She did home visits and prenatal care; she was the one who came for the labor and delivery. With the change to hospital confinement the mother saw a number of people in another setting. The investigator, by the way, had expected an improvement when everyone went to the hospital. I love studies when they are like that. In a large British study,[5] plain low-risk home births had the lowest perinatal mortality; the home birth group transferred to the hospital were highest. Planned hospital deliveries showed moderate mortality, which was significantly greater than the low-risk home births.

Recently, Dr. Warren Pearse[6] of ACOG said that home births are "maternal trauma and child abuse." The current president, Dr. Martin Stowe[7] has agreed. Pearse relied on state health department data on out-of-hospital births that showed more than a sevenfold increase in mortality in some states.[8] That category includes 28-week accidents, precipitous deliveries in cars and in the bathroom, and even car accidents. Some states use newborn, some use perinatal, and some use infant mortality rates, but ACOG just took the raw incidence data for home and out-of-hospital births, and compared them to the whole state. When ACOG claims six to seven times worse outcome for home births and calls the whole thing a fad, they confuse *accidental* out-of-hospital and *planned* home births. They also treated transfers to hospitals as failures. But it is really a screening process.

CHOICE

Such misrepresentation affects social policy. Social policy affects the situation of birth. Attitudes of birthing mothers and of caregivers influence the course of labor. The course of labor affects the management of the labor, and both affect the outcome. Current obstetrical practice and policy do not in most institutions reflect women's needs in childbirth. Little research attention has been paid to the needs of the women; much work has been done to attend to the needs of the hospital. Two studies—one by a graduate student in midwifery at Yale, Jane Pittenger, and one by a sociologist, childbirth educator and long-time friend to mothers, Lester Hazell—discuss attitudes of birthing parents.

Pittenger[9] compared the attitudes of women who chose to have their babies at home, using my patients as the home birth group, with a matched group of mothers selecting the birth room at Yale New Haven Hospital. At home there was less fear for physical safety and more acceptance of death. That is, the home birth people told the investigator what things they thought they might die of if they were going to die of something. All the home birth people, but only 50% of the hospital people, mentioned God. The birth-room people did not want to talk about death. One of the questions posed to the parents was, "Who is responsible?" The home birth people said, "We are responsible." The birth-room people did not understand the question. With a more direct question the hospital people said, "The hospital's safe," or "Nothing's going to happen," or "I trust my doctor." Almost all of the home and most of the hospital patients resented routine hospital practice. Half of both groups would have liked the father to deliver the baby. All of the home birth mothers breast fed, while 60% of the hospital mothers did so.

Lester Hazell[10] carefully documented why people choose to have their babies at home: a relaxed personal atmosphere; the presence of people of the mother's choice; avoidance of unsupportive staff and others; female attendants; avoidance of routine procedures; choice of position; labor and delivery in the same room and bed; no separation of family or baby and mother; breast-feeding immediately and whenever desired; freedom to eat and drink and walk in labor; decreased infection; participation of the father; and, overall, family control.

The most significant problem in trying to adapt the hospital to families, is that whatever flexibility you build into your system, it still looks and feels as though you are giving people permission to do "crazy things." Changes are deviant to the institution. Neither the hospital nor the caregivers have any real *right* to tell sane healthy adults what they *may* do.

Since closing my home birth practice I have joined a private practice of two ob/gyns and three nurse-midwives. We tend 40 deliveries a month. I have been astonished at how very nice the hospital can be. Although I do not think I will ever feel that it is the most comfortable place for the human event of birth, I am discovering with joy that the system that exists—the one that all but the 43,000 out-of-hospital people experience—can be what the women want and need. We as a practice agree to implement the families' wishes for labor and delivery. We can prevent, most of the time, the small and large insults a mother might receive from the institution. We do not do anything routine. The hospital at this point has only two absolute policies that we cannot help the families get around. Children may not attend delivery (though they can be there for labor and return immediately after delivery, and they can hold and dress the baby or whatever the family or child wants). The second policy is that the father may not deliver the baby.

I was not able to take care of more than seven deliveries a month in my home birth practice because of distance and time; now I can participate in all 40 that our group practice averages. I think I am better used. I am proud of our practice. We provide a good, satisfying service and are very successful in the ways that other obstetricians and the hospital notice. This too produces change. In New Haven more practices are hiring nurse-midwives and more deliveries are occurring out of the delivery room. The hospital provides a place for the others to see that we don't have problems because we do not monitor a mother or because she goes home after delivery, and so on.

Another agent for change over the past few years in New Haven has been the Consumers for Choices in Childbirth (CCC). They formed just to protect the nurse-midwives three years ago. The private midwifery service at Yale Medical School was pulling more patients than any other private service in the medical school, and so the medical school tried to close the midwifery practice. The consumer group forced them to back off. Recently, through the Connecticut Health and Hospital Commission, the CCC delayed a certificate of need for a 60-million dollar addition to the hospital and medical school until Yale-New Haven Hospital agreed to meet with the consumers and to put them on the planning committee for the development of the maternity service.

Some doctors think the best health care is given when everything known to medicine is applied to every individual by the highest trained medical scientist in the most specialized institution. The actions of specialists are evaluated and continue to be supported because of the number of such actions, not because the problem is solved. But in my opinion, in the direct one-to-one provision of care, the best program is no program. The best health-care for a pregnant woman simply allows the discovery of her particular physical and emotional needs, and ensures a dignified, self-directed resolution to those desires, wishes, and needs.[11]

A Native American Response

Katsi Cook

THE CIRCLE

I came here to try to be helpful, because whenever we have a women's council or women getting together to talk about anything, there's a whole lot of power in that. I want to set before you a whole concept that exists in our world, as Native American women. I know that for you women to see a Native American woman is rare—it's not common in your everyday experience. I want to ask you to bear with me through this time; I'm not used to making up notes or reading from papers, so what I say, I know it here in my heart.

I've noticed your science: you've got a method where each one of you may specialize in a certain specific aspect of a particular system. Each reaches an end point, and each reaches a truth—a scientific truth. This method is known in our prophecies. Thousands of years ago our people knew that at some time there was going to come a people who would think that way, who would look for truth that way. We knew your people would be so blind about how to get back to the center that our very survival would be at stake. Because we're women, because we're mothers that's what we've got to talk about here: survival.

Native American people are a different kind of scientist. We're the kinds of scientists who work in a circle; we don't have linear ways. So before I can speak to you about childbirth, I need to give you a sense of that circle, the woman within it, what control is, what all those concepts are.

I come among you as a representative of Women of All Red Nations. I'm not here as an individual. I have behind me my grandmothers, my aunts, my sisters, my children, and even the little ones who haven't been born yet. As mothers, as the women native to this land, we greet you. As mothers and women, we bring a message to you that goes beyond the ethical questions and the individual details of human reproduction that are raised here. We bring these words to you here, because we're looking for ways that we can put our minds together to see what kind of life we're going to make for our children. Not only our children, but our grandchildren's grandchildren, whose faces are yet coming out of the ground.

People like to talk about traditional Indian culture as if it's a romantic museum curiosity. The reality is that Native Nations still carry in our memories the duties we have been charged with as human beings, by the Creator and the Creation. Our government, our medicines, our ceremonies, our art, our cosmology, our way of life continue to function on this land. We carry a commitment of truth to the natural world.

These are concepts that come out of Western civilization that have been functioning within the framework of this conference. Technology, control, policy making, feminism, male domination... those are some of the words that I've been hearing that I shall address within a framework of the reality of our traditional world. It's our primary message to you women that you must look through your societal microscopes and focus on the Native American experience. And, in doing so, observe the process of your own oppression and destruction. Native People are the miner's canary. When you see us dying, you know that your own people are the next to go.

This conference is filled with factual information of how women are oppressed. My impression is that feminism blames much of that oppression on the men. Looking at the history of and the very nature of Western civilization, it's understandable why. But our observations are that oppression in the American way knows no sex, no class, no race, no religion, whatever. Where I come from, our communities are really suffering. We're the microcosm, in Indian communities, of everything that's bad in the American way of life. That's why, when we come to you, it's really hard for us to talk—because it's your very way of life that's oppressive. Every one of us here participates in it. We're all oppressed. We are all oppressors.

It's our hope that women throughout the earth will continue to strengthen and take on the duty and privilege of being a woman. In our traditional way of life, women don't isolate themselves from the man, the child, the natural world. The woman is the base of the culture. She carries the language, the home, and the children. She provides the political, spiritual, and social direction for her people. It's the women who decide when there will be war, for we're the ones who suffer in the community when the men don't return. A nation isn't conquered until the hearts of its women are on the ground.

It's a pitiful community where there are few men, and those men must be strong. In our society, it's a difficult task to be a leader. Leadership takes on a different quality. A leader is the one who is put in by the women, because we are the mothers, and we've watched our sons grow into men. We see which of them are kind, which of them eats last, and which of them pities the people. When a leader is put into the leadership position, he isn't installed to freely express his will and his opinion and his attitudes. He's there as a spokesman for the will of the clan, for the will of the people.

Women are the base of the generations. Our reproductive power is sacred to us, and it is that spiritual power that connects us to the earth and to the moon—whom we refer to as our mother and our grandmother. It's not a romantic notion. It's scientific. It's as simple as this: we have a natural world and an unnatural world. We have a definition of a woman within the Creation, and of a woman within this Creation that the white man brought here. The effects of the damages and devastation that Western technology has brought to native nations throughout the world are reflected in the women, because we are the people.

Something feminists need to understand is the relationship between the suffering of our Mother Earth and the suffering of women. It shows just how real our connection is, as women, to the Mother Earth. She's being raped for her natural resources—coal, uranium, gold, silver—so that less than 15% of the human beings on this earth can live a standard of life that's based on extractive technology. We're living in the wealthiest society ever assembled in the history of the world. We are beneficiaries of that, at least materially, as much as we might try to deny it.

We have been taught—or rather, our minds have been colonized—to fit into a system that bases itself on extractive technology. This system pulls resources, materials, and labor from many different parts of the world, processes them for us, and brings them to our tables and our clothes racks. It allows us to be fed and housed in ways that we have no way of understanding. This means that we have been taught to be on the recipient end of the system, which at the other end—the extractive end—really exploits people and destroys the natural world. This is a reality—something everyone needs to understand. It's very confusing, and it's meant to be confusing. Confusion and misinformation are tools of oppression.

Colonization of Indian lands—the process that is destroying our nations—has already wiped out whole nations of people. The process that broke the circle of the nations continues to take its toll on our lives—all of us here, not just Indian people. First the nations were fragmented, then the families, and nowadays we come up against the fragmentation of the very individual. We see that reflected in mental diseases that have never been heard of before. People with different personalities, people with images in their minds that they know not how to control. From the very moment we're born to the day we die we're barraged with images, with conflicting arguments, with thousands of choices. Whole ways of being are laid before us, yet we have no way of judging whether they're good or bad.

In this conference, we're trying to make a judgment about what is good and what is bad, what is useful and what is not. The technology we've been talking about so far, I feel, is inappropriate technology to a people who still participate in a sovereign community. It was stated that technology can make our lives freer and richer—free us from backbreaking toil. At a particular level of human technology, I couldn't agree more. But, it's not true that *all* lives are freer and richer. We don't *see* the backbreaking toil. Other people are exploited to make us more free, and those people are the Native People, the people of South Africa, the people in South America, the people in Mexico, the people we don't see everyday. We just see each other: privileged people.

I appreciate Western medicine for its surgical technique and germ theory. But it creates new pathology in place of what it hopes to eradicate. When you look at the history of medicine, you can't deny that fact. So you can wipe out polio and you can wipe out syphilis, but new kinds of diseases have taken their place: cancer, leukemia. And none of your technology is going to find the answer to that, because you're not looking at your world in a whole way. You can't come and just talk about ethics and human reproduction.

I want to talk to you about uranium, because *the* technology right now that most threatens our survival is this nuclear power cycle. Uranium is crucial to the nuclear fuel cycle. Uranium is the raw material that is processed to produce the energy for nuclear power plants. Over two-thirds of the uranium reserves in this country are on Indian land. Indian land supplied 100% of the uranium produced in the United States in 1974. The total uranium reserves on Native American land rank sixth in the world. We are the source of the nuclear fuel cycle, but not by our choice. That's another word that's come up here often: choice.

Less than three hundred miles away from Three Mile Island, here we sit talking about reproduction and women's health, and no one except Ina May Gaskin—because that's real in her community—has brought up the health effects of low-level radiation on women and children. You may know the history of the oppression of women in your history, but do you know the history of the oppression of your children?

When you produce something that you think is going to solve all problems in one way, you don't take the rest of the circle into consideration. I don't care how scientific you've been, how much research you've done, how many control groups you've had. We're scientists, too, and we know that you're going to ruin something on the other end of it. Maybe when they started using DES they thought they would do a good thing for women and help save them from having miscarriages. But now the effects of DES can never really be taken into consideration until all those DES sons and daughters are buried, and they're in the earth again. Who's going to study their lives for the rest of this time? I know that scientists will look at us and say, "Well, there's nothing in the traditional worlds of Native People that's appropriate for the 1980s." That's complete racism.

Even your agriculture has its drawbacks—European agriculture and technology, as it was transplanted to America and then to the world. European agriculture is distinguished by the process of clearing the land and turning the soil, and then setting forth to accomplish the biological simplification of the land until only one life form remains on the fields. It's the European farmer's objective that only one thing is left standing in a field of cabbages, and that's the cabbages. That process has led to a lot of problems for the farmer. Plowing the land and planting it to one crop will rapidly decrease the fertility of the soil, requiring that the land be refertilized with animal dung. A whole other set of processes arises. And in turn, you have plants that contain smaller quantities of nutrients for the people who eat them than do plants raised in naturally fertile soil. Because you're women, I think you would be interested to know about the Hodenosaunee, the Iroquois people. We had in our society a community of men and a community of women, and it was the duty of the women to care for the agriculture. It was our part of our tradition that we had to do this job. With the new kind of agriculture, that part got disrupted because it took so much more backbreaking toil to farm the European way than it did our own traditional way. We didn't even need to plow.

I want to tell you a little bit about our information from our own science—our prophecies. (Three of the main powers on this land right now are: the Hodenosaunee—the Iroquois people: these are the Six Nations just next door to you in New York State; the Hopi people, together with the Navajo; and the Lakota, whom you know as Sioux.) We've all got common prophecies. When they dropped that bomb on Hiroshima, the Hopi people in their sacred meeting areas, the kivas, said, "We've carried this series of songs and stories and ceremonies for years, from the elders, and we didn't know what it was meant for. But since this thing in Hiroshima, we think the time has come to tell people about it. To tell the world about it." It takes days to talk about these prophecies. They said: "It's very explicit. We knew that there would be houses in the sky. We knew that a time would come when the white man would try to go to the moon, and that it would interfere with our women's ability to bear children."

A scientist would look at that and say, "Oh, how superstitious. Isn't that cute?" But it's true, because the process that provides the ability for that human being to get to the moon requires a ripoff. And the earth, she's a woman, too. She's being ripped off. And so, if we're women, we've got to worry about her. Let's stop being selfish. I see so many bullshit struggles that have nothing to do with our survival as human beings on this planet.

That's what we're talking about. We're talking abour survival. And all these midwives here—they're scientists in their communities, and that's what childbirth has to come out of. That's why I'm telling you all this about the circle. Because even though Helen Swallow has a good practice where she is—and I'd have my baby with her any day— the fact is that she's not buttressed by the whole community, and that she does not have a say about how the food is.

Our purpose as women should be to give direction to the kind of food our children eat, to the way they're educated, to the way their health-care is taken care of. Those are the processes of sovereignty. Keep that word in your mind, because individuals have to learn how to be sovereign. And that's our way—the way of the Native People right now. We're trying to get self-sufficient communities going and to use that sovereignty.

We have midwives, too. But we don't listen to the state. They have no control over us, because of our sovereignty. We want to control our food, our reproduction, the reproduction of the four-leggeds. Who is thinking about them? Who has even talked about them here? These plants outside—they are our medicine. And who's thinking about them?

Even in our Longhouse, when the chiefs have to make a decision, even now they make decisions about the Six Nations and how we're going to go about on this earth among human beings. They say, "How is this decision going to affect our children seven generations from now?" I never read that in your *Congressional Record.*

I don't believe that this society loves its children. I don't believe it. Because how could you love your children and still put up with nuclear power plants? Do you know what that does to our children? The ones who aren't even born yet? And here we are, just sitting here.

You want to have your power as a woman back? It's yours. Right there. But it's a hard struggle. It's hard. Our women know that. Our men are sitting in prison. We're seeing our kids die. And all of this has come to the Native People. It's horrible, and I really wish you women would start working on something *real.*

MIDWIFERY

I'm probably dealing with some of the highest risk women in the population of the country, because there's a lot of alcoholism, diabetes, poor nutritional status, and everything. But in the kind of midwifery we're practicing, we aim towards the restructuring of traditional communities to that sovereign, self-sufficient model we're talking about. That's the only way we see it working effectively. I think Ina May's practice is probably the ultimate model for that—her community is a sovereign nation. They have control over those life processes. We may not agree with some of their local customs, just the same as if a doctor came to me, he might not agree with mine.

We use our Indian medicines in birth. We use them all through the prenatal care. In our prenatal and our birth work, we believe in spiritual midwifery, too, not the same kind of spirituality that Ina May talks about, but spiritual in the Indian way. Some of the other midwives (my mother-in-law in South Dakota, who's a member of the Native American Church) use peyote in their practice. Peyote, among the Lakota people, or at least a population of them, is a strong medicine, and it's used in a lot of different healing. It puts a woman in a mind that's just right for birth.

We don't use any kind of intervention. Sometimes I won't even do a vaginal, becuse if you're close enough to that woman, you know by the way she's acting how dilated she is. You can see that if you're close to her. Sometimes you'll do it because she wants to know where the baby is, how much she's got to go.

We've got a good backup system worked out in Minneapolis and St. Paul. But we work on that woman's mind with the prenatal care, and talk to her about what being a woman means. We don't do anything for pain in labor. There are different herbal medicines that women use to try to alleviate pain, but we tell them: there are so many ways that, as women, we suffer—and some of those are real. That's part of the process of being a woman. I'm not saying that it's good that women suffer. I'm saying that that's a reality within birth. I'm not trying to lie to that woman. If you want to call your contraction a pain, then you've got to have an attitude about that. You've got to work with them, because on the other side of that pain is some knowledge that's going to help you. We know that, because in our fasts and in our vision quests, we suffer a lot of ways in our ceremonies, in our ceremonial life. And birth is a ceremony. I know that myself. I delivered at home. I come from a long line of women who have never even been on the inside of a hospital.

My grandmother delivered me and about half the kids on our

reservation, and I always knew I was going to have my babies at home. Midwifery is a job that I had to do. It wasn't even my own choice. It is just something I've got to do. There are many different areas to being a midwife that go beyond just catching a baby. You have to be a lot of different things. We use our own ceremony if a woman's having a problem, if her baby is a breech. We pray for them. We know how to pray. We still have a way. It's nothing like the Christians. But we have a real kinship to the Spirits on this land. We've got thousands of years of information about what life is here, on this great Turtle Island that you know as your United States.

The medicines that are here outside, we know about them. Those medicines are gifts of the Creation. They're gifts of the Mother Earth. We make use of that, and that's what our midwifery involves. You know, I know how to use a Doppler; I know how to read deceleration variables. I know that. But in my own practice, the most important aspect of birth—about 75% of it—is just your hands, and your heart, and knowing how to use that spirit.

I know that in Western science, you don't have much access to that. That's why you'd better really appreciate the midwives here. Because a birth is a ceremony. It's the biggest ceremony you people have. I don't see very many others in your lives that make much sense.

An Obstetrician's Perspective

Mary Jane Gray

That labor and delivery constitute a period of high risk for women is confirmed in every graveyard of Colonial America. Traditionally, the obstetrician was concerned with preserving the life and health of the mother. As pregnancy became safer, concern shifted to the intrauterine patient and to ways of lowering perinatal death rates and insuring that the babies who survived were normal.

We have often heard the complaint that women feel deserted in the impersonal hospital setting because attention has focused on the fetus as a patient. Each presentation of the childbirth session has shown us a different pattern for supporting the woman in labor. As an obstetrician old enough to have delivered women at home and one who has worked outside a hospital in the Kentucky Mountains, I share with you the fact that the more experience I had with obstetrical hemorrhage and other crises, the closer I wanted laboring women and newborn babies to the life support systems of modern hospitals.

The data that Ina May Gaskin has presented are very impressive. There are several things that you must remember as you interpret these data. In our society, the health of the newborn relates more to general health and nutrition, age at child bearing, diet and the use of drugs, alcohol and tobacco than to any particular facet of medical care. Thus, in an intentional community of dedicated people, eating farm-grown produce, Gaskin is starting with a very low risk group. Second, fear is known to stimulate the release of epinephrine. This compound inhibits uterine contractions so that the loving reassurance that she and the other groups practice is good obstetrics. Finally, when she tells us that she has eight midwives, two physicians, a "crew" of nurses, incubators, oxygen, and 24-hour emergency service with two ambulances and a two-way radio, she is obviously not talking about "simple home deliveries."

The issue is not in-hospital versus out-of-hospital deliveries, but how we can best support the woman in labor and her infant both emotionally and medically. A difficult issue for those doing home deliveries is how to allocate responsibility and backup so that in time of trouble help is available. Furthermore, if home delivery returns for the higher risk poor in addition to the middle class women who are involved at present, how can we insure that the poor are not once more exploited by those who are incompetent?

The most important problem facing obstetrics today is that of how to give the safest care modern technology can devise in a loving and personal way in order to reach the goal of us all—a healthy happy mother with a normal infant.

Response

Norma Swenson

We have tried to present both the rationale and the means by which the experience of childbirth as we now understand it might be transformed so as to strengthen the individual woman's sense of autonomy, mastery, and fulfillment, while simultaneously restoring her sense of community and connection with other women.

Ethics without politics or political analysis is inadequate, if not unethical. All of us want to affect policy about childbirth, but we cannot do this without a more accurate knowledge about how policy is made; nor can we do it without full access to knowledge about our bodies or full knowledge of medical technology. We need to return to the concept of medicine as an institution of social control in more detail.

Medicine as an institution in the West mediates a woman's experience of her body to a degree not experienced by males or by women in other parts of the world. Normal female bodily function appears to require frequent medical intervention, almost by definition. In the case of childbirth, the control by allopathic medicine is a virtual monopoly on indispensable resources. Childbirth is the eye of the needle, through which all of society passes under medicine's direction. Despite the recent upsurge in out-of-hospital births, hospitalized birth is still estimated at 98.5% of all US birth. In many states physicians must sign birth certificates, and attendance at birth is defined as the practice of medicine. To test the social control hypothesis, we need to look at what happenens when women or birth attendants do deviate from the prescribed norms established by medicine.

In Santa Cruz, California, several years ago, when physicians failed to cooperate with women who requested natural childbirth, the women refused to come to the hospital for birth. The physicians, in turn, refused to give women prenatal care. The women then created their own prenatal care and delivery system; the physicians then called out the law to entrap and arrest the lay midwives. Although the ensuing legal process was ultimately inconclusive, the power of medicine to enlist the law, to charge the midwives with practicing medicine without a license, and ultimately to destroy the midwifery service, was clear. Last year another lay midwife in California, Marianne Doshi, delivered a baby who subsequently died in hospital. Though Marianne was ultimately acquitted, she was tried in court, not simply for malpractice or manslaughter, or practicing medicine without a license, but for murder. That trial also served to end her career.

The same year, the state of Illinois, through the Consumer Protection Division, charged the Association for Childbirth at Home International (ACHI) with consumer fraud, at the instigation of prominent national obstetricians in Chicago, simply for giving out information on emergency childbirth at home. Again the law was invoked by mobilizing the Organized Crime Division of the Los Angeles Police Department to harass women at the California office of ACHI, which was in their homes, demanding records and information. The women have refused to answer the 72 inquiries in the subpoena. But whether such a violation of the right of free speech could have withstood a detailed legal test is not the point. The point is that the energies and the meager financial resources of these women are used in fighting their harassment. The effect of such harassment is obviously to punish and deter.

Earlier in this conference we heard about three women in different parts of the country who were taken from their homes forcibly by local police, while in labor, and made to give birth in hospitals against their wills. This action was also at the instigation of physicians, who charged that the parents were committing child abuse. The violation of civil liberties in these actions is also clear, but that did not prevent this from happening. The intent of the harassment is what requires examination, as does the deliberate dissemination of misleading propaganda to the public by the American College of Obstetricians and Gynecologists (ACOG), as described by Helen Swallow.

"Child abuse" and "maternal trauma" are terms that have been used by both the Executive Director and the current President of the ACOG to describe out-of-hospital birth. The monopoly over information is also becoming more complete. In Philadelphia recently, a community-based class was labeled inadequate by a hospital that wished to require its own childbirth classes, a trend that promises to continue. There are further, more subtle instances where physicians have been denied hospital admitting privileges for supporting out-of-hospital births, and nurse-midwives have lost their jobs for giving prenatal care to couples planning home births, or for assisting physicians at home births. In several states, new and restrictive legislation has been introduced against lay midwives. Thus far lay midwives have received the brunt of discrimination and harassment, by being denied training, licensing, or medical backup, but even within the fraternity of physicans there have been several refusals by obstetrical staffs to permit family practice physicians to deliver babies in their hopsitals; sometimes obstetricians have denied colleagues referrals, and even caused them to be censured for participation in out-of-hospital births.

At a different level, insurance companies and physicians recently have been collaborating in denying reimbursement for nurse-midwifery services unless the physician is physically present in the same room, a crippling waste of resources and an insult to all nurse-midwives. As we go to press, there are fresh illustrations.

One conclusion that could be reached on examining these incidents and many others concerned with practices within hospitals is that the infant belongs primarily to the state, not to the parents. The power of the state has been delegated to physicians, or to medicine, to the point where not only in the case of alternatives, but in the ongoing creation of policy, expert opinion is frequently the only source consulted by government, fused, in effect, with public policy. The voices of professional and corporate interests are heard, but women's and families' are not.[1] We have also been shown repeatedly that this professional behavior is not seen as a conflict of interest by our government. Also, reform in medicine usually is voluntary; we have few mechanisms to require it even when abuses are flagrant.

Although these medico-political actions do represent responses to a clear economic threat as well, it is important to recognize the attitude and the tone of those who harass parents and midwives. Their source of righteous entitlement could only come from the sure knowledge that they have been ceded the power to direct the elimination of these challenges to their hegemony. This hegemony extends to the health planning process as well. In most states, physicians and provider interests dominate the process, actively working to eliminate all maternity care options except those within established hospitals, under licensed physicians. In some instances they have shut off reimbursement to families who refused to attend the "designated" facility for their care.

What this struggle also represents is an illustration of how slender our legal hold on alternatives is. In many ways we take our presumed legal rights for granted and do not fully engage in the struggle when they are threatened. In other ways, we are romantic about the law, feeling that unless we have an express legal right to particular services or the right to perform certain services, we are helpless. What is needed is some of the same sure sense of entitlement on the part of parents and birth attendants that is being expressed by the physicians and professionals. What is needed is a better understanding of the ethics of civil disobedience.

Women have always attended other women at birth, in abortion and contraceptive practices, and they always will. When women want and need services that institutions cannot or will not provide, other women will create them. Most of the political action toward alternative maternity care so far has been taken by those women whose calling and work is the direct care of mothers and babies. To fight the harassments and to be active advocates for mothers, families, and these alternative services is also a calling and a specialized kind of work. What is needed is a stronger commitment to this growing division of labor. If we are not prepared to take direct political action ourselves, it is critical that we support those who do. If we are not prepared to be the caregivers, we must support those who are. The childbearing population is much too small—the smallest ever in the history of this country—and the scale of the resources of professionals much too large—the largest in history—to make this a fair contest. But let us make no mistake that it is a contest. Without a commitment by those who want to oppose monopoly and preserve the right to alternatives as a part of our system of health care, and not just opposition by those who need the services at the time, the monopoly will continue. Without open, public, and legal demands for a cessation of harassment, it, too, will continue. For my part, I am always amazed, and very heartened, that women, and men, continue to come forward out of each generation to fight for those rights despite the stiffening opposition. I salute them all.

Policymaking and Projections

Organized by
Helen B. Holmes

Policymaking and Projections Overview

Helen B. Holmes

It is helpful to look at ways in which some women have made and changed policy, in order that women everywhere become better able to plan their own methods of influencing and revamping policy. The three approaches here described are those used by an administrator in a state department of health, by a consumer special interest group, and by a member of an advisory board. (Other suggestions, organized by Margaret Kohn, comprise the Appendix.)

First, Joyce Lashof describes the interplay of six forces that influence policy development through her story of the creation of abortion legislation in Illinois in the 1970s. Her account implies that we women who believe that any woman should be permitted to choose when and whether she shall assume the responsibility of motherhood have two distinct groups working at counter purposes to our stance: those who oppose abortion categorically and those who hope to make a quick buck from abortions. (Each of these groups, of course, is also opposed to the other.) The Illinois State Department of Public Health persuaded the Illinois legislature to implement the Supreme Court abortion decision, with the full support of the local press, on the basis of regulating abortion for safety. Naturally, neither group of potential opponents could publicly oppose *safety*. This legislative success raises in my mind a disturbing question: is the best way for us to achieve our goals to attempt to couch our interests in terms acceptable to males in authority?

Dedicated, concerned women are needed on many fronts. In response Ilene Wolcott notes that each of Lashof's six forces is in itself diverse—in opinion, in values, in objectives. She urges us to influence each of these from women's perspectives.

Then, Beth Shearer relates the intriguing story of C/SEC, an interpersonal special interest group that has had local and national impact on policy surrounding cesarean births. As in the case of RESOLVE, later to be described by Barbara Menning, concerned

267

consumers have banded together to effect change. If we wish to make changes within the system, Shearer has advice for us as women with essentially no power at present. We should join together not only for group force, but also for the psychological power that comes from believing in our cause and from assuming responsibility. We should have very specific goals in mind and be willing to begin with small steps in a few institutions. Also, it is important to try to get the support of at least one "insider" politically acceptable to the institution. Finally, persistence is essential. The chance to change one's anger, hurt, and frustration into constructive action to benefit others may well provide the necessary persistence.

Finally, Karen Lebacqz describes her work as the designated ethicist on advisory boards. She points out several ways in which a feminist Christian ethics already differs from a traditional male-structured ethics, suggesting that "'the good life' consists not in the future ideal state in which we will be in control of everything, but in the very struggle that we are going through . . . to fight for liberation and justice for oppressed peoples."

Forces Impacting on the Policymaker

Joyce Lashof

As someone who forms policy, I have been asked to share with you some of my observations on the multiple forces impacting upon and influencing the decisions of a policymaker. Today I will review some overall forces and then illustrate the decision-making process by describing a specific case, namely the enactment and implementation of abortion legislation in Illinois.

Let me start by identifying the six principal forces I see as the major factors affecting policy formation: personal ideology, legislation, interest groups, courts, the press, and the budget.

First and foremost, the policymaker's own ideological orientation and commitment, and that of the administration for which she works, is or should be the primary determining factor in any decision. It is important to keep one's own ideology in mind when interacting within and without any administration. In the health field today there are a number of key issues that must be thought through: the role of regulation, government responsibility versus individual responsibility, consumer involvement in decision-making, and governmental accountability. It is not my purpose to elaborate on these, but rather to point out that one's position on these and other issues will impact on the decision the policymaker reaches. Knowing when one's ideological position meshes with the administration and when not is essential if one is to work effectively toward one's goals.

The second force is legislation. The policymaker must clearly identify what legislative support exists for her position, how that support can be obtained, what compromises will be needed, and what the political cost will be in relation to the goal being sought. Therefore, it is essential to understand the legislative process and the forces impacting that process. Legislative decisions may be made on the basis of the issue itself, but they are also made on the basis of other related and nonrelated factors. It is not always easy to determine when decisions are the result of political tradeoffs and when they are based primarily on principle. Deciding when and when not to accept half a loaf, or no loaf at all, is probably one of the most difficult decisions for a policymaker.

Third is the role of interest groups, especially the "special" or "vested" interest groups and the public interest groups. The special or vested interest groups have an economic interest in the outcome of specific governmental actions. Hospitals, health professionals such as nurses and doctors, and the pharmaceutical and medical devices industry are representative of special or vested interest groups.

Public interest groups, in contrast, are not motivated primarily by specific economic incentives, but rather by a public concern. Like the special interest groups, they can define their missions either broadly or narrowly. Examples of broadly concerned groups are the Consumer Federation, the League of Women Voters, Common Cause, and such environmental groups as the Environmental Defense Fund. Some public interest groups may have more narrowly defined concerns and have elements of specific economic interest. Examples of these are the Hemophiliac Foundation and the Kidney Foundation. Not fitting clearly into either of these categories are groups that look at issues broadly, but with some element of self-interest, such as the women's groups and civil rights organizations. The impact of the well organized Right to Life Group on recent Congressional elections is testimony in itself to the power of interest groups and, indeed, it influences the position now being taken by members of Congress and other elected officials facing re-election in 1980.

Fourthly, the role of the courts is growing in importance all the time; yet it tends to be overlooked. The courts are an important resource for the individual fighting for her rights, but are equally important, if not more accessible, to industry in fighting government intrusion and protecting its property rights.

Fifth, the power of the press, especially investigative reporting, is well known in this country. On the other hand, investigative reporting is not necessarily completely responsible, unbiased, and balanced. One of the difficulties with the emphasis on investigative reporting is that certain problems of government, such as scandals, inaction, and lack of responsiveness are always highlighted; others rarely mentioned are the successful accomplishments of an agency. I stress this because, frankly, the focus on "incompetence," scandal, and corruption has a demoralizing effect on many government servants. In fact, it is popular now to refer to government employees not as civil servants, a term that once connoted a kind of respect, especially in England, but rather as bureaucrats. The term bureaucrat has come to have a demeaning and derogatory connotation that politicians themselves have popularized. This adverse environment is beginning to influence the number of people willing to accept governmental positions. So the press can be a powerful ally, but also a powerful adversary.

The sixth, and possibly the most critical, major impact on the policymaker is the budget. Governors, Secretaries, agency heads, all come to their offices committed to certain goals. They soon find themselves constrained more by the budget process than by any other single factor, primarily because the major part of the budget is devoted to the so-called uncontrollable items. The policymaker soon learns that she has much less flexibility and much less ability to re-order priorities and to reallocate resources than she thought. For instance, in 1978, the federal health budget was 52 billion, $45 billion or 87% of which was devoted to Medicare and Medicaid. These programs provide for reimbursement for services rendered, over which one has little control. Thus, the amount of funds that might be available that can be restructured or reallocated is quite small—less than 13% of the budget in this example. Further, within this amount the majority of the programs are mandated by law. A great many of the policy decisions are made during the budget making process and will constrain other decisions that one can make throughout the rest of the year.

Now, the force that overrides all of those listed above is the complexity of our society itself. The number of issues that need to be addressed, the range of issues, and the amount of information one needs to adequately understand the complexity of these issues are indeed overwhelming. The growth in the complexity of the organization of our society and the growth of technology—the impacts of those technologies, some foreseen and some not—have led to a steady growth in the staffs of members of Congress, Congressional committees, and government agencies themselves. Because it is so difficult to get enough information analyzed appropriately, we have seen the growth of all types of special assistants, special councils, advisory groups, policy analysts at every level of government—be it local, state, or federal. This has often led to the concern that our policy is being made not by the elected officials, but by their staffs. There are no easy answers to this issue or indeed to any of the other issues I have raised above.

Let us look at the case of abortion legislation, one of the first issues I faced on assuming the Directorship of the Illinois State Department of Public Health in 1973, shortly after the Supreme Court decision on abortion. The issue facing the Department was how to guarantee the availability of safe abortions while preserving the free choice and privacy of the individual. Was legislation going to be necessary at the State level? If so, how could that legislation be framed in a way to gain the kind of broad support that would be necessary to guarantee passage? To try to tackle this problem we brought together several key State legislators who had been strong advocates of abortion, several who were experts in constitutional law, and a key woman Catholic legislator whose religious commitments obviously strongly influenced her position. In addition, the representatives of women's groups, the medical society, and the hospital association were also involved. The timing was important. This group was brought together shortly after the Supreme Court decision had been handed down, when the mood was one of accepting the decision and protecting women rather than one of trying to reverse the decision and prevent its implementation.

From the outset our premise was that the Supreme Court decision would be our guidepost. We would not pass any legislation that was not in keeping with that decision. The legislation would be geared to trying to assure that any woman who wanted an abortion got a safe abortion under excellent medical conditions. We finally evolved a package of three laws. (1) The Abortion Statute defines the first, second, and third trimesters of the pregnancy period, and sets certain conditions for performance of abortions. It also permits abortions to be performed only by licensed physicians, and specifies that all abortions be reported to the Illinois Department of Public Health for confidential statistical usage. Another clause provides that any physician who refuses to perform an abortion would not be liable to civil or criminal action. (2) The second bill amended the Medical Practice Act to restrict abortions to licensed hospitals or ambulatory surgical facilities. Any physician who performed an abortion in any other facility could be subject to revocation of his or her license. (3) The third bill defines ambulatory surgical treatment centers as approved facilities for performance of abortion or any other surgery that normally would not require overnight hospitalization for the patient's recovery and well-being. The bill also requires that all such centers be licensed and supervised by the Illinois Department of Public Health.

This approach was taken to assure the constitutionality of the bills as much as possible. We considered most likely for constitutional challenge the second bill providing that out-of-hospital abortions should be done only in ambulatory licensed centers. Should that bill subsequently be found unconstitutional, the other two bills would remain intact. We then could try by education to convince women to have their abortions at licensed centers rather than in private physicians' offices.

We announced these three bills at a joint press conference held with the President of the Illinois State Medical Society and the Associate Director of the Illinois Hospital Association. It was sponsored by a highly respected Catholic State Senator. The major groups lobbying for the legislation were the Planned Parenthood Association and a number of Abortion Rights groups, a coalition made possible by emphasizing the need to "provide a comprehensive means of restricting abortions in order to safeguard the physical, mental and emotional welfare of the patients involved" (Press Release IDPH). With this as the basic premise we were able to defeat any amendments that we could show were not in keeping with the Supreme Court decision on the basis that the law would be declared unconstitutional and women would be left unprotected. There was also strong editorial support from the major newspapers.

This package of legislation was passed and has been fairly successfully implemented. Implementing regulations were developed with the aid of a board that included representatives of women's groups. The major problem for the Department of Public Health has been to maintain an adequate inspection force to see that all centers are in compliance with the regulations.

One role of the courts and the press in articulating policy is visible in the treatment of violations. In early 1976 the state went to court requesting a temporary injunction restraining the operation of an abortion center until the facility obtained a license. This order was granted, but the Medical Director of the abortion center immediately filed suit against the Director of the Department of Public Health first challenging the constitutionality of the Ambulatory Surgical Treatment Center Act as being overly broad in that it purports to regulate facilities in which first trimester abortions are performed and secondly, seeking money damages from the Director and two other employees of the Department. At that time, there were no laws in Illinois to protect state employees against such suits and money damages. (Such legislation has since been passed.) The court finally dismissed the complaint. In the interim, despite the suit, the Medical Director proceeded to meet the licensure requirements and did receive a license to operate the center. However, in late summer of 1978 the Department of Public Health commenced procedures to revoke the center's license because of the Medical Director's refusal to allow inspection of the facility. By October 1978, the license was revoked, but the center's Director immediately went into court and obtained a temporary restraining order against the Department and resumed operation.

That temporary restraining order was not lifted until a series of articles in the *Chicago Sun Times* in November, 1978, exposed poor practices at four abortion centers—including the one described above. All four clinics had at one time or another been cited by the

Department. The allegations contained in the newspaper articles included abortions on nonpregnant women, inadequate counseling, abortions done in two to five minutes without anesthesia, in unsterile conditions, with inadequate recovery facilities.

Besides the action of the courts, the Governor reacted by appointing a task force and making more staff available for inspection and enforcement of the regulations. The Department of Public Health revoked the license of one center and was not challenged. A second center was given a summary suspension for extensive use of untrained personnel. When the facility went to court to obtain a temporary restraining order, it failed and remained closed for several months. The Department then issued a six-month suspension, but the center obtained a temporary restraining order and reopened one month later. The Department also started the process of revoking the license of a third clinic, following which the clinic voluntarily closed and surrendered its license.

Are there negative aspects of the press coverage? Certainly there was little written about the excellent facilities that do exist. The articles supplied fuel for the fire of the Right-to-Life groups. Further, in my view, the Department of Public Health became a scapegoat and little attention was paid to the legal problems the Department faced.

The legislative climate was in flux throughout this period. In 1975, just two years after the first legislation, a new Abortion Statute was passed in response to lobbying by the Right-to-Life groups, concerned mainly with informed consent, requirements for describing the appearance of the fetus, and requirements for obtaining parental and spousal consent. Immediately upon passage, an injunction was obtained to prevent its implementation. Although the act has since been struck down, further appeals are still possible. Currently, several bills are pending in the state legislature. One provides for better statistical surveillance, especially of complications. A second bill amends the 1975 Abortion Act to make it more consistent with the Supreme Court decision. A third bill known as the Abortion Act of 1979 is apparently more unconstitutional than the 1975 act. Suffice it to say, the coalition and mood of 1973 has given way to the battles of 1979 with which you are all familiar. Meanwhile, the 1973 legislation remains in place.

This story of abortion legislation in Illinois I believe illustrates the broad array of forces at play in our governmental process. The lessons to be learned I leave to you.

Response

Ilene Wolcott

I wish to set the stage for translating the issues with which we've been grappling into public decisions about human reproduction technology, influenced by women. For such translation, we need to know: how decisions are made; who makes these decisions; and, as Joyce Lashof notes, what values and ethical judgments influence the policymakers that in turn influence the medical care providers, health researchers, and FDA bureaucrats. We have to remember that policy is made in response to and in reaction to the pressures from all the external forces, such as public and private interest groups, the press, and the courts. Policymakers' power comes only from their ability to educate and to influence compromises, and from the use of their personal position and their prestige to manipulate these outside forces. We have illustrated the diversity of opinion, philosophy, values, demands, and objectives of these outside forces.

Our concern and mission is to influence these values from a women's perspective. How can we as women create change and effectively participate in the development of the practices that affect our reproductive health? How can we decide what risks, benefits, values, and ethical considerations there are that must be addressed? How can we become the decision makers?

It is our task to impose our women's perspective on policymakers, to define the standards and values that influence decisions, to assure that decisions affecting our health are based on considerations that reflect adequate attention to questions of safety, efficacy, responsibility, sensitivity, informed consent, and information.

C/SEC: A Special-Interest Interpersonal Group Brings About Change

Beth Shearer

I shall describe the efforts and successes of a special interest group in bringing about changes in attitudes, policies, and practices on a local level. Hospital policy tends to be even more engraved in stone than is federal legislation. C/SEC, or Cesareans/Support, Education, and Concern, is an organization of and for cesarean parents. For many people, the first question may be "Why a special organization for cesarean parents?"

Two parallel trends have been taking place in American obstetrics over the past 20 years. The first is a dramatic development of, and reliance on, technology in childbirth, including antenatal testing, induction, routine intravenous infusion, and electronic fetal monitoring. Women who have cesareans sometimes benefit tremendously from technology, but also suffer from it. Technologies related to birth are very much connected to the dramatic rise in the cesarean rate. Nationally, the cesarean rate in 1978 was over 15%, up from 4.5% in 1965. Furthermore, there is every indication that rates have continued to rise since 1978. One in every four or five births in the greater Boston area is now by cesarean.

At the same time, parents' expectations about the birth experience and their desires to retain control over that experience have been changing dramatically as well. The spread of the prepared childbirth movement to help women participate with dignity in giving birth, the rightful inclusion of the father, Leboyer's popularization of "gentle birth," and the burgeoning literature on parent/infant attachment have made everyone much more aware of the psychosocial dimensions of childbirth. Thus, parents may find the gap between their expectations and wishes and the reality of a cesarean delivery very hard to accept.

Women feel deprived; they feel cheated; they feel frustrated; they feel terrified. The primary emotion that I carry with me from my first child's birth is one of overwhelming loneliness. Women feel a sense of loss of control. I realized afterwards that having my child's birth be something *I* did, rather than something that was done *to* me, was a metaphor for my ability to retain control of my life after she came into it; having my husband actively involved in her birth had become for me a metaphor for how well he was going to be involved after. I felt a great sense of loss, for both of those things.

Women who have undergone cesareans feel a sense of failure that their bodies have let them down. It's not only that "I didn't do it 'right'" in the sense that "I didn't have that wonderful Lamaze birth, that peak experience." I think it goes deeper than that. I have had a concern that a woman's desire to have a baby was being attributed by some to men, as if men had given that desire to us to keep us in our place, and I do not believe that is true. The restriction of a woman's role to childbearing is actually recent. I suspect a desire to participate in creation goes back much further—to the days of the mother goddesses, long before men invented God the Father. And so women giving birth by cesarean feel a loss somehow of an essential part of their identity, in that they did not do what other women could. And finally, some women feel, or are made to feel, guilty by people who say "What's the matter with you? It doesn't matter how your baby was born. You just had a healthy baby and that's all you need." By that reaction women are separated not only from their bodies, but from their feelings, as well.

C/SEC grew out of one woman's personal struggle to deal with these feelings, her refusal to see them all as necessary, and her determination that a cesarean birth could be a more affirming experience for others than it had been for her. In 1972, Nancy Cohen was delighted with her new son, but couldn't shake her frustration and disappointment, her sense of loss, over the circumstances of his birth, an unexpected cesarean. She wrote a letter to the newsletter of the organization that had sponsored her childbirth classes, and at once was inundated by calls and letters from other women who said, "Yes, I felt the same way, but I thought I was the only one." Nancy and co-founder Jini Fairley called together a group of these women locally, and C/SEC was born. With the rapidly increasing numbers of parents experiencing this form of birth, C/SEC was clearly an idea whose time had come. While Nancy was still in the process of forming a local organization, an unknown person wrote about her efforts to a national magazine, and suddenly C/SEC was a national organization. It incorporated in early 1975, and now has about 1800 members around the country, with more than a dozen affiliate groups in other states.

C/SEC is also in contact with over 150 other cesarean support groups that have since been formed.

I am always amazed when I go around to childbirth education conferences at how often people come up afterwards and want to tell me their sad stories. They are heartbreaking, some of them, and I always think, "that's really too bad, for this woman in Kansas City to have to wait for a woman to come from Boston to be able to tell her story, and to have that validated."

From the beginning, C/SEC has had three principal goals: offering support, providing education, and affecting hospital policy. We provide support by offering a place where parents can share feelings and know they will find understanding and acceptance because the listener has "been there." We receive many thousands of letters and phone calls; it is not uncommon to receive several thousands of pieces of mail directly attributable to a specific mention in a national publication. Locally we also offer open discussion meetings.

Our second major goal is education. We first began cesarean prepared childbirth classes in conjunction with Boston Hospital for Women in January 1976, and our own classes in early 1977. We have also produced an instructional slide/tape presentation about family-centered cesarean birth, as well as written materials for parents and professionals. These include a survey of contemporary literature on vaginal delivery after a cesarean and a comprehensive survey of maternity practices at all hospitals with obstetrical services in Massachusetts. We also see part of our educational function to be increasing the awareness of providers about the emotional needs of cesarean parents. We try to encourage traditional childbirth educators to include more and better preparation about cesarean delivery, not only so that parents will know what to expect and what their options are, but also so that they will be fully informed about the risks and benefits of other obstetrical interventions, and how they may affect the course of labor and the need for a cesarean.

Our third major thrust, one that has been important from the beginning, has been bringing about changes in attitudes and policies relating to cesarean childbirth so that: (1) all those coming into contact with birthing families are aware of the special stresses that may accompany a cesarean birth, especially an unexpected one; (2) family-centered options and extra support for initial bonding, early parenting efforts, and breastfeeding are extended to all families, but especially those experiencing difficult births; and (3) parents know their birthing options and have the confidence to exercise them responsibly.

The first change that is necessary is in attitude. We no longer permit a cesarean to be treated primarily as surgery that happens to result in a baby, but rather as a birth that happens to be by a surgical method. The mother is changed from a surgical patient back into a birthing woman. Thus, a major target of C/SEC has been hospital policies that separate parents during cesarean births, and parents from their newborns. Nancy and Jini spent untold hours calling, writing, and meeting with many people at Boston Hospital for Women before the first fathers were allowed to share in their infants' cesarean births in 1974. The current policy allows a father to be present with the agreement of the obstetrician, anesthesiologist, and head nurse.

What is interesting is that the C/SEC women chose the hardest hospital in Boston to change. It does 6–7000 births a year, is a Harvard Teaching Hospital, and a very conservative institution. They chose it only a few months after fathers had been allowed to be present for vaginal births, for the first time. Rationally you would never have picked that hospital to start in, but rather some other institution with a long history of family-centered care. But they just determined that that hospital was *going* to change, and that they were going to struggle with it until it did. And they did, and it did, and then many others began to change for economic reasons. So I think the lesson is that sometimes it is worthwhile trying to change things that are obviously impossible to change, and trying to do what is obviously impossible to do. It is important to identify clearly the changes wanted and the specific first steps. And it takes unending patience. Another lesson, one women know well, yet one that sometimes needs to be reiterated: there is much more power in a group than just the additive powers of the individuals, and a group empowers individuals. Thus although the practice is still more common for elective than for emergency cesareans, I have not had a father, either student or client, refused admittance to a cesarean in Boston in over two years.

C/SEC also worked to make changes in the treatment of the infant by eliminating the automatic 24-hour observation of all cesarean babies in a special care nursery, where they were totally unavailable to their mothers. This has usually been easier to accomplish.

How to bring about similar changes is still one of the most common questions I am asked when I speak to childbirth groups around the country. Although each situation has its unique aspects, several points stand out:

(1) The power individuals have to effect change increases exponentially when they band together as a group. A group can wield considerably more economic, political, and moral power. The group also has a psychological effect on its members. One of the necessary steps is for parents to come to believe fully that it is appropriate for

them to take responsibility for decisions about their birthing experience, and their health care in general. The result when parents have gone through this process is a relationship with physicians and hospitals that is forever changed.

(2) It is important to know exactly what changes are wanted, and to be willing to limit them to one or two initial steps. Once the door is open, other changes will come more easily. It is unwise to try to remake the entire obstetrical service, or every hospital in town, simultaneously.

(3) It is helpful to understand the politics of the hospital and community as much as possible—who are the opinion leaders, who has the power, what issues and concerns will have leverage. Opposition to the kind of changes that C/SEC has tried to bring about has been on political and emotional grounds, not on empirical, medical data. If the assistance of at least one "insider," preferably a physician, can be enlisted, s/he can be enormously helpful, talking informally to colleagues, providing a bargaining point (someone who will implement the new policy, perhaps on a trial basis), giving insight into the politics of the particular institution. Such assistance is not essential, however.

(4) Above all, unending patience and persistence are prerequisites.

Parents in groups such as C/SEC derive two benefits. One is the initial support or information immediately before or after a cesarean birth. The other is a chance to turn the anger, frustration, and disappointment into constructive action, to make things better for themselves next time, or for those who come after. This is the motivation that provides the drive to keep at what is often a long process.

Although most cesarean groups focus on the issue of father's presence at the birth, the broader issues are parent choice, informed consent, and parental control over the birth experience, regardless of the method. We have been accused of trying to make a cesarean such a wonderful experience that everyone will want to have one, and that as a result women will not resist unnecessary cesareans. Having experienced the risk and discomfort of two cesarean births, I find that argument a strange one. In my experience, this argument is generally offered by women who have had vaginal deliveries and apparently have not had major abdominal surgery, so that they do not know what it's like to stand up and be sure all your guts are going to fall out on the floor in front of you when you are trying to go to feed your hungry baby. And I am also not sure how keeping a woman ignorant, and terrified, and psychologically powerless can help her resist an unnecessary cesarean.

Of course we are all concerned about a 20, 25, 30% cesarean rate, about its causes and costs. But denying parents a positive, fulfilling birth experience if they have a cesarean birth does nothing to reduce the rate. Parents *do* need as much information as possible about the processes of labor, the variations of labor that are not pathological, and the full risks and benefits of all obstetrical interventions, including cesarean delivery. Women should not ever feel that they have to give birth in a certain way or a certain place. Although we are enthusiastic, and I very much share that enthusiasm, about more and more opportunities for out-of-hospital birth and alternatives in birth, let's not forget that there will always be some women who will give birth in the hospital, and who will *need* to give birth in the hospital. There will always be some women who need cesareans (though not 25%). We need to mount a parallel effort to assure that our institutions routinely provide humane care during the birth process.

The more information parents have, and the more they are encouraged to take responsibility for their babies, and their health in general, the more they will be able to participate meaningfully in decision-making all along the way. This may be the most important and far-reaching change of all.

The Ethicist in Policy Making

Karen Lebacqz

I am a white woman—middle class—born and raised in the United States, but in the minority here in this conference of mostly first-born women since I am the second child in my family, with an older brother.

I am also a teacher by profession and a token woman in my institution. This has given me a grave concern for issues such as preferential hiring. Indeed, I propose that one cannot do ethics in the biomedical field unless one is also doing ethics around such issues as preferential hiring. What we do in one arena spills over into another.

I am a trained Christian ethicist with a focus on bioethics—a field on which I have worked, now, for more than ten years. Believe it or not, that makes me one of the old people in the field. Knowing that I am a trained ethicist, you will also then know that I was trained in male-dominated institutions because there were not—and I believe today still are not—places where one can go to study ethics in anything other than a male-dominated institution.

To be a "Christian" ethicist means that I was trained to look at theological as well as philosophical issues. Also, I have become, over the last few years, by personal conviction, a Christian—which I believe is intimately connected with my feminism.

Finally, I have had some experience as a woman in a policymaking or policy-recommending position, in the California State Department of Health in 1976–77. (The Department of Health has been completely restructured since that time.) Also, I have served on the National Commission for the Protection of Human Subjects, which has now issued some ten reports to the Secretary of DHEW on the proper treatment of human beings as research subjects.

I wish to address two questions. First, what does ethics or the trained ethicist bring to policymaking? And second, what difference does it make to be either a feminist or, in my case, a Christian feminist ethicist, or a woman ethicist in this role?

First, what does an ethicist do? Not all of my male or female colleagues will agree with my interpretation. Ethical questions are

283

"ought" questions—questions about what we should or ought to do. Ethical dilemmas arise when we feel that there are several courses of action, each of which has reasons that support it, but that are mutually incompatible in some way. I "ought" to do this, but I also "ought" to do that—for different reasons—and somehow I must reconcile that conflict.

In that kind of a situation the ethicist locates the value presuppositions that lie behind the reasoning and the proposal for action and observes the logic or illogic of the arguments that are used. For example, do the person's conclusions really follow from her/his premises, or was there some kind of a jump—some kind of hidden premise or hidden assumption? In the debate about population and food policy, for example, proponents of different positions often begin with a different metaphor for understanding our current situation. Some assert that we are on a "lifeboat" from which we must cast some persons into the ocean lest we all drown. Others speak of "spaceship earth," suggesting a model in which there is no option of casting some out in order to survive. The ethicist exposes the hidden assumptions in these models and argues for certain value premises or interpretive frameworks.

Finally—something that I think is very crucial and largely ignored in my field—an ethicist should make arguments about the criteria for validity of data and its interpretation. We have heard several people say here that there is no such thing as simply giving data. Every time you give data, you put it in an interpretive framework as you give it. I think that's true, and that there is a very serious question about whose interpretive framework should count, which interpretive frameworks are better than others.

Now, these tasks of locating value presuppositions, observing the logic and illogic of arguments, and proposing and defending our own arguments and presuppositions are not exclusive to the ethicist. I resonate with something that Gena Corea has said, and would also like to quote here one of my favorite passages from the Danish theologian and philosopher Sören Kierkegaard. He asked, rhetorically, "Why did Socrates compare himself to a gad-fly?" Kierkegaard answered his own question this way: "Because he only wished to have ethical significance. He did not wish to be admired as a genius standing apart from others. ... No, he only did what every man can do. ..." (Journal, 1846) In that sense yes, it is true that all of us can be and should be ethicists. The difference between the trained ethicist and the untrained ethicist has to do partly with those male-dominated institutions and partly, one hopes, with increasing ability to locate presuppositions quickly, observe logic quickly, and so on.

For example, as an ethicist, I served as a consultant to the

Department of Health for the State of California. I envy Joyce Lashof when she describes what was done with the abortion law in Illinois. When I arrived at the Department of Health in California in 1976, one of the first things that I observed was that the California abortion statute pre-dated the 1973 Supreme Court decisions, and there was no revision of that law to make it consonant with those decisions. With several other people, I worked on drafting a new law, and was then frustrated to find that nobody would submit it to the legislature because it was an election year, and nobody wanted to alienate his or her constituents. Therefore, to date—so far as I know—the California abortion statute retains such provisions as: no abortions beyond the twentieth week and committee decision before a woman may have an abortion.

Clearly, nobody is practicing medicine in accord with this statute. Women are able to obtain abortions. But one of the interesting fallouts from this disparity—this state of limbo in which California exists—is that we cannot even gather data on how many abortions are done, at what stage of pregnancy, and by what means, because the law provides for the reporting of therapeutic abortions, and the abortions that are done today are not considered "therapeutic."

I also dealt with the issue of Medi-Cal payments for abortion. Most arguments in the Department of Health on this issue—and on most others!—centered on a cost–benefit analysis. I was able to convince the Director of Health that the central question was one of justice—of equal access to medical care for women of all socioeconomic positions.

Similarly, the ethicists on the National Commission for the Protection of Human Subjects played an important role in introducing concerns for justice into the protection of human subjects of research. Before this time, most research on human subjects operated under a principle that I call "respect for persons." The most common form in which we see this principle is the requirement of "informed consent." Obtaining consent from participants provides important protections. But it does not guarantee that subjects who are invited to participate are equitably distributed among population groups. Women and other persons from disadvantaged positions in society may be used disproportionately. So the National Commission has made a number of recommendations related to the justice of selection of subjects for research.

The Commission exposed our reasoning process to public scrutiny, which in itself was a significant contribution. We operated under the "sunshine" laws. The record is therefore available to anyone willing to read through the voluminous materials accumulated.

My second question was, what difference does it make to be a feminist (in my case, a Christian feminist) doing ethics? I have said that the task of the ethicist is, in part, to propose and defend value premises, interpretive frameworks, and the like. The central difference in doing ethics as a feminist (or as a woman concerned with women's issues) is that one operates out of different premises, proposes different frameworks, models, and metaphors for doing analysis, and proposes, very significantly, different criteria for the validity of data.

Let me demonstrate this in terms of what we have done during these discussions. First, in terms of premises: a feminist, or a woman concerned about women's issues, will examine the assumptions that are made by others in policymaking and challenge those assumptions from the perspective of women's experience—making women's lives and concerns and experience central. This leads to the development of new categories of thought, new categories for sorting out data, new interpretive modes. We have seen some examples of that here. For example, unlike most work in bioethics—which tends to be individualistic and ahistorical—a feminist will bring an historical dimension, because women are concerned about patterns or structures of meaning. And you cannot have a pattern or a structure without some kind of a history of repeated action. And so here, in this meeting, as we have asked such questions as, "Should we have in vitro fertilization?" we have not asked "What is the immutable human nature that we are trying to protect?," which is one traditional approach. Nor have we simply asked: "What are the consequences of doing this?" Instead, we have approached the question by asking, "How does in vitro fertilization fit into a larger framework of the development of technologies that are impacting on the lives, capacities, and choices available to women?" We do not all agree on the answer to that question, but we are asking a different question. Eventually, in my view, that will change the shape of how we do ethics.

I wish to close with a proposal for us. The field of bioethics has been very decision-oriented. We ask, "What should I do?" or, "What should our policy be?" We are action-oriented. This orientation ignores two other aspects of ethics that I believe are central, and that are being re-addressed with some seriousness in Christian and feminist ethics today.

The first of these is character. If, indeed, we think that the personal is political—as I do—then surely we need to ask questions about what it means to be a good person, what our character should be. What is the nature of virtue? For any of you who think that question is unimportant, I refer you to some of Adrienne Rich's beautiful work on honor in women. Why is it that a woman is honorable if she confines her sexuality to one man, whereas a man is honorable if he keeps his word, meets his contractual obligations, and the like? Why is honor, for women, determined by sexuality, whereas for men, it is determined by truth-telling and promise-keeping? We need much more analysis of these kinds of issues.

We also need more analysis of what "the good life" is. This conference has exhibited a basic tension. On the one hand, we see "the good life" as increased control and self-determination for women. And yet, each of us in some way is struggling and sacrificing, not for the sake of our own reward (my guess is that few of us will reap the rewards of the feminist and women's movement). We are struggling and sacrificing for the sake of others—be they our children or other women who will come after us. So the other image of "the good life" is this struggle for liberation and justice for women and oppressed peoples. There is no liberation or justice on the personal level alone, as we can sometimes talk about control or self-determination as though it were on the personal level alone. Liberation and justice require empowerment.

I would propose to you that we need to look carefully at how we understand the nature of "the good life," and that it just may be that "the good life" consists not in that future ideal state in which we will be in control of everything, but in the very struggle that we are going through, that brings us together in this room, and in our own communities, in those voluntary organizations that we have spoken of here, to fight for liberation and justice for oppressed peoples.

Appendix

Action Possibilities
Margaret A. Kohn

ACTION POSSIBILITIES

I. Interaction with the FDA

A. Patient Labeling of Medication. Press for the Food and Drug Administration (FDA) to require patient labeling for all prescription drugs. Urge that such labeling contain warnings of special concern to women, e.g., instructions not to use medication during periods of pregnancy and lactation. Notice of proposed patient package labeling requirements is published in the Federal Register, available in many public libraries, and in virtually all libraries with a decent reference collection, with at least 30 days for public comment. In addition to the submission of comments, it may be possible to work with the FDA prior to publication of such notices in the Federal Register.

B. Advisory Committees of the Food and Drug Administration. 1. Monitor committee activity and participate as consumers/experts on issues of concern to women. The Obstetrics and Gynecology and the Anesthesia advisory committees are of special importance.

2. Increase representation of feminist views in committee membership as well as in the number of women serving in both consumer and professional capacities.

C. Periodic Consumer Meetings with Senior Food and Drug Administration Officials. These periodic meetings, announced in the Federal Register and held several times a year, provide an opportunity for relatively small meetings with key decision-makers. Consumers may add topics to the agenda.

D. Congressional Lobbying on the New Drug Bill.   Congress is still considering several different bills to change the Food and Drug laws. Issues of special importance to women and consumers are raised by these bills. Persons interested in lobbying may contact two sources for additional information about the implications of the bill for women and consumers in general: Marcia Greenberger, Center for Law and Social Policy, 1751 N Street, N. W., Washington, D.C. 20036, or Women and Health Roundtable, Suite 403, FOPW, 2000 P Street, N. W., Washington, D.C. 20036.

E. Petitions to FDA.   Any citizen, group of citizens, or organization may petition the FDA for actions within its authority. This offers a way to force the agency to deal with issues it has not attended in the past. The process of filing a petition is simple; indeed, the FDA has prepared a pamphlet with directions. Assistance from a lawyer may be helpful, but is not essential. Certain petitions have been published in the Federal Register for comment. The filing offers an opportunity for publicity around the issue. Be forewarned, however, that the agency may never address the issues raised by your petition in depth or to your satisfaction. It is not a mechanism that will necessarily bring quick results.

F. Participation in Agency Hearings.   There is provision for third parties to challenge FDA actions and participate in FDA hearings. There is also provision for the FDA to reimburse groups for expert witness and attorney costs in those proceedings.

G. Law Suits.   It is possible to challenge FDA decisions in court if they are not consistent with the law or regulation.

II. Interaction with and Participation in Activities of HSAs at the Local Level

The National Health Planning Act requires states and communities to engage in health planning with federal funds. Consumer input is required, but has been ineffective in communities where the providers and the institutions have control over the planning units for various political and economic reasons. *Consumer and feminist input and pressure are essential.* Those structures will be and are effecting decisions on such matters as:

- which maternity units remain open or are permitted to expand
- availability of sterilization and abortion services
- purchase of equipment costing over $150,000
- distribution of health facilities geographically
- identification of health needs which are unmet and priorities for serving unmet needs
- health provider distribution and training priorities geographically and by professional mix

For more information in general on the Health Service Agencies (HSAs) that conduct these planning activities and on how to be actively involved in these processes, excellent contacts are the Consumer Coalition for Health, 1751 N Street, NW, Washington, D.C. 20036, (202) 638–5828, and Judy Norsigian and Norma Swenson, who have been involved in the Boston area planning process, at the Boston Women's Health Book Collective, Box 192, West Somerville, MA 02144, (617) 924–0271.

Notes and References

REPRODUCTIVE TECHNOLOGIES, Helen B. Holmes

1. Raymond, J., "Response," in *The Custom-Made Child?*, Holmes, H. B., B. B. Hoskins, and M. Gross, eds., Humana, Clifton, New Jersey, 1980.
2. Pearse, W. H., quoted in *Ob. Gyn. News* **19**, 1, 33 (1977).
3. Swallow, H., "Midwives in Many Settings," elsewhere in this volume.
4. Luce, J., "Ethical Issues Relating to Childbirth as Experienced by the Birthing Woman and Midwife," elsewhere in this volume.
5. Ampola, M., "Prenatal Diagnosis," in *The Custom-Made Child?*, Holmes, H. B., B. B. Hoskins, and M. Gross, eds., Humana, Clifton, New Jersey, 1980.
6. Carlton, W., "Perfectability and the Neonate," in *The Custom-Made Child?*, Holmes, H. B., B. B. Hoskins, and M. Gross, eds., Humana, Clifton, New Jersey, 1980.
7. Cook, K., "A Native American Response," elsewhere in this volume.

HISTORICAL STYLES OF CONTRACEPTIVE ADVOCACY, Joyce Avrech Berkman

1. Gordon, L., *Woman's Body, Woman's Right,* Penguin, New York, 1977, pp. 40–49; without the clarity of vision that informs this entire study of the American birth control movement, my paper would not have been possible. Reed, J., from *Private Vice to Public Virtue,* Basic Books, New York, 1978, pp. 5–15. Busfield, J., and M. Paddon, *Thinking About Children,* Cambridge University Press, Cambridge, 1978, p. 226.
2. Sanger, M., Introduction, in *For Legalized Birth Control,* The New Republic, New York, 1934, pp. 4–5. This volume also includes: Smith, H. H., *Wasting Women's Lives,* and Garrett, E. H., *Birth Control's Business Baby.*
3. Reed, J., *op. cit.,* p. 215. Fryer, P., *The Birth Controllers,* Secker and Warburg, London, 1965, pp. 246–249. Gaular, J. M., "Women Rebel: The Rhetorical Strategy of Margaret Sanger and the American Birth Control Movement, 1912 to 1938," PhD Dissertation, Indiana University, August, 1978, p. 12. Stopes, M. C., *Mother England,* Bale,

Sons, and Danielsson, London, 1929, pp. 184–189. Smith, H. H., "Wasting Women's Lives," in *For Legalized Birth Control.*

4. Rowbotham, S., *A New World for Women: Stella Browne-Socialist Feminist,* Pluto Press, London, 1977, p. 27. See also Gordon, L., *op. cit.,* p. 62.

5. Rowbotham, *op. cit.,* p.45.

6. Gordon, L., *op. cit.*

7. Sanger, M., *An Autobiography,* Dover, New York, 1971, (Norton, 1938), p. 414;
_____*Motherhood in Bondage,* Brentano, New York, 1928, pp. 293–295.

8. Gordon, L., *op., cit.,* pp. 62–63.

9. Stopes, M. C., *Wise Parenthood,* Fifield, London, 1918, p. 6. Gordon, L., *op. cit.,* p. 62. Sanger, M., *Motherhood in Bondage,* pp. 322–324.

10. Rosenberg, C. S., "The Female World of Love and Ritual...," *Signs* **1,** 1–29 (Autumn, 1975).
Degler, C. N., "What Ought To Be and What Was: Woman's Sexuality in the Nineteenth Century," *American Historical Review* **79,** 1467–1490 (1974).

11. Gordon, L., *op. cit.,* p. 107. Masters, W., and V. Johnson, *Homosexuality in Perspective,* Little Brown, Boston, 1979. Hite, S., *The Hite Report,* Dell, New York, 1976. Rowbotham, S., *Woman's Consciousness, Man's World,* Dell, New York, 1971, chapter 18.

12. Stopes, M., *Wise Parenthood,* pp. 21–25.

13. Rowbotham, S., *Stella Browne—Socialist Feminist,* p. 62. Chafe, W. H., *The American Woman,* Oxford University Press, Oxford, 1972. "Introduction": see too, Woolf, V., *Three Guineas,* Harcourt, New York, 1966.

14. Gordon, L., *op. cit.,* pp. 109–115. Stopes, M., *Radiant Motherhood,* Putnam, New York and London, 1921, passim. Stopes, M., *Wise Parenthood,* pp. 1–2, 7. Sanger, M., *An Autobiography,* pp. 193–195, 361–362.

15. Reed, J., *op. cit.,* pp. xi, 68. Fryer, P., *op. cit.,* pp. 240–249.

16. Gordon, L., *op. cit.,* pp. 179–185, 190–206, 364–365, 411.

17. Fee, E., and M. Wallace, "The History and Politics of Birth Control: A Review Essay," *Feminist Studies* **5**(1), 201–215 (1979).

18. Reed, J., *op. cit,* p. 364. Corea, G., *The Hidden Malpractice,* Morrow, New York, 1977, p. 143.

19. Corea, G., *op. cit.,* pp. 143–145.

20. Westoff, C. F., and N. B. Ryder, *The Contraceptive Revolution,* Princeton University Press, Princeton, 1977, pp. 18–22.

21. Corea, G., *op. cit,* pp. 136–138, 180–183.

22. Ibid., pp. 140–141, 157, 160–167.

23. *Ms.* **7**(12), 32 (1979).

24. *Ibid.,* p. 43.

25. *Sparerib,* "If the Cap Fits...," Issue 57, 45–47 (April 1977).

ETHICAL PROBLEMS IN GOVERNMENT-FUNDED CONTRACEPTIVE RESEARCH, Belita Cowan

1. The publication *Inventory and Analysis of Federal Population Research* (DHEW) covers all grants and contracts in which population and contraceptive research constitutes a major category. The *Inventory* also includes objectives and recommendations for federally funded research. The latest *Inventory* available is for fiscal year 1977, includes nine federal agencies, and covers grants and contracts from 1973–1980.
2. In 1971, the FDA issued a warning to all physicians that the use of DES in pregnancy was linked to a rare form of vaginal and cervical adenocarcinoma in the female offspring. The carcinogenicity (cancer-causing ability) of DES and other estrogens has been known for almost four decades. In 1976, evidence from the University of Chicago linked *in utero* exposure to DES with genital tract abnormalities in the sons. In 1978, the reevaluation of data from the University of Chicago showed an increased risk of breast cancer among DES mothers.
3. Testimony before the US Senate Subcommittee on Health and Public Welfare, February 27, 1975. Edward Kennedy, Chair.
4. DHEW no. 77-3138.
5. Jones, J., L. DelRosario, and A. Soeiro, "Adrenal Function in Patients Receiving Medroxyprogesterone Acetate," *Contraception* 10, 1, (1974).
6. Rosenberg, K., "Human Experimentation." *Health/PAC Bulletin* 8, 1979.
7. In December, 1979, HEW published an announcement that it would fund efficacy studies on the cervical cap. This comes on the heels of testimony by the National Women's Health Network before the US Senate Health Sub-Committee charging FDA with trying to suppress the cap for lack of efficacy data.
8. "FDA Asks Upjohn to Revise Label on Anti-Cancer Drug," *Wall Street Journal,* June 8, 1979.
9. "Birth Control Shot Gets New Scrutiny," *San Francisco Chronicle,* June 8, 1979.

VALUE CONFLICTS IN BIOMEDICAL RESEARCH INTO FUTURE CONTRACEPTIVES, Carol C. Korenbrot

1. Gordon, L., *Woman's Body, Woman's Right: A History of Birth Control,* New York, Viking Press, 1977.
2. Lowrance, W. W., *Of Acceptable Risk: Science and the Determination of Risk,* Los Angeles, California, Kaufman, 1976.

3. Korenbrot, C., "Facts and Values in Testing Risk of Toxic Substances; Experiences with Systemic Contraceptives." In *Decisions and Values II. Testing Toxic Substances.* Technical Information Project, Washington, D.C.

4. Carl Djerassi, a research chemist at Stanford, is the head of his own drug company which does not produce contraceptives. He worked for Syntex Drug Company during the 1950s, where he was involved in developing progestin, a synthetic estrogen used in the first oral contraceptive, Enovid®. Syntex sponsored clinical trials of Enovid in both Puerto Rico and Mexico.

5. Norsigian, J., "Redirecting Contraceptive Research," *Science for the People,* January/February, 27 (1979).

6. Green, K., M. Bygdeman, K. Bremme, "Interruption of Early First Trimester Pregnancy by Single Vaginal Administration of 15-Methyl-P6F$_2$-Alpha-methyl ester," *Contraception* **18,** 557 (1978).

7. Chvapil, M., T. Chvapil, S. Jacobs, T. A. Owen, H. L. Horton, M. W. Heine, "Laboratory and Clinical Testing of Collagen Sponge as Intravaginal Contraceptive," *Contraception* **15,** 693 (1977).

8. Chvapil, M., C. W. Lischer, T. B. Campbell, M. Kantor, T. A. Owen, T. Chvapil, "Ultrastructure of the Vaginal Tissue of Rabbits Treated with Collagen Sponge Alone and Medicated with Zinc and Copper Salts and Copper Wire," *Fertil. Steril.* **30,** 461 (1978).

9. Djerassi, C., *Politics of Contraception,* Palo Alto, Stanford University Press, 1979, chapter 7. I am grateful to Dr. Djerassi for his permission to use the galley proofs of his book.

10. Although cottonseed oil had been a staple of the diet for generations without any sign of associated disease, modernization of the production of cottonseed oil removed a boiling step which apparently had been inactivating the entity causing the side effects described.

STATUS OF CONTRACEPTIVE TECHNOLOGY DEVELOPMENT, Linda E. Atkinson and Jacki Ans

1. Greep, R. O., M. K. Koblinsky, and F. S. Jaffe, *Reproduction and Human Welfare: A Challenge to Research,* MIT, Cambridge, 1976.

2. Djerassi, C., "Birth Control after 1984," *Science* **169,** 941 (1970).

3. Atkinson, L. E., In *Contraception: Science, Technology and Application,* National Academy of Sciences, Washington, D.C., 1979.

4. Segal, S. J. In *Contraception: Science, Technology and Application,* National Academy of Sciences, Washington, D. C., 1979.

WOMEN-CONTROLLED RESEARCH,
Laura Punnett

1. Lennane, K. J., and R. J. Lennane, "Alleged Psychogenic Disorders in Women," *New England J. Med.* **288** (6), 288–292 (1973). There is a medical diagnostic computer at Duke University programmed automatically to award 10 points towards "psychosomatic" for any female patient; information from Barbara Ehrenreich's lecture, "Medicine and Social Control of Women," Hampshire College, Amherst, Mass., April 30, 1975.

2. For examples, see Sturgis, S. H. "Primary Dysmenorrhea: Etiology and Management," *Progress in Gynecology,* **5,** Sturgis, S. H., and M. L. Taymor, eds., Grune & Stratton, New York, 1970, p. 149; Rogers, J., *Endocrine and Metabolic Aspects of Gynecology,* Saunders, Philadelphia, 1963, p. 88.

3. Schneiderman, Lawrence, Univ. Calif./San. Diego Medical School, in "Women [sic] Say Men Doctors Are Sexist," *Daily Hampshire Gazette,* Northampton, Mass., June 2, 1979.

4. See *Hastings Center Report* **5**(3), 11–46 (1975). Section B of the Report of the Commission is primarily concerned with the fetus, "its health condition, benefits and risks (accruing) to that fetus, and . . . that subject's own welfare." The Report acknowledges, as if an afterthought, "the necessary involvement of the woman in such research" (p. 42). See also *Hastings Center Report* **5**(5), 9–16 and **5**(2), 8–10 (1975).

5. So the Health/PAC Bulletin described research by Goldzieher's group in an editorial "AIDing the Poor," *Health/PAC Bull.* **40,** 11(April, 1972).

6. J. W. Goldzieher administered placebos instead of oral contraceptives to half of 398 poor Chicana women who had come to his center in Texas seeking effective birth control and who were not informed that they had been incorporated into the study. In four months, ten had become pregnant—an unplanned "side effect" for which no provisions had been made. At that time abortion was still illegal in Texas and these women had no choice but to carry the pregnancy to term. Goldzieher stated that he was attempting to prove that side effects of the Pill about which many women complain were largely "psychosomatic" or imaginary, a result of suggestion. Goldzieher, J. W., et al., "A Placebo-Controlled Double-Blind Crossover Investigation of the Side Effects Attributed to Oral Contraceptives," *Fertil. Steril.* **22,** 609–623 (Sept. 1971); and "Nervousness and Depression Attributed to Oral Contraceptives: A Double-Blind, Placebo-Controlled Study," *Amer. J. Obstet. Gynecol.* **111,** (8), 1013–1020 (1971). He has been criticized by Seaman, B. *Free and Female,* Fawcett, Greenwich, Connecticut, 1972, pp. 180–183; by Brown, L. K., "Feminist Controlled Research," April 1974, available from the Oakland Feminist Women's Health Center, 2930 McClure St., Oakland, CA 94609; and by Veatch, R. M., " 'Experimental' Pregnancy," *Hastings*

Center Report **1** (1) (June 1971). The supercoil is, according to Brown and Mattingly, an extremely dangerous, experimental second-trimester abortion method developed by Harvey Karman, in which coils are packed into the uterus until it contracts to expel them along with the fetus. Of 15 procedures done on poor, black women in Philadelphia (5/15/72), all the women suffered complications, including one hysterectomy owing to perforation and one requiring exploratory surgery. Between February and May, 1972, he performend 41 procedures on women who had been raped by soldiers in Bangladesh and whose social status, already jeopardized, would be even more hazarded by births following from the rapes. Karman's supercoil abortions in Bangladesh are documented in Mullick et al., "Termination of Pregnancy with Intrauterine Devices," *Amer. J. Obstet. Gynecol.* **54** (3), 305ff. (1973). He has been criticized by Brown, L. K., op. cit.; and in "Synopsis of the Activities of Harvey Karman," from the FWHC, 1112 Crenshaw Blvd., Los Angeles, CA 90005. [Also see Karman, H. O., "The Paramedic Abortionist," *Clin. Obstet. Gynecol.* **15**, 379–387 (1972), and response (same title) by R. F. Mattingly, *Obstet. Gynecol.* **41**, (6), 929–930 (1973).]

7. For examples see Beecher, H. K., *Research and the Individual: Human Studies,* Little Brown, Boston, 1970, p. 77; Lasagna, L., "Special Subjects in Human Experimentation," pp. 262–275, and Moore, F. D., "Therapeutic Innovation: Ethical Boundaries in the Initial Clinical Trials of New Drugs and Surgical Procedures," p. 376, both in *Experimentation with Human Subjects,* Paul A. Freund, ed., Braziller, New York, 1969; Morris, R. C., "Guidelines for Accepting Volunteers: Consent, Ethical Implications, and the Function of a Peer Review," *Clin. Pharmacol. Therapeut.* **13**, 783 (1972); "Experimentation and Consent: Special Questions of Consent," in the *Hastings Center Bibliography of Society, Ethics and the Life Sciences,* compiled by Sollito, S., and R. Veatch, 1975.

8. For further information, see Punnett, L., "Women-Controlled Medicine: Theory and Practice in 19th-century Boston," *Women and Health* **1** (4), 3–11 (1976).

9. Williams, J. W., "Medical Education and the Midwife Problem in the United States," *JAMA* **58**(1), 1–7 (1912).

10. *Center for Disease Control Abortion Surveillance 1975,* US DHEW, Public Health Services, CDC, issued April 1977.

11. For more information, see Rothman, L., "Menstrual Extraction: Procedures," *Quest: a feminist quarterly* **4** (3), 44–48 (1978).

12. Frankfort, E., *Vaginal Politics,* Bantam, New York, 1973, p. 203.

13. There are numerous examples of political opposition to the self-help movement. In 1972, Carol Downer and Colleen Wilson were arrested in Los Angeles for practicing medicine without a license, on counts of inserting a speculum into another woman, applying yogurt to a woman's vagina, etc. Many other women have taken their own plastic specula into practitioners' offices only to be told that they will "damage" themselves by using such a device. And plastic specula are now packaged in bags that label them as prescription devices, a move clearly aimed at lay women

since we are the only group other than practitioners who use specula in the first place.

14. Gordon, L. "The Politics of Population: Birth Control and the Eugenics Movement," *Radical America* **8**(4), 62 (1974).

15. van der Vlugt, T., et al., "Menstrual Regulation Update," Population Report series F, #4, Population Information Program, George Washington Univ. Medical Ctr., May 1974, p. 49.

16. Brown, L. K., personal communication. Brown attended this conference and listened to such discussions; there is not (yet) any documentation of this statement in the literature.

17. Dixon, R. B., "Women's Rights and Fertility," Reports on Population/Family Planning #17, The Population Council, New York, Jan. 1975, p. 12. Reprinted with the permission of the Population Council.

18. Ibid., p. 18.

19. Population control advocates often argue that their programs are necessary to solve problems such as world hunger and environmental quality by linking them to overpopulation and the resulting strain on global resources. Such arguments in depth are beyond the scope of this paper, but it is appropriate to refute them briefly by pointing out that world hunger, poverty, and pollution are not direct results of global population size and growth, but of control by economic interests and the priorities of profit-making. The "radical social, political or economic reforms" referred to above must include corporate responsibility for environmental impact, redistribution of economic resources, and an end to the Western exploitation of the land, food and raw materials of the Third World. The world's population could all be adequately fed if land was used to grow food for home consumption needs rather than as nonnutritional cash crops or cattle feed for the developed nations. (See Mass, B., *Population Target: The Political Economy of Population Control in Latin America,* The Latin America Working Group and the Canadian Women's Educational Press, Toronto, Ontario, 1976; and Lappe, F. M., and J. Collins, *Food First: Beyond the Myth of Scarcity,* Houghton Mifflin. Boston, 1977.

WOMAN-CONTROLLED BIRTH CONTROL,
Women's Community Health Center

1. Rice, F. J., C. Lanctot, and C. Garcia-Devesa, "Effectiveness of the Sympto-thermal Method of Natural Family Planning: An International Study," in press.

2. Billings, E. L., J. J. Billings, J. B. Brown, and H. G. Burger, "Symptoms and Hormonal Changes Accompanying Ovulation," *Lancet,* **1,** 282–284 (Feb. 5, 1972).

3. Rice, F. J., C. Lanctot, and C. Garcia-Devesa, *op. cit.*
4. World Health Organization. Special Programme of Research, Development and Research Training in Human Reproduction: Seventh Annual Report, Geneva, Nov. 1978. Reported in *Family Planning Perspectives* **2**(1), 41 (1979).
5. Lawler, R., "An Address to the Clergy," *Bulletin of the Natural Family Planning Council of Victoria* **6**(1), 7 (1979).
6. Billings, J. J., "Overview of the Ovulation Method—1977," Third Annual Institute on the Ovulation Method. Available from Natural Family Planning Centre, c/o Family Life Centre, 86 Wellington Parade, East Melbourne, 3002, Australia.
7. Hite, S., *The Hite Report,* Macmillan, New York, 1976, p. 291.

Annotated Bibliography

This list concentrates on some basic studies in the development and testing of the ovulation method, some sources of scientific information, and good sources of ovulation method information (see especially Guren and Gillette, 1977; and *Ovulation Method Newsletter*). This is not a complete list of references. There are many books available on natural birth control methods and programs of different sorts; we do not recommend any of the books not listed below. Please contact Fertility Consciousness Group, Women's Community Health Center, 639 Massachusetts Ave. #210, Cambridge, MA 02139, for more information.

Billings, E. L., J. J. Billings, J. B. Brown, and H. G. Burger, "Symptoms and Hormonal Changes Accompanying Ovulation," *Lancet* **1**, 282 (Feb. 5, 1972). The initial publication on the correlation of cervical mucus observations by 22 lay women ("housewives") and hormonal changes. The study demonstrates that "normal" women can predict and identify ovulation by noting the pattern of their vaginal mucus, without recourse to temperature measurement or more specialized tests.

Klaus, H., et al., "Use–Effectiveness and Analysis of Satisfaction Levels with the Billings Ovulation Method: Two–Year Pilot Study," *Fertil. Steril.* **28** (10), 1038 (1977). A two-year study of 135 women using Billings Ovulation Method. There were 1381 exposure cycles during the first year and 580 during the second year. Total conception rates were 1.303 per 100 woman-months for the first year and 1.896 per 100 woman-months for the second year. Biologic failure (method failure) rates were 0.072 per 100 woman-months for the first year and 0.517 per 100 woman-months for the second year. Continuation rate 51.8%. Compares some studies of use effectiveness of other contraceptives to the ovulation method (the following is an excerpt from a chart in this paper):

	Use-Effectiveness	
Contraceptive	Duration of use, Mo.	Pregnancies per 100 woman-months
Oral	6	3.9
Intrauterine device	6	2.36
Diaphragm and jelly	12	1.9-2.2
Ovulation Method		
Biologic Failure	12	0.072
	24	0.517
Personal Failure	12	1.231
	24	1.379
Total	12	1.303
	24	1.896

Weissmann, M. C., L. Foliaki, E. L. Billings, and J. J. Billings, "A Trial of the Ovulation Method of Family Planning in Tonga" *Lancet* **2,** 813 (Oct. 14, 1972). A study of 282 women using the Billings Ovulation Method for 250.3 months total (average approximately 8.8 months for each woman). Of the 81 pregnancies occurring, 28 resulted from couples dropping the method because they wanted more children; 50 women ignored indications of possible fertility (user failure); two pregnancies were from teaching failures and one from method failure.

Billings, J. J., and E. L. Billings, "Teaching the Safe Period Based on the Mucus Symptom." *Linacre Quarterly* **41**(1), 41 (1974). Another review of the ovulation method including teaching experiences and the philosophy of the Billingses.

Wolf, D. P., L. Blasco, M. A. Khan, M. Litt, Human Cervical Mucus, II. Changes in Viscoelasticity During the Ovulatory Menstrual Cycle. *Fertil. Steril.* **28**(1), 47, (Jan. 1977). Correlates high mucus viscosity with favorable sperm penetrability and with the ovulatory phase of the menstrual cycle.

Kerin, J. F. P., C. D. Matthews, J. M. Svigos, and M. Makin, "Migration of Stored Human Spermatozoa Through Cervical Mucus in Relation to the Preovulatory LH Surge," *Reproduction Fertil.* **46,** 499–500 (1976). Cervical mucus is most favorable to the penetration of sperm on the day preceding the day of the LH surge, and thereafter decreases rapidly.

Marshall, J., "Cervical–Mucus and Basal Body–Temperature Method of Regulating Births," *Lancet* **2,** 282 (Aug. 7, 1976). In this study, 84 women used the method for 1195 cycles. There were 22 unplanned pregnancies per 100 woman cycles. No distinction was made between method failure and user failure.

World Health Organization, *Special Programme of Research, Development and Research Training in Human Reproduction: Seventh Annual Report,* Geneva, Nov. 1978. Reported in *Family Planning Perspectives* 2(1), 40 (1979). In this study 890 women contributed 2685 cycles, resulting in 19.4 pregnancies per 100 woman-years use effectiveness; 98.5% method effectiveness.

Rice, F. J., C. Lanctot, C. Garcia-Devesa, "Effectiveness of the Sympto-thermal Method of Natural Family Planning: An International Study," in press. Sympto-thermal method used basal body temperature, mucus, and calendar calculations. Here 1022 couples contributed 21,736 cycles and reported 128 unplanned pregnancies, a rate of 7.47 conceptions per 100 woman-years. Only 16 pregnancies occurred when the couples were following instructions, giving a theoretical effectiveness of 0.93 pregnancies per 100 woman-years using the Pearl formula. Couples trying to prevent any pregnancies had a failure rate of 4.13%; those only delaying a pregnancy had a failure rate of 14.83%. The sympto-thermal method used alone had a failure rate of 6.24%, while use of contraceptive devices with the Sympto-thermal method had a failure rate of 10.33%. Method failure using the Pearl index was 0.75 over 24 months for couples using STM only. User failure 5.49. STM with barrier methods during a portion of the fertile period: method failure 1.36; user failure 8.97.

Guren, D., and N. Gillette, *The Ovulation Method: Cycles of Fertility,* 2nd ed., 1980. Available in bookstores or from Ovulation Method Teachers Association, P.O. Box 14511, Portland, OR 97214. Clear, concise, without religious orientation; best presentation of the ovulation method in print.

Ovulation Method Newsletter. Available from Ovulation Method Teachers Association, P. O. Box 14511, Portland, Oregon 97214. An excellent newsletter, including new information about the ovulation method, program reports, reviews of books and articles.

World Health Organization. *Cervical Mucus in Human Reproduction,* Copenhagen, Scriptor, 1973. Available from Human Reproduction Unit, WHO, 1211 Geneva 27, Switzerland. Scientific and medical information on the physiology of mucus and its relation to fertility.

Bell, S., et al., "Reclaiming Reproductive Control: A Feminist Approach to Fertility Consciousness," *Science for the People* 12(1), 6 (Jan./Feb. 1980), and corrections in 12(2), 31 (Mar./Apr. 1980). Available from Science for the People, 897 Main St., Cambridge, MA 02139 at $1.50 per issue. The most thorough feminist analysis of natural birth control currently in print. More comprehensive discussion of information and issues raised in this article, including international strategies of the Catholic ovulation method hierarchy, cooptation of feminist issues, mechanization of the method, and issues to consider in choosing a program to learn a natural birth control method. By the authors of this article.

RESPONSE, Judy Norsigian

1. Lasagna, L. C., as reported in *Medical World News,* June 11, 1979, p. 12.
2. *People* 4(6) (1979).
3. Schearer, B., The Population Council, personal communication, June, 1979.

DEPO-PROVERA AND STERILIZATION ABUSE OVERVIEW, Marie M. Cassidy

1. Naierman, N., "Sex Discrimination in Health and Human Development Services." Under contract to Office O.C.R., H.E.W., June 1979.
2. Huston, P., *Third World Women Speak Out! Interviews in Six Countries on Change, Development and Basic Needs,* Overseas Development Council, Praeger, New York, 1979.
3. Newland, K., *The Sisterhood of Man,* A Worldwatch Institute Book, Norton, New York, 1979.

THE DEPO-PROVERA WEAPON, Gena Corea

Hearing transcripts are coded in the following way in the footnotes:

Transcript A. "Fertility and Contraception in America, Domestic Fertility Trends and Family Planning Services," Hearings before the Select Committee on Population," February 23, 1978.

Transcript B. "The Depo-Provera Debate," Hearings before the Select Committee on Population, US House of Representatives, August 8, 9, 10, 1978.

Transcript C. "Use of Advisory Committees by the FDA," Subcommittee of the Committee on Government Operations, March 6, 7, 8, 12 and 13; April 30 and May 21, 1974.

Transcript D. "Quality of Health Care—Human Experimentation," Hearings before the Subcommittee on Health of the Committee on Labor and Public Welfare, US Senate, February 21, 22, 1973. Part I.

1. The argument that the Department of Defense should stop world population growth might seem reasonable to the US Agency for International Development (AID), which is conducting an inundation campaign to flood the Third World with the Pill. Critic Stephen Minkin describes the campaign as "the equivalent of the U.S. military's saturation bombing of Vietnam." (See: Minkin, S., "Bangladesh: The Pop Con

Game," *Healthright* **5**(1), 3 (1979). Available from HealthRight Inc., 41 Union Square, Room 206-8, N.Y., N.Y. 10003.

At those Congressional hearings, Dr. Charles Cargille, director of the Division of Population Studies in the Department of Community Medicine at the University of North Dakota, strongly supported Mumford: "The United States will collapse not from the growth of the American population, but from the growth of foreign populations..."

Expressing a fear reminiscent of that of eugenicists in the early 20th century, he added: "The American future will not be determined chiefly by the growth of the American population—unless they are Mexican immigrants and other Latins entering illegally across the Southern border. From 60 to 80 million Mexican immigrants over the next 20 to 30 years may well change the nature of this country."

To solve the population problem, Cargille told Congress, the US needed an agency "which is already incredibly large, well manned, well funded, and possessing worldwide transportation capabilities." Such an agency exists, he declared: "The Department of Defense." Cargille, however, was willing to give the job to NASA or a NASA-type agency provided its internal structure followed the vital military model.

For Cargille's testimony, see: Transcript A, Volume I, pp. 171–183. For Mumford's testimony, see: p. 197. Also see: pp. 366–416.

The paper I referred to that uses such terms as "vaginal delivery system" is entitled "Role of Controlled Drug Delivery in Contraception." Authors are F. G. Burton, G. W. Duncan, and W. E. Skiens. It appears in Transcript A, Volume III.

2. For the full Ravenholt interview, see: Wagman, P., "U.S. Goal: Sterilize Millions of World's Women," *St. Louis Post-Dispatch,* April 22, 1977.

Dr. Ravenholt listed the protection of US economic interests as one reason why the US should lead world population control effects. He explained: "Without our trying to help these countries with their economic and social development, the world would rebel against the strong US commercial presence. The self-interest thing is a compelling element."

3. Even though Depo-Provera has not been approved as a contraceptive, it is available to physicians because it is FDA-approved for palliative treatment in cancer.

For an acknowledgement that Depo-Provera "is being used for contraceptive purposes by a significant physician population," see p. 448, Transcript C. Also see: Corea, G., *The Hidden Malpractice,* Jove, New York, 1978, pp. 174–178.

In clinical studies conducted on Depo-Provera, a disproportionate number of women of color seem to have been subjected to the experimental drug. Between February, 1965, and July 1, 1968, studies were conducted on 2926 women, 88% of whom were clinic patients. Of these clinic patients, almost half (47.5%) were women of color. There were 2266 clinic patients and 660 private patients in the studies. Of the private patients, 86.8% were white. Hispanic women may have been included in the "white" category. This point is not clear from the data. Source:

"DepoProvera 50 MG/CC, 150 MG. Every Three Months as a Female Contraceptive, Summary of Clinical Data Submitted Through July 1, 1968."

Statements on who Depo-Provera targets are or should be appear in the following sources: comment by Dr. C.-R. Garcia, Medical Tribune, March 22, 1978; *The Lancet,* August 27, 1977; Harne, L., *Spare Rib,* April, 1978; Transcript D, testimony by R. H. Hutcheson, Jr. and Dr. N. Kase.

In 1973, FDA stated that it intended to permit the use of Depo-Provera as a contraceptive, not for all women, but "for the patient who accepts the possibility that she may not be able to become pregnant after discontinuing the drug, and *who refuses or is unable to accept the responsibility* demanded by other contraceptive methods, *or is incapable or unwilling* to tolerate the side effects of conventional oral contraceptives, or is one in whom other methods of contraception are contraindicated or have repeatedly failed" (emphasis mine).

It is argued that Depo-Provera would be appropriate for women who cannot tolerate the estrogen-induced effects of the Pill. But Depo-Provera induces menstrual abnormalities that physicians usually treat by administering estrogen to suppress irregular and excessive bleeding. Dr. Mokhtar Toppozada testified to that effect at the August, 1978, Depo-Provera hearings. The administration of estrogen obviates any advantage of a progestin-only contraceptive, as FDA Commissioner Donald Kennedy acknowledged at the hearings.

I doubt that physicians are obtaining truly informed consent from the women into whom they inject Depo-Provera.

Dr. Nathan Kase, chairman of the ob/gyn department at Yale University School of Medicine, reported to Congress on his investigation into Depo-Provera use in Cumberland County, Tennessee: "Informed consent was not obtained, nor was an attempt made to achieve awareness or acceptance of this issue. In particular, the potential short and long term hazards of the drug were not discussed in any instance studied..." Transcript D.

Dr. Robert H. Hutcheson, Jr., assistant commissioner of the Tennessee Department of Health, testified at the same hearing. Some doctors failed to inform women that Depo-Provera was not FDA-approved as a contraceptive, he acknowledged. Furthermore, the drug's non-approved status was not mentioned on the Depo-Provera consent form. Senator Edward M. Kennedy asked Hutcheson if he thought that fact *ought* to be on the consent form. Hutcheson replied by asking Kennedy if *he* thought it should be. Kennedy said, "Yes." Hutcheson responded: "Okay, you have talked me into it." The hearing transcript records: "(Laughter)."

The assertion by many population control experts that women in the Third World freely "choose" Depo-Provera is open to question. In a paper written for a seminar at the Ministry of Health in Botswana, July 1978, Barbara B. Brown, now of Boston University, wrote:

"According to figures in *Medical Statistics 1976,* there is very wide variation in Depo-Provera use from clinic to clinic. In some clinics as many as 42 percent of all women family planning users were using Depo-Provera, while in other clinics no women were using the drug. The most likely explanation is one offered to me by some clinic staff themselves, who told me, "'I favor Depo' or 'I am a Pill person.'"

It appears that the clinic personnel, rather than the women themselves, may be choosing the type of contraceptive used. (See Brown's paper: "Some Aspects of Women and Health." I obtained the paper from the Boston Women's Health Book Collective, Box 192, West Somerville, Mass. 02144.) Brown added: "Unfortunately, in poor countries where women have little education and limited knowledge of physiology and also have an unquestioning respect for authority, women are forced to put their trust in the medical staff."

4. In the 1930s, eugenicists argued that the poor were irresponsible and stupid and could not practice contraception, L. Gordon writes in *Woman's Body, Woman's Right* (Penguin Books, New York, 1974, pp. 308–313). She adds: "The eugenic conclusion that the poor were stupid and immoral provided ammunition for a renewed campaign for sterilization during the Depression."

   As Gordon points out, both organizationally and individually, eugenicists became population controllers between 1930 and 1950 (p. 396). For more information on the eugenics and population control movements, see: Gordon's book; Howard, T., and J. Rifkin, *Who Shall Play God?*, Dell, New York, 1977, pp. 47–82; Corea, G., *The Hidden Malpractice,* pp. 144–155.

5. Rosenfield, A. G., "Injectable Long-Acting Progestogen Contraception: a Neglected Modality," *Amer. J. Obstet. Gynecol.* **120**(4), 537–548 (Oct. 15, 1974).

6. Dr. Juan Zanartu, professor of Human Reproductive Endocrinology at the University of Chile Medical School, has stated that in a test of Depo-Provera, "All subjects were informed as well on expected side effects. To a certain level, these are the cost for reliable contraception. Thus, our subjects accepted the risk of headaches, amenorrhea, irregular uterine bleeding, some diminution of libido and/or orgasm, etc."

   Should a male contraceptive become available that would diminish the man's "libido and/or orgasm, etc.," I wonder whether Dr. Zanartu would take it lightly, passing off the loss as merely "the cost for reliable contraception." See Transcript B.

7. No one knows whether there are metabolic or hormonal changes related to prolonged amenorrhea, Toppozada observed. Nor does anyone know what impact changes in menstrual cycles might have on women with endemic diseases or metabolic disorders. See Toppozada's testimony in Transcript B.

8. *Maturation of Fetal Body Systems,* World Health Organization Technical Report, Series No. 40, 1974, p. 27. Cited in paper by Stephen Minkin, "Depo-Provera: A Critical Analysis," May, 1979. To be published in *Women & Health* **5**(2), in press.

As Dr. Juan Zanartu has stated: "...the effect of DMPA (Depo-Provera) on the nursed infant is unknown." Transcript B.

9. Harfouche, J. K., in *Fertility Regulation During Human Lactation,* Parkes, A. S., ed., IPPF, London, 1976, p. 170.
10. Gray, R., in *Fertility Regulation During Human Lactation, op. cit.,* p. 174.
11. Satahasthit, N., et al., *J. Reproductive Fertil.* **46,** 411–412 (1976). Cited in Minkin, "Depo-Provera: A Clinical Analysis."

Prolonged exposure of infants to the transferred steroid in milk, Toppozada has testified, "may have serious consequences in later life particularly with respect to reproductive performance, metabolic disorders or neoplastic potential." See Transcript B.

12. McDaniel, E. B., and T. Pardthaison, "Use Effectiveness of Six-Month Injections of DMPA As a Contraceptive, *Amer. J. Obstet. Gynecol.,* **119**(2), 174–180 (1974).

In his review of published literature on the teratogenic effects of female hormones, Samuel Shapiro, co-director of the Drug Epidemiology Unit at Boston University Medical Center, concluded that female hormones may cause cardiac deformities, and perhaps other deformities as well, when used in early pregnancy. He added that "there are reasonable scientific grounds for suspecting that exogenous female hormones, medroxyprogesterone (Depo-Provera) included, may be harmful to the fetus." Transcript B.

13. See Transcript C, p. 324.
14. Dr. Victor Berliner of the FDA, who attended the meetings, confirmed that fact for me in a telephone conversation June 6, 1979.

Either the beagle dog is an adequate model for testing the long-term effects of sex hormones on the human breast or it is not. In either case, at this stage of our knowledge, we have no business giving this drug to human beings.

If the beagle is not adequate and if no adequate model exists, then it is not possible to guarantee, even minimally, that this drug is safe for women. If this is the case, we have no right to inject it into women, especially when the drug's purpose is merely to prevent conception, not to treat a life-threatening disease.

But evidence suggests that the beagle dog is indeed an appropriate model, and, since studies on the beagle implicate Depo-Provera as a carcinogen (as do studies in the monkey), we are not justified in using this drug as a contraceptive.

In a 1976 report, Anita Johnson of the Health Research Group (HRG) dealt with the "inadequate test model" argument in this way: She pointed out that there is no evidence that beagles are more susceptible to progestins than humans, and that beagles excrete progestins at a rate remarkably similar to humans. (Transcript of the FDA Ob-Gyn Committee, February 22, 1973, p. 143. Comments of Dr. Victor R. Berliner, FDA.)

Control dogs not given the drug do not have a high incidence of breast tumors, Johnson notes. In fact, two industry scientists pointed out that they have a "remarkably low" incidence. Hill, D., and H. Dumas, "Use of Dogs for Studies of Toxicity of Contraceptive Hormones," in Briggs, M. H., *Pharmacological Models in Contraceptive Development,* World Health Organization Research and Training Center in Human Reproduction, Stockholm, 1974; also Berliner, *op. cit.,* p. 84; and Huggins, "Steroids, Growth and Cancer," in *Biological Activities of Steroids in Relation to Cancer,* Pincus and Vollmer (1959).

Johnson further observes that beagles do not get tumors from all progestins. Although some synthetic progestins cause cancer in beagles, others such as norethindrone, do not. Johnson concludes with a quotation from *Acta Endocrinologica* **supp. 185,** 252 (1974), that there is "no reason of value to disregard the results obtained in the beagle studies for the tumorigenic or carcinogenic potential of hormonal contraceptives..." (See: A. Johnson, "Depo-Provera—A Contraceptive for Poor Women," December, 1976. A Health Research Group report. Available from: Health Research Group, 2000 P Street, NW, Washington, D.C. 20036.)

In discussing the risk of breast cancer posed by Depo-Provera, then FDA Commissioner Donald Kennedy also commented on the beagle question: "Although there has been much debate over the appropriateness of the beagle as a test model, an ideal animal model for this risk assessment simply does not exist... Although we still do not know whether the increased occurrence of breast cancer in dogs can be extrapolated directly to humans, the Bureau views the drug as posing a significant potential risk to users. No contraceptives currently approved for marketing have shown a similar carcinogenic potential in the beagle assay." Transcript B.

Furthermore, the Ad Hoc Committee on Evaluation of Environmental Chemical Carcinogens noted in its 1970 report to the Surgeon General: "Any substance which is shown conclusively to cause tumors in animals should be considered carcinogenic and therefore a potential cancer hazard for man... No level of exposure to a chemical carcinogen should be considered toxicologically insignificant for man." ("Evaluation of Environmental Carcinogens," Report to the Surgeon General of the Ad Hoc Committee on Evaluation of Environmental Chemical Carcinogens," April 22, 1970.)

15. In Depo-Provera studies reported to FDA, from 9 to 16 women (depending on whether Upjohn or FDA figures are used) developed cervical carcinoma *in situ.* Thirteen women developed Grade III pap smears, which are defined as "cytology suggestive of, but not conclusive for, malignancy." There is no indication that the 13 women were followed up to see if they developed cancer.

It was impossible to compare the 9 to 16 cases of cervical carcinoma *in situ* among the Depo-Provera group with the cases in the control group because Upjohn had no control group. So a Congressional committee compared those figures with the cancer rates in the general population as measured by the Third National Cancer Survey (3NCS)—36 per 100,000.

The rates in the Depo-Provera group were 235 per 100,000 if Upjohn's figures were used, and 410 with FDA's figures.

When the gross excess of cervical carcinoma *in situ* figures for the Depo-Provera users were reported, FDA objected to the comparison with the 3NCS on the grounds that it might have under-reported the real incidence of cervical cancer among women. Depo-Provera users were screened periodically by pap smear so all cases of cancer would be found, the argument went, while women in the survey were not screened and might have undetected cancer.

To meet this objection, the Health Research Group found groups of women who had been repeatedly screened after they'd been diagnosed as normal with a preliminary pap smear. Using one study, it found that black Depo-Provera users had a 2.67-fold excess of cervical cancer above black women in Memphis. The excess in white Depo-Provera users was 6.1-fold. Depo-Provera users also had a 4.4-fold excess of cervical cancer over women in a British Columbia study.

Anita Johnson, author of the HRG report, commented: "These comparisons meet the objections of the Third National Cancer Survey raised by FDA and the results are consistent with the 3 NCS comparison... Even when the control group is screened so as to increase the potential for detecting early cervical cancer, there is still much more cancer found in Depo-Provera users than in non-users." (See: "Depo-Provera—A Contraceptive for Poor Women," op cit., pp. 5, 6.)

Upjohn issued a 35-page rebuttal to the HRG report. "They never once attacked those statistics or the appropriateness of those comparisons," Johnson, now an attorney with the US Justice Department, told me on June 5, 1979. "My report has never been rebutted by anybody. Immediately after it came out, FDA decided not to approve Depo-Provera."

I asked Upjohn for a copy of its rebuttal to Johnson's report for use in this paper, but I have not received it.

16. Stephen Minkin told me he had put in a Freedom of Information Act request to the FDA for documents detailing FDA's reasoning behind approval of the protocol. FDA, he said, supplied him with just one memo with one paragraph mentioning that it was okaying the hysterectomies. But there was no explanation for the decision. Minkin commented: "I said to the FDA over the phone and I'll put it in writing: Am I to assume that this was done and there was not a single record kept on the whole matter?"

17. Minkin, S., "Depo-Provera: A Critical Analysis," May, 1979. Available through the National Women's Health Network, 224 7th Street, S.E., Washington, D.C. 20003.

18. Minkin notes that the claim that the beagle uterus is especially susceptible to progestins is similar to the claim that the beagle breast is especially susceptible to tumors. He has completed a computer search of the medical literature to see whether there are any studies proving or suggesting that the beagle uterus is particularly susceptible to progestogens. He reports: "There is no documentation in the modern literature regarding this." He

plans to do another computer search going some years back to see if there are any studies in this area.

19. Anita Johnson made this observation to me in conversation. Formerly an attorney with HRG, Johnson now works for the US Department of Justice.

20. Minkin is requesting from FDA any records relating to why FDA did not consider the risk of uterine cancer in followup studies.

21. Discrepancies in reports on the monkeys who developed endometrial cancer (at least two out of 10 by one calculation, and two out of 12 by another) owe to difficulties encountered in making accurate calculations when animals have been added to and removed from the study while it was on-going.

22. Wyrick, R., "Contraceptive Tied to Cancer," *Newsday,* June 3, 1979. For details on the monkey study protocol, see: "Long Term Intramuscular Study in the Monkey (Twenty-four Month Interim Report)" September 4, 1970. Copy available through the National Women's Health Network (NWHN), 224 7th St. S.E.. Washington, D.C. 20003.

23. Conversation with Upjohn spokesperson, Terry G. Kelley, June 5, 1979.

24. Wyrick, R., *Newsday,* op. cit.

Former FDA Commissioner Donald Kennedy has also answered the general charge that in FDA animal test protocols, scientifically inappropriate doses are used to test for carcinogenicity. He wrote: "We have to begin from the premise that humans share most basic biological mechanisms with other animals, and that among those mechanisms is that responsible for susceptibility to cancer. With the possible exceptions of arsenic and benzene, *all* known human carcinogens are also carcinogenic in lab animals. In the design of animal experiments, we are faced with the problem that many types of cancer in humans do not show up for 30 years or longer—by which time the small laboratory mammal, along with ten or more generations of its descendants, has passed into history. And if we are looking for something that causes, say, a cancer in one of every 10,000 persons exposed, it will be necessary to use several times 10,000 animals in the experimental group alone. Yet an incidence of 1/10,000 is the equivalent of 23,000 new cases of cancer in the United States population. There just are not enough laboratories, toxicologists, animal handlers, money, or time to do this for each of the thousands of chemicals that must be tested. So, we compensate for the shortness of the test animal's lifespan and the necessary smallness of the sample by compensating on the other end of the test equation: we increase the dose. That rationale is based on substantial experience with the form of the relationship between dose and response. Despite the impression widely held in the lay public, we are not inducing cancer by excess. In such experiments most compounds do *not* turn out to be carcinogenic." D. Kennedy, Ten medical myths about FDA, *West. J. Med* 127(12), 529-534 (1977).

25. International Research and Development Corporation (IRDC), "Long Term Intramuscular Study in Beagle Dogs—Twenty-Four Month Interim," September 4, 1970. Available through NWHN (see note 22).

26. FDA, "Pharmacology Supplemental Review," April 19, 1977. FDA noted: "The onset of diabetes and eventual death of two dogs receiving DP (Depo-Provera) could also be attributable to the treatment."
27. IRDC, "24-Month Interim Report," September 4, 1970, op. cit.

   FDA's Pharmacology Supplemental Review dated April 19, 1977 refers to two dogs in the first study who developed widely metastasized breast adenocarcinomas. One dog died in the 42nd month of the study and the other was killed *in extremis* during the 40th month. The review notes: "These dogs developed malignant mammary tumors at a relatively early age, which would suggest their development was compound-related rather than an inherent spontaneous development . . . The incidence of benign mixed tumors and lobular hyperplastic lesions in both treatment groups was very high, when compared to the control group, and certainly can be attributed to DP."

   The incidence of mortality during the first dog study was: 6% for the control group; 50% for the low dose Depo-Provera group; and 100% for the high dose Depo-Provera group.
28. Minkin, S., "Depo-Provera: A Critical Analysis," op. cit. Minkin noted in his paper: "At 24 months, mortality in the high dose monkeys was three times greater than in controlled monkeys. The IRDC report attributed the monkey deaths to sub-acute gastric dilation, pneumonia and enteritis. These findings do not rule out the possibility that Depo-Provera, by interfering with the immune response system, makes the treated animals more susceptible to fatal illness."
29. I am endebted to Judith Dickson Luce, Boston midwife, for this insight.
30. See: Form 8, Amendment to Application, Securities and Exchange Commission (SEC), Act of 1934. Received by SEC on July 30, 1976. Sent by Gerard Thomas, vice-president, secretary and general counsel of Upjohn. We do not know which Upjohn products the company was attempting to promote by making these payments.

   Minkin notes: Besides bribed officials, others deciding to import non-FDA-approved drugs into their countries would often be western-trained bureaucrats whose PhDs have been paid for by Western governments or institutions. They are given various incentives to judge issues through the eyes of powerful westerners.

STERILIZATION ABUSE AND HISPANIC WOMEN,
Sandra Serrano Sewell

1. California Department of Health Services memorandum, July 8, 1977, p. 3
2. "Physician Attitudes: MD's Assume Poor Can't Remember to Take Pills," *Family Planning Digest,* no. 13 (January, 1972).
3. Coalition for the Medical Rights of Women, San Francisco, California, 1978.

4. *Stop Forced Sterilization Now,* The Committee to Stop Forced Sterilization.
5. *Madrigal vs Quilligan,* Civil Action no. 75 2057, U.S. District Court Central District of California, filed, June 18, 1975.
6. "10 Lose Their Fertility and Their Case," *Los Angeles Times,* September 28, 1978.
7. *Ibid.*
8. *Ibid.*

CHILDBIRTH OVERVIEW, Norma Swenson

1. Most modern women do give birth, however, and most feminists find the event an enormous personal and political struggle, whether or not a father is intimately involved. We are vulnerable to the idea that we must justify having a child. The older morality that made unmarried sexual intercourse the primary sin has been transformed: to have unprotected intercourse or to have an unwanted child—these have become the sins. Many of us will have no more than one birth in our lifetimes. Increasingly it is an intentional act. For many, it is an event that has long been postponed and may never be repeated. Firestone, S., *The Dialectic of Sex:* The Case for Feminist Revolution, Bantam, New York, 1971.
2. Questioning the values on which our system is based is still not generally thinkable, particularly about birth. In this, as Brigitte Jordan and Sheila Kitzinger have pointed out, we resemble all other societies. (For Jordan's work, see Susan Ekstrom's account in this book; see also, Kitzinger, S., and J. Davis, eds., *The Place of Birth: A Study of the Environment in Which Birth Takes Place,* Oxford University Press, Oxford, England, 1978. Also, *The Experience of Childbirth,* 1974 and *Women as Mothers,* Random House, 1979.
3. Sociologist Irving Zola identified medicine as an institution of social control; it has remained for the Women's Health Movement to analyze and explore the extent to which modern medicine serves as an institution of social control over contemporary women in industrial society. Zola, I. K., "Medicine as an Institution of Social Control," *The Sociological Review,* new series (England) **20** (4), (November, 1972). Also in *Sociology of Medical Practice,* Cox, C., and A. Mead, Collier Macmillan, New York, 1975, pp. 170–185.

MAN-MIDWIFERY AND THE RISE OF TECHNOLOGY, Dorothy C. Wertz

1. Nash, C. E., *The History of Augusta, Including the Diary of Mrs. Martha Moore Ballard, 1785–1812,* Augusta, 1904.

2. Demos, J., *A Little Commonwealth: Family Life in the Plymouth Colony*, Oxford University Press, New York, 1970.
   Greven, P. J., *Four Generations: Population, Land and Family in Colonial Andover, Massachusetts*, Cornell University, Ithaca, N.Y., 1970.
3. The midwife was Margaret Stephens in London in the 1790s (Aveling, 1892, p. 127)
4. Nihell, E., *A Treatise on the Art of Midwifery: Setting Forth Various Abuses Therein, Especially as to the Practice with Instruments*, London, 1760.
5. Aveling, J. H., *English Midwives, Their History and Prospects*, London, 1892.
6. Anonymous, *Remarks on the Employment of Females as Practitioners in Midwifery*, Boston, 1820.
7. Kobrin, F. E., The American Midwife Controversy: A Crisis in Professionalization, *Bull. Hist. Med.* **40**, 356 (1966).
8. New York Academy of Medicine Committee on Public Health Relations, *Maternal Mortality in New York City: A Study of All Puerperal Deaths, 1930-1932*, New York, 1933.
9. White House Conference on Child Health and Protection, *Fetal, Newborn, and Maternal Mortality and Morbidity*, New York, 1933.
10. DeLee, J. B., The Prophylactic Forceps Operation, *Am. J. Obstet. Gynecol.* **1**, 34 (1920).
11. U. S. Bureau of the Census, *Statistical Abstract of the U.S.*, 1978.
12. Baird, D., Sociological Considerations of Maternal and Infant Capabilities, in *Horizons in Perinatal Research*, Kretchmer, N., and E. G. Hasselmeyer, eds., New York, 1970.

THE ELECTRONIC FETAL MONITOR IN PERINATOLOGY, Henry Klapholz

1. Benson, R. C., et al., Fetal Heart Rate as Predictor of Fetal Distress, *Obstet. Gynecol.* **32**, 259 (1968).
2. Haverkamp, A. D., et al. A Controlled Trial of the Differential Effects of Intrapartum Fetal Monitoring, *Am. J. Obstet. Gynecol.* **125**, 310 (1976).
3. Hon, E. H., The Electronic Evaluation of the Fetal Heart Rate, *Am. J. Obstet. Gynecol.* **75**, 1215 (1956).
4. Paul, R. N., et al., The Evaluation and Significance of Intrapartum Baseline Variability, *Am. J. Obstet. Gynecol.* **123**, 206 (1975).
5. Schitrin, B. S., et al., Fetal Heart Rate Patterns as Predictors of Apgar Score, *JAMA* **219**, 1322 (1972).

DRUGS, BIRTH, AND ETHICS, Yvonne Brackbill

1. *Bibliographic reviews of studies of the effects of prescription and nonprescription drugs:* American Pharmaceutical Association, *Handbook of Nonprescription drugs,* 5th ed., American Pharmaceutical Association, Washington, D.C., 1977.
   Gottlieb, G., ed., *Studies on the Development of Behavior and the Nervous System,* vol. 4, *Early Influences,* Academic, New York (1976).
   Mofenson, H. C., J. Greensher, and R. Horowitz, Hazards of Maternally Administered Drugs, *Clin. Toxicol.* **7,** 59 (1974).
   Schardein, J. L., *Drugs as Teratogens,* Chemical Rubber Co., Cleveland, 1976.
   Shepard, T. H., *Catalog of Teratogenic Agents,* 2nd ed., The Johns Hopkins University Press, Baltimore, 1976.
   Stewart, R. B., L. E. Cluff, and J. R. Philp, eds., *Drug Monitoring: A Requirement for Responsible Drug Use,* Baltimore, Williams & Wilkins, 1977.
   Warkany, J., *Congenital Malformation,* Yearbook Medical, Chicago, 1975.
   Wilson, J. G., and F. C. Fraser, eds., *Handbook of Teratology,* vol. 4, Plenum, New York, 1977.
2. The Food and Drug Administration's new Committee on Anesthesiology and Life Support Systems met for the first time March 19 and 20, 1979. Its priority deliberation was to evaluate the data from the studies shown in Table 2. Although the committee unanimously agreed that adverse effects of obstetric drugs had been demonstrated in neonates, it did not agree to make this information available to consumers.
3. "Use of Drugs for Unapproved Indications: Your Legal Responsibility," *FDA Drug Bulletin,* Oct. 1972.
4. The GAO 1976 Report to the Congress, "Federal Control of New Drug Testing Is Not Adequately Protecting Human Test Subjects and the Public" shows that 74% of clinical investigators failed to comply with one or more requirements of the law and regulations.

BENEFITS AND RISKS OF ELECTRONIC FETAL MONITORING, David Banta

1. Banta, H. D., and S. B. Thacker, *Costs and Benefits of Electronic Fetal Monitoring: A Review of the Literature,* Hyattsville, MD, National Center for Health Services Research, Department of Health, Education, and Welfare, April, 1979 (DHEW Publication No. PHS 79-3245).

2. Banta, H. D. and S. B. Thacker, *Obstetrics and Gynecological Survey*, August 1979.
3. Haverkamp, A. D., H. E. Thompson, J. G. McFee, et al., The evaluation of continuous fetal heart rate monitoring in labor, *Amer. J. Obstet. Gynecol.* **125**, 310–317 (1976).
4. Haverkamp, A. D., M. Orleans, S. Langendoerfer, et al., A controlled trial of the differential effects of intrapartum fetal monitoring, *Amer. J. Obstet. Gynecol.* **134**, 399–408 (1979).
5. Renou, P., A. Chang, I., Anderson, et al., Controlled trial of fetal intensive care, *Amer. J. Obstet. Gynecol.* **126**, 470–476 (1976).
6. Kelso, I. M., R. J. Parsons, G. F. Sawrence, et al., An assessment of continuous fetal heart rate monitoring in labor, *Amer. J. Obstet. Gynecol.* **131**, 526–532 (1978).
7. Roux, J. F., M. R. Neuman, and R. C. Goodlin, Monitoring of intrapartum phenomena, *CRC Critical Reviews in Bioengineering* **2**, 119–131 (1975).
8. National Institute of Child Health and Human Development: Task Force on Predictors of Fetal Distress (Draft), Consensus Development Conference on Antenatal Diagnosis, prepared as a working document for discussion on March 5–7, 1979, Bethesda, MD, National Institutes of Health.
9. Johnstone, F. D., D. M. Campbell, and G. J. Hughes, Has continuous intrapartum monitoring made any impact on fetal outcome?, *Lancet* **1**, 1298–1300 (1978).
10. Paul, R., and E. Hon, Clinical fetal monitoring. V. Effect on perinatal outcome, *Amer. J. Obstet. Gynecol.* **118**, 529–166 (1977).

ETHICAL ISSUES IN CHILDBIRTH TECHNOLOGY, Sheryl Burt Ruzek

1. See, e.g., Cochrane, A. *Effectiveness and Efficiency: Random Reflections on Health Services*, London, Nuffield Provincial Hospitals Trust, 1971; Illich, I. *Medical Nemesis: The Expropriation of Health*, New York, Pantheon Books, 1976; McKeown, T. *The Role of Medicine: Dream, Mirage, or Nemesis?*, London, Nuffield Provincial Hospitals Trust, 1976; *Medicine in Modern Society: Medical Planning Based on Evaluation of Medical Achievement*, London, George Allen and Unwin, 1965; and Reiser, S. J., *Medicine and the Rein of Technology*, Cambridge, Cambridge University Press, 1978.
2. Banta, H. D. and S. B. Thacker, "Costs and Benefits of Electronic Fetal Monitoring: A Review of the Literature," NCHSR Research Report Series, DHEW Publication No. (PHS) 79–3245, April, 1979.
3. See, e.g., Friedman, E. A. "Obstetrical Anesthetics and Analgesics: What are the Real Risks to the Fetus?" *Medical World News*, March 19, 1979, p.

93, and Kolata, G. B., "Scientists Attack Report That Obstetrical Medications Endanger Children," *Science,* **204,** 391, (April 27, 1979). Y. Brackbill (personal communication, June 1979) argues that she and S. Broman did not, as alleged, take their findings to the press before publishing in scholarly journals; the press sought them out.

4. The efforts of these groups are documented in S. Ruzek, *The Women's Health Movement: Feminist Alternatives to Medical Control,* New York, Praeger, 1978.

A REPORT ON BIRTH IN THREE CULTURES,
Susan Cope Ekstrom

1. Jordan, B., *Birth in Four Cultures,* Eden Press Women's Publications, Montreal and St. Albans, Vermont, 1978.
2. Ibid., p. 67.
3. Ibid., pp. 3–4.
4. Two of the most pervasive misconceptions about "primitive" childbirth are that it is painless and that it is easy (or at least that it is much easier than "civilized" birth). Both of these beliefs are clearly false. For example, in the Yucatecan system, the most "primitive" of the three systems described here, having a baby is clearly regarded as work, and some pain is an expected part of birth. The Yucatecans say, in fact, that the baby is born "in the very center of the pain" (*en el centro del dolor*). Although some women in any society seem to give birth without experiencing pain, it is also clear that pain is a recognized and expected part of the birth process in almost all societies. See also: Freedman, Z., and V. M. Ferguson, The Question of "Painless Childbirth" in primitive cultures, *Amer. J. Orthopsychiat.* **20,** 363 (1950).
5. Jordan., B., op. cit., p. 85.
6. Although there will of course be variations even within this system, there is every reason to believe that the majority of American women give birth under conditions similar to those described here. Jordan adds that "it is true that natural childbirth has made some inroads in the last decade, especially in smaller community hospitals; however, there are still many hospitals, particularly hospitals with a large volume of low-income patients, who provide no more than token accommodation to the philosophy of natural childbirth." (Jordan, p. 98). See also: Shaw, N. S., *Forced Labor: Maternity Care in the United States,* Pergamon, New York, 1974.
7. Other locally invariable features of birth would include who is permitted to be present, where the birth is properly located, what kinds of tools and equipment are seen as being necessary, and local methods of preparing the woman for the course and experience of labor and birth (see the Appendix).
8. Treating birth as a medical event is "consistent with the fact that in contemporary U.S. society physiological processes in general fall into the

medical domain. Thus, nutrition, sexual adjustment, sleeping patterns, mood swings, obesity, learning difficulties, alcoholism, drug abuse, violence, dying, and all sorts of 'deviance,' are considered proper subjects for medical attention" (Jordan p. 35).

9. Parsons, T., *The Social System,* The Free Press, Glencoe, Illinois, 1951.
10. I use masculine pronouns to refer to physicians—and feminine pronouns to refer to midwives—to reflect the fact that in the cultures under discussion most physicians are in fact male and most midwives are female.
11. The assumptions about who is responsible for birth in our culture are revealed, for example, in the kinds of questions that are put to women (or couples) who declare their intention to give birth at home. Inevitably someone will ask, "But what if something (unspecified) goes wrong? Wouldn't you feel terrible?" The assumption obviously is that in the hospital the woman (or couple) is *not* responsible, in some important way, for what happens (though presumably she/they will still feel "terrible" if something does go "wrong").
12. "Complications during pregnancy, for example, or with a previous birth will channel a woman to the hospital and so will crowding at home, substandard housing conditions, absence of help postpartum, and the like. If a woman prefers to go to the hospital but does not qualify according to these criteria she can do so but is charged for the cost of her hospital stay. Otherwise all perinatal services are free." Jordan, p. 100.
13. Jordan, B. op. cit., p. 49.
14. Ibid., p. 86.
15. Ibid.
16. A significant increase in maternal satisfaction will be accompanied by an improvement in infant outcome statistics. This improvement will occur, Jordan argues, "not necessarily because the new methods will be 'better' in any objective sense but because they reduce the dissonance between the woman's conception of herself and the treatment she is accorded." (Jordan, p. 100) An article by Rosengren, despite significant methodological problems, is of interest in this context. Rosengren classified doctors and parturient women according to whether they saw pregnancy as 'illness' or not. Those women who held the same view of pregnancy as their obstetricians, regardless of whether this was a 'sick' or a 'well' view, had amazingly shorter labor times. They took an average of 6.7 as compared to the 'discrepant' group's 13.7 hours. Rosengren, W. R., Some Social Psychological Aspects of Delivery Room Difficulties, *J. Nerv. Ment. Dis.* **132,** 515 (1961).

MIDWIVES IN MANY SETTINGS,
Helen Swallow

1. Interprofessional Task Force on Health Care of Women and Children Joint Position Statement on the Development of Family-Centered Maternity/Newborn Care in Hospitals, Chicago, 1978.

2. Rosengren, W. R. Some Social Psychological Aspects of Delivery Room Difficulties, *Journal of Nervous and Mental Disease* 1961h, **132**, 515.
3. Levy, B., et al., Reducing Neonatal Mortality Rate with Nurse-Midwives, *Amer. Coll. Obset. Gynecol.* 1971, **109**, 50.
4. Chalmers, I., et al, Obstetric Practice and Outcome of Pregnancy in Cardiff Residents, 1965–1973, *British Med J. 1976*, **1**, 735.
5. Fryer, J. G., and J. R. Ashford, Trends in Perinatal and Neonatal Mortality in England and Wales 1960–69. *British J. Prevent. Social Med.* 26, *1*, (1976).
6. Pearse, W. *Ob-Gyn News* **12**, 1; 33 (1977)
7. Stowe, M., Pearse, *op. cit.*
8. Pearse, W. *Ob-Gyn News* **13**, 1; 35 (1978).
9. Pittenger, J. Consumer Characteristics: Attitudes of Connecticut Home Birth and Birthroom Populations, unpublished Masters Report, Yale School of Nursing, New Haven, 1979.
10. Hazell, L. *Birth Goes Home,* Seattle, Catalyst Publishing, (1974).
11. Stewart, A., and L. E. Mehl, A Rebuttal to Negative Birth Statistics Cited by ACOG, *in* Stewart, L. and D. Steward (Eds.), *21st Century Obstetrics Now,* Chapel Hill, NAPSAC, 1977.

RESPONSE, Norma Swenson

1. Illich, I., I. K. Zola, J. McKnight, J. Caplan, and H. Shaiken. *Disabling Professions,* Marion Boyars Publications, London and Salem, New Hampshire, 1978.

Biographies

The following biographies outline the personal histories of those of our authors with substantial contributions in this volume. Discussants' biographies that do not appear here will be found in the companion volume, *The Custom-Made Child?.*

Barbara Hilkert Andolsen: I am currently completing a PhD in Theological Ethics at Vanderbilt University, Nashville, TN. My dissertation is an analysis of the problem of racism in the 19th and 20th century American feminist movements. I am an instructor in religion at Douglass College–Rutgers University. I am married; my husband, my 11-year old son, my infant daughter, and I live in New York City. I enjoy the new "women's novels," theatre, swimming, and jogging.

Jacki Ans: My present position is as the administrative person for grants in the Population Office of the Ford Foundation. Previously, I was involved with a world-wide, historical survey of the funding of reproductive science and contraceptive development for the Ford and Rockefeller Foundations. I spent my first nine professional years as a Family Planning Research Assistant/Counselor in the clinical services of the Columbia Presbyterian and Flower Fifth Avenue Medical Centers in New York City. I presently live in Queens, New York, with my two daughters, aged 18 and 13, and assorted pets. I enjoy playing the piano and being outdoors. I have recently completed my Bachelor's Degree at Adelphi University in the evenings; I plan to continue my education toward a Master's in Health Care.

Linda Atkinson: Population Office, The Ford Foundation, New York City

Byllye Y. Avery: I grew up in the South and have lived here all my life. In 1959 I received an AB degree in psychology and in 1969 earned an MEd from the University of Florida in Special Education. Married in June, 1960; birthed two children; widowed in 1970. For 6½ years I worked with autistic children as the Head Teacher in Child Psychiatry at the University of Florida. In May 1974, I was one of the founders of the Gainesville Women's Health Center. This center provides well-woman gynecological and abortion services. In October 1978, we opened a free-standing Birth Center—Birthplace—where I am currently having fantastic experiences. At home we are currently trying to figure out how to build a deck and hot tub!

H. David Banta: My academic training includes an MD from Duke (1963), internal medicine residency at the University of Washington, an MPH degree from Harvard (1968), and an MS degree from Harvard (1969) in health services administration and medical sociology. I was on the faculty of community medicine at Mount Sinai School of Medicine in New York City from 1969 to 1974, and have now made the transition to government bureaucrat after almost three years with the Office of Technology Assessment. I administer a research group of about 17 people, and we do studies for Congress on health issues of public policy importance. My wife Sandy and I share a passion for travel and for ballet. My four children (and our two) seem to have both enthusiasms. I first became interested in obstetric care because of experiences I had during the birth of those four children (I was present at the birth of three).

Helen B. Barnes: I was born in 1928, and did my undergraduate work at Hunter College before completing medical school at Howard University and serving residencies at Kings County Hospital in 1959–1960, and in 1963–1965. I was a Clinical Assistant at the Brooklyn Cumberland Medical Center in 1965–1968, and have been on the faculty at the University of Mississippi Medical Center since 1969. I entered private practice in Jackson, MS, in 1976, and have remained an Associate Professor at the University of Mississippi Medical Center, Department of Obstetrics and Gynecology, on a part-time basis since that time.

Joyce A. Berkman: With a long single braid over my left shoulder, I am Associate Professor of History at the University of Massachusetts (Amherst). I teach courses in American and British women's history for graduate and undergraduate students. My recently published monograph on the feminist writing of Olive Schreiner is being followed up by a comprehensive critical study of the many sides of her genius. The historical context for human thinking and behavior intrigues me whether on issues of reproductivity or patterns of initiating relationships leading to friendship. Bi-coastal, I was born in San Jose, California, and received my BA from UCLA; then I moved East, attended Yale for my MA and PhD, and finally settled in Amherst in 1965, where I live with my husband and two sons.

Yvonne Brackbill: I grew up on the west coast and got my BA from Berkeley and PhD from Stanford. I've worked as a child psychologist in Denver and Washington, DC, and am currently at the University of Florida, Gainesville. In addition to maternal and child health, my professional interests include bioethics and behavioral teratology. My favorite hobbies are swimming, sailing, gardening, and traveling.

Marie M. Cassidy: As a professor of physiology, I administer a graduate program for 32 MS and PhD candidates in physiology, and teach medical students, residents, and allied health professionals. My main research areas are cell membrane transport mechanisms in cardiac, eye, and gastrointestinal tissues—specifically in the diseases of cardiac hypertrophy and glaucoma— and the role of dietary fibers in health. I teach sex physiology and reproductive mechanisms to a spectrum of students. A dedicated inner city resident, I am married to an architect, have two sons and two daughters, am an active feminist in several organizations, and a veteran of PTA, community, and church affairs.

Katsi Cook: I am a 28-year-old wolf clan woman from the Mohawk Nation at Akwesasne and member of the Central Council of Women of All Red Nations. I am a lay midwife and mother of two children, Wahiahawi, 5, and Tsiorasa, 3. My husband José Barreiro and I are co-directors of the Circle of Life Survival School, and our work in women's health, anti-nuclear mobilization, education for survival, self-sufficiency, and our family, is our curriculum development. We are currently involved in a book project called Women's Dance, a health book for Native American women, and I am director of the Women's Dance Health Program in Minneapolis—St. Paul.

Gena Corea: Between reporting jobs for *The Berkshire Eagle* and *The Holyoke Transcript,* I attended the University of Massachusetts, graduating in 1971. I spent a year teaching English in Athens, Greece, and later wrote a book, *The Hidden Malpractice,* and a weekly newspaper column for The New Republic Feature Syndicate. Recently I spent two years in Germany with my husband. I enjoy bicycling, reading mysteries in German, and telling stories to my pre-school neighbors.

Terry Courtney: Representative of Women's Community Health Center.

Belita Cowan: I am Executive Director of the National Women's Health Network; author of *Women's Health Care: Resources, Writings, & Bibliographies* (1977); Medical Editor of *her-self* newspaper (1972–1977); Health Care Instructor, Washtenaw Community College, Ann Arbor, Mich. (1974–1977). My research on the drug, DES, and testimony as an expert witness before the US Senate Health Subcommittee (Edward Kennedy, chair) brought the DES issue to the attention of the Congress and the public. In my capacity as director of the only national women's organization devoted exclusively to women and health, I monitor federal health policy and assist the Women's Health Movement with grassroots organizing efforts.

Rosa C. Cuéllar: Since 1975 I've been an organizer for the Texas Farm Workers Union. Recently I worked with Texas Rural Legal Aid as a paralegal.

Susan Cope Ekstrom: Although I have been active in various feminist groups since the early 1970s, it was not until I began working in 1977 with Dr. Brigitte Jordan, an anthropologist at Michigan State University studying childbirth cross-culturally, that I satisfactorily combined my involvement in the Women's Movement with my academic interests [I have a BA in philosophy (1968) from Kalamazoo College and an MA in philosophy (1971) from MSU]. I have since given birth to my first child, trained to become an instructor for a local (Lansing, MI) childbirth education group, and begun my dissertation (in philosophy) on the value systems underlying alternate ways of doing birth. I am also interested in medical self care, alternative education for children, and Chinese philosophy.

Ina May Gaskin: I was born and raised in Marshalltown, Iowa, and have my BA in English from the State University of Iowa, Phi Beta Kappa. I participated in a 650-mile walk for peace with the Committee for Nonviolent Action, ending in Vallejo, California, in 1961, and later spent two years teaching English in Malaysia with the Peace Corps in 1963–1965. I obtained an MA in English from Northern Illinois University in 1967, and then left immediately for San Francisco to become a hippy. I taught English to adult Chinese immigrants for a few months. I became a self-taught midwife in 1970, and my book, *Spiritual Midwifery,* is a product of eight years of delivering babies at home and of training midwives. My husband and I have 10 children including biological and foster.

Mary Jane Gray: After graduating from Swarthmore College and Washington University Medical School, I spent five years as an OB/GYN resident at Columbia Presbyterian Hospital in New York. The usual academic–research–practice career followed, ending with me as Professor of OB/GYN at the Unversity of Vermont. My interest in abortion and other women's issues led to my involvement in the then developing Vermont Women's Health Center. A series of health crises caused me to reassess my priorities and led me to accept a job at the University of North Carolina, where I continue to teach medical students and serve as gynecologist for the Student Health Service. In my "spare" time, I write, edit, and maintain my interest in women's health.

Michael Gross: As a graduate student in the history of science (at Princeton) I focused on biomedical thought since the nineteenth century. During some five years of teaching at Hampshire College I have developed concurrent interests in problems of biology and society, especially theories of biological determinism and uses of science for social control. Although gay men are not necessarily sympathetic to feminism, for me that evolving body of political and philosophical thought continues to be of great inspiration. I am also interested in the theories of, and periodically a participant in, various forms of therapy or meditation that strive toward body-mind integration.

Helen Bequaert Holmes: I was born in Boston, raised in Cambridge, Massachusetts, and received a BA in chemistry from Oberlin College in 1951 and an MS in zoology from Cornell University in 1953. Then I moved to Amherst, Massachusetts, gave birth to and raised three children, was active in Girl Scouting and the Quaker meeting, and taught in high school. Later, at the age of 40, I completed a PhD in zoology (population genetics) at the University of Massachusetts. I have had an assortment of temporary college teaching posts and two year-long sojourns in The Netherlands. My hobbies are reading, canoeing, and hiking. I prefer to be called "Becky."

Betty B. Hoskins: Constitutionally I'm a generalist with a series of careers. I was trained as a biologist at liberal arts colleges (BS 1956, Goucher; MA 1958, Amherst College; PhD 1973, Texas Women's University—small children rearing in US and Europe in between.) At present I'm an Editor of Science Publications at a textbook publishing house. That midlife career change followed six years as a faculty member at an engineering–science college. The diversity of my interests in biology, bioethics, academic advising, and program development led to administrative training and the experience of institutional sexism. I have enjoyed working within professional, womens', and community groups to clarify choices in the applications of our newer biological knowledge, helping people of diverse backgrounds to hear and understand each other. Folkdancing, gardening, friends, and my two teenagers are also enjoyments.

Jeanne Hubbuch: Representative of Women's Community Health Center.

Renée Rosiland Jenkins: I am currently an assistant professor in Pediatrics at Howard University College of Medicine. I arrived there in 1975 via Wayne State University and residency training in New York City. I direct the Adolescent Services within the University Hospital, including the General Adolescent Service, Adolescent Prenatal Service (in cooperation with OB/GYN), and a Family Planning Program that is being restructured. We are encouraged to become active in the community; hence I serve on the Medical Advisory Board of Planned Parenthood, the Board of Directors for a group home, and the DC Task Force on Adolescent Sexuality and Parenting. My newest venture is appearing as a regular in the health segment of PM Magazine TV Show. My hobbies are tennis, horseback riding, and skiing.

Henry Klapholz: After completing two degrees in electrical engineering (1963 and 1965) and working as a project engineer for Sperry Rand and Bendix, I received my MD from the Albert Einstein College of Medicine (1971). I was a medical intern at Montefiore Hospital in the Bronx and a resident in OB/GYN at Beth Israel in Boston, where I served as a Fellow of the American Cancer Society. I have also been Chief of Family Planning Services at Walter Reed Medical Center (1976–1977), Assistant Professor of OB/GYN at the Uniformed Services University of Health Sciences and Harvard Medical School (1977–1978), and currently am Chief of Clinical Fetology and Director of Medical Education in OB/GYN at Beth Israel Hospital. My primary interest is perinatal medicine.

Margaret A. Kohn: I practice law at the Center for Law and Social Policy, a public interest law firm in Washington, DC. After graduating from Swarthmore College in 1969 and Columbia University Law School in 1972, and a year at the Center working on health and mental health law issues, I provided civil legal services for New York City inmates for a year and a half. Since returning to the Center in 1975, I have focused on health and women's rights issues, especially in the areas of federal policy development and enforcement regarding education, health, and employment.

Carol C. Korenbrot: As a reproductive endocrinologist in the research laboratories of medical schools at Duke University and the University of California, I investigated the production and effects of sex steroid hormones. This increased my awareness of the potential difficulties of hormonal technologies. In 1977, I became co-organizer of a national conference on "Contraceptive Hormones and Human Welfare" sponsored by the University of California (Berkeley) Women's Center and gave birth to my second child. Acutely aware of the serious difficulties faced by scientists and physicians dealing with the risks and benefits of systemic contraceptives, I left the laboratory to work in Bioethics and Health Policy at the University of California at San Francisco. In the Department of Obstetrics and Gynecology and with the Health Policy program there, I now teach and do research on the problems with the use of technologies in obstetrics and gynecology.

Joyce C. Lashof: I received my MD in 1950, and specialty boards in Internal Medicine in 1955. After teaching medicine and preventive medicine at three medical schools, I left the ivory tower and developed a neighborhood health center in Chicago and later became Director of the Illinois Department of Public Health. I came to Washington in 1977, first as a Deputy Assistant Secretary in HEW, and currently as an Assistant Director at the Office of Technology Assessment. I am married to a professor of Mathematics. We have two daughters, ages 25 and 23 and a son 20. We enjoy hiking, biking and traveling.

Leslie Laurie: (Observer) Executive Director, The Family Planning Council of Western Massachusetts, Northampton, Massachusetts.

Karen Lebacqz: I am an Associate Professor of Christian Ethics at the Pacific School of Religion, where I teach ethical theory, social ethics (with a focus on bioethics), professional ethics, and feminist ethics. I have been a consultant in Bioethics to the California State Department of Health and a member of the National Commission for the Protection of Human Subjects of Research. My special interests are professional ethics, distributive justice, and liberation theology. As a new homeowner, I also do a lot of painting, pruning, and puttering!

Carol Levine: I received a BA in history from Cornell University in 1956 and an MA in public law and government from Columbia University the following year. While raising my three children, I was a free-lance writer and editor. For the past three years I have been Managing Editor of the *Hastings Center Report;* in addition, I am Managing Editor of *IRB: A Review of Human Subjects Research,* also published by The Hastings Center. If I had more time, I would pursue my "side career" of photography.

Judith M. Levy: Program Director, Birthplace, Gainesville, Florida.

Judith Dickson Luce: As a student, I was told that my strong point was integrating various disciplines. This "strength" has kept my life anything but simple. I taught for two years, organized farm workers, and worked with the elderly. My husband, Tom, and I put down roots in Boston and started our family. My work in childbirth stems directly from my own birthing experience with my three children. Midwifery has connected me to other women and issues of women's health care. Other current concerns include nuclear power and the careful use of the earth to sustain our lives. Tom and I hope our children are happy and learning their connectedness to others and to the earth. We love to sail (a quiet, nonpolluting, fun use of wind power).

Kristin Luker: I got my PhD from Yale University in 1974, and then spent a year at Berkeley in postdoctoral research on social psychology, focusing on male contraceptive patterns. I am presently an assistant professor of sociology at University of California, San Diego, where I am researching abortion activism. My overall research interests are concerned with how people experience, internalize, and are shaped by and shape the external environment—in other words, how people negotiate that delicate boundary between self and society.

Julie Melrose: (Conference Assistant) Oral History Research Office, Columbia University, New York City.

Judy Norsigian: After graduating from Radcliffe College in 1970 (BA), I lived in an intentional rural commune with seven other adults and two children. Upon returning to the Boston area I joined the Boston Women's

Health Book Collective, taught auto mechanics to women, and co-directed a juvenile delinquency program (LEAA-funded) in North Cambridge, MA. Over the years I have concentrated more and more on women and health concerns and currently work full-time for the Collective. I am also a Board member of the National Women's Health Network and the Health Planning Council of Greater Boston. My favorite leisure-time activity is playing the cello in informal chamber music groups, occasionally in orchestras.

Laura Punnett: I began my full-time involvement in the self-help women's health movement in 1973 on the staff of the Oakland Feminist Women's Health Center. Since then, I've worked in western Massachusetts with various women's health groups and other feminist projects in organizational, educational, and administrative capacities. I received my BA in the Politics of Women's Health from Hampshire College. In 1978 a grant from the National Endowment for the Humanities supported a portion of my ongoing research on the history of the New England Hospital for Women and Children (Boston, 1862–1969). Currently I am in a public health graduate program studying the epidemiology of occupational health problems, particularly those affecting women.

Helen Rodriguez: I graduated from University of Puerto Rico Medical School in 1960, and was in academic medicine in a conventional mode until 1970 as a pediatrician and clinical investigator. I discovered the women's movement, myself, New York, and social pediatrics in 1970, directed the Department of Pediatrics at Lincoln Hospital in the Bronx for four years, and until 1978 was working there. I have become involved in patients' rights issues in the past few years, especially on sterilization and am a founding member of the Committee to End Sterilization Abuse. I have four children who have grown beautiful and involved, and three grandchildren in San Francisco. Presently I am Director of The Children and Youth Program at The St. Lukes-Roosevelt Hospital Center in NYC.

Sheryl B. Ruzek: I am a medical sociologist with a PhD from the University of California, Davis. Currently I am a Continuing Education Specialist, Program for Women in Health Sciences, University of California, San Francisco. In recent years I have taught courses on women on the San Francisco, Davis, and Berkeley UC campuses. My recent book, *The Women's Health Movement,* analyzes contemporary feminist discontent with medicine and medical technology. Previous publications are in the areas of client–professional relations, ethics and accountability, careers, and occupational development. My daughter, Jennifer, and I live in Piedmont on the sunny side of San Francisco Bay, where we swim and garden.

Hilary R. Salk: I am a founding member of the Rhode Island Women's Health Collective, a statewide organization providing support and information on women's health, serving as an organized consumer voice for women, and linking women to each other with mutual concerns. My involvement in the women's health movement developed directly from the birth of my first child (Nikki) thirteen years ago and my subsequent work with the Boston Association for Childbirth Education. I have worked for these two consumer organizations in a number of capacities: as childbirth educator, as a fundraiser and grant writer, as an editor of pamphlets, as conference coordinator, and as a project director. To make a living I work as a real estate agent. In addition to my daughter, I live with my son Daniel and my husband Stephen.

Sandra Serrano Sewell: I am national president of Comision Femenil Mexicana Nacional, a national Chicana feminist organization. My interest is in health care for Hispanic women, with a special emphasis on reproductive freedom. I have spoken on behalf of the organization on abortion rights, and on sterilization abuse. I am an administrator of bilingual bicultural child development centers in Los Angeles and the mother of two young children.

Beth Shearer: After an undergraduate major in music, I went on for an MEd, and taught in the Philadelphia public schools. The births of my daughters in 1972 and 1975, changed the direction of my life again. I became involved in the childbirth education movement, primarily for what it offered to help women regain control over their bodies and their lives. I have been teaching prepared childbirth classes for the Boston Association for Childbirth Education and developing a private practice as a labor assistant for over three years. I was also an original board member of C/SEC, a support, education, and advocacy organization for parents experiencing cesarean birth, and was appointed to a NIH-sponsored consensus development task force on cesarean childbirth, which presented its report in September, 1980. In January 1980 I received an MPH degree from Boston University.

Margaret O'Brien Steinfels: I grew up in Chicago where I graduated from Loyola in 1963. I then moved to New York, and began writing, editing, and going to graduate school. My graduate work was in American history, particularly history of the family. After finishing my Master's, I began work on my book, *Who's Minding the Children? The History and Politics of Day-Care in America,* which is a useful combination of history, social policy, and family studies. In 1972, I joined my husband in working at the Hastings Center, where I am now editor of the *Hastings Center Report* and have organized several projects on childbirth, medicine, and the family. I live in New York City with my husband and two children, Gabrielle and John.

Helen H. Swallow: In 1961 I graduated from Wells College with a major in French Literature. From 1961–1968, in New York, I was a frame maker, an usher at Lincoln Center, a waitress in the Village, a weaver, and a textile designer. We also had two girls in 1965 and 1967. In 1968–1969, I was in nursing school, which was followed by three years of lay midwifery in a general practice in California. For professional training I went back to Yale for nurse-midwifery and a master's. Since 1975, I have been on the Yale faculty, worked at the Maternity Center Association in New York, and opened and closed my own homebirth practice in New London. Now I am in private practice with an obstetrician and gynecologist and three nurse-midwives, and am active in legislative midwifery affairs, a consumer group, and the development of alternatives in childbirth.

Norma Swenson: A native New Englander, I've lived, worked, and gone to school in Boston since 1941. Through the childbirth movement (I was

President of ICEA—International Childbirth Education Association—from 1966-1968) and now the women's movement (I've been part of *Our Bodies Ourselves* since 1971), I've been an activist and community organizer around women's health issues since 1962. This conference is probably the 300th or so I've either helped plan or participated in. I got my MPH from Harvard in 1973 and have been working on a doctorate in medical sociology, off and on, currently at Brandeis. I have a 22-year-old daughter Sarah, and have been married since 1956.

Dorothy C. Wertz: My career has been interdisciplinary from the start. I received my AB in Social Relations from Radcliffe (1958), spent a year at the London School of Economics in Social Anthropology, and completed my AM and PhD from Harvard in Religion and Society in 1966. I have taught sociology full-time since 1965 at ten different institutions, including Suffolk University in Boston, where I am now Associate Professor. I have also held an NEH fellowship, and done research on the history of social science research about women as workers. My current research interests are (1) women and midlife career change; (2) social changes in childbirth from 1960 to the present in the US and England, which continues the social history from my book, *Lying-In,* which was co-authored with my husband, an American historian; and (3) the ethical aspects of genetic counseling. In the future I hope to do full-time research in areas of concern to women.

Ilene Wolcott: Formerly Project Director of the Women and Health Roundtable, a project of the Federation of Organizations for Professional Women in Washington, DC, I am currently living in Australia and continuing to work in the area of women's health at the Social Biology Resource Center in Melbourne. My background includes years as an elementary school teacher and school counselor. In 1974, I received a Masters Degree in Educational Counseling from American University. I have been a volunteer counselor with Planned Parenthood for 12 years. My other roles include being the wife of a Foreign Service Officer and the mother of a 13-year-old daughter.

Jill Wolhandler: Representative of the Women's Community Health Center.

Women's Community Health Center: Women's Community Health Center in Cambridge is the only women-worker-owned and -controlled licensed free-standing clinic in Massachusetts. We are committed to feminism and self-help. Through self-help women share information and skills, demystifying health care and encouraging each woman to take control of her body and her life. Self-help demonstrates that all women have the right, and, given adequate information, the ability to make responsible decisions about our own health care. Women's Community Health Center offers a wide range of educational and medical programs, works politically on local and national levels to empower women, and struggles to create a viable workspace for those who work at the center.

FIG. 1. Members of the contraceptives panel (clockwise from left): Laura Punnett, Kristin Luker, Carol Korenbrot (behind Luker), Jacki Ans, Judy Norsigian, Margaret Kohn, Michael Gross, Belita Cowan, Joyce Berkman, Jeanne Hubbuch, Jill Wolhandler, Rosa Cuéllar.

Index†

†Topics marked with an asterisk * are treated at much greater depth in our companion volume, *The Custom-Made Child?*. Page numbers in **boldface** indicate the major contribution of an author or the major treatment of a topic.